Crisis Management for
Law Enforcement

Crisis Management for Law Enforcement

SECOND EDITION

James Smith

CAROLINA ACADEMIC PRESS
Durham, North Carolina

Library of Congress Cataloging-in-Publication Data

Names: Smith, Jim, 1954- author.
Title: Crisis management for law enforcement / by James Smith.
Description: Second edition. | Durham, North Carolina : Carolina Academic
    Press, [2019]
Identifiers: LCCN 2019032220 | ISBN 9781531013240 (paperback) | ISBN
    9781531013257 (ebook)
Subjects: LCSH: Law enforcement. | Crisis management.
Classification: LCC HV7935 .S565 2019 | DDC 363.34/8--dc23
LC record available at https://lccn.loc.gov/2019032220

CAROLINA ACADEMIC PRESS
700 Kent Street
Durham, North Carolina 27701
Telephone (919) 489-7486
Fax (919) 493-5668
www.cap-press.com

Printed in the United States of America

Contents

Foreword

This text explores the knowledge base and procedures necessary for a law enforcement leader to plan, mitigate, and respond to a crisis and the subsequent consequences. A feature of the textbook is that actual events are explored in a Lessons Learned section at the end of some chapters. This provides the law enforcement leader or law enforcement officer with lessons in not only what he or she should do, but also addresses those actions he or she should not take.

Situational awareness is explored from the strategic and tactical standpoint to provide the leader an understanding of the value of both strategic and tactical intelligence. The textbook also provides tactical situational awareness and guidance for the onsite leader in tactical decision making.

Essential information is provided to allow the law enforcement leader to function in the dynamic and evolving environment of terrorism, weapons of mass destruction (WMD), and natural disasters, along with public disorder. The dynamics of leadership during a crisis are discussed.

The issue of novel toxic substances is explored. This provides the law enforcement leader information as to how operations potentially involving these substances should be handled. More important, the text provides information to recognize a potential event involving a novel toxic material.

Events involving emerging diseases, animal, and plant terrorism are reviewed. The law enforcement role in epidemiology involving both human, zoonotic, and plant diseases is discussed. The disease threat for law enforcement engaged in operations and the vectors of diseases are provided, as are countermeasures to exposure to mosquito and tick-borne diseases.

The problems inherent with evacuations, emergency sheltering, sheltering in place, and access issues are discussed. Issues such as interagency interfaces, Law Enforcement Incident Management System, and NIMS are addressed with emphasis on pre-existing mutual aid agreements and memoranda of understanding. Decision making is explored with an emphasis on making decisions during a crisis. Legal concepts involving jurisdictional disputes, forcible evacuations, scene access, interagency operations, and incident management are addressed. This textbook provides an overview and essential information for the law enforcement leader to identify the areas in which additional information, study, planning, and education are required. The text emphasizes IMS but also explains the areas in which IMS does not perform well and encourages the law enforcement leader to use the portions of IMS which work well for the agency and event, while discarding the components not needed.

Introduction

Law enforcement personnel will face multiple crises during a career. Most will be self-resolving or require minimal actions on the part of the responders or leaders. However, almost every responder and leader will face a challenging crisis which will test his or her resolve and abilities. A crisis consists of the events preceding or during a disaster, and a disaster is the consequence of a crisis. However, the terms may be used interchangeably in some instances.

The key to resolution in an amenable manner is prior planning and the ability to operate in a stressful environment, making decisions in a time-limited manner with conflicting data. Two occupations perform these tasks routinely: emergency physicians and law enforcement officers.

Mental preparation is crucial. One must be mentally prepared, have resolved any issues in the use of deadly force, and be prepared to make decisions with long-range, life-changing potential. Anecdotal reports from responders and leaders demonstrate that even a short amount of time to prepare mentally for an event is valuable in facilitating coping skills and in facing critical decision making. Drills and exercises are another important aspect of mental preparation for crises. These allow the "what if" scenarios to be portrayed in a safe setting.

Simply considering "If A happens, how would I react?" is the beginning of a mindset which allows one to consider the myriad of scenarios one might face. Those leaders and responders failing to consider the unlikely are doomed to failure should the event occur. Mental and emotional overloads during a crisis are common, and during the crisis is not the time to consider what to do. One should have sorted out and determined many of the options of the more common crises one can expect. This should be accomplished prior to their occurrence. This mindset provides a framework for decision making.

Leaders should consider the following poem, as the poem is prophetic about law enforcement events.

Far-stretching, endless time
Brings forth all hidden things,
And buries that which once did shine.
The firm resolve falters, the sacred oath shattered;
And let none say, "It cannot happen here."

Sophocles, *Ajax*, 400 B.C.

This textbook addresses the facets of mental preparation, development of risk matrices, identification of threat spectrum, and probability of crisis event occurrence. Common events along with some more esoteric issues are discussed. Decision making and analytical skills are reviewed along with resources to obtain information regarding threats and threat periodicity.

Crisis Management for
Law Enforcement

Chapter One

Planning

Overview

Every agency will face a major incident that requires crisis management techniques. The event is not a matter of if, but when. Preparations and planning may assist in the mitigation of the incidents. Prior planning is needed to identify risks, methods to mitigate the incidents, and available resources, along with plans that are exercised, reviewed, and updated annually.

The events that should be planned for include natural events, such as severe weather, flooding, earthquakes, and conflagration, and man-made incidents, such as hazardous materials release, utilization of weapons of mass destruction, civil disorder, or major crimes. The focus of crisis management of major incidents will remain the same regardless of the event.

An area of concern is incidents involving weapons of mass destruction. These involve chemical weapons, biological weapons, radiological weapons, nuclear weapons, and explosives (bombs) or incendiaries. The acronym CBRNE is used to describe these weapons. Chemical agents may be nerve agents such as sarin, blister agents such as sulfur mustard (H or HD), or improvised agents derived from commercial insecticides or toxic industrial chemicals such as chlorine or anhydrous ammonia. Biological weapons involve toxins derived from living creatures or plants, bacteria, and viruses. Ricin has become one of the preferred toxins. Abrin is another naturally derived toxin obtained from *Abrus precatorius*, rosary pea, or jequirity bean. These agents can be used to attack humans, animals, or plants. A radiation attack can involve the detonation of a nuclear device (low probability) or dispersion of radioactive material using an explosive such as a pipe bomb containing radioactive material, which is more likely. Incendiary devices tend to be simple devices used in arson, which can range from an ignition source used to ignite a forest or hand

An incendiary device using homemade thermite burns atop a 55 gallon metal drum. Photograph by Jim Smith.

delivered Molotov cocktail. Explosives can range from a simple pipe bomb (IED) to a vehicle-borne improvised explosive device (VBIED) with several hundred pounds of explosives. Other concerns are the use of computers to attack various automated systems such as those which control power, water, and sewer systems (SCADA), or denial of service attacks to government sites. This could include the introduction of a virus that disables the system or causes the loss of data; even simpler are denial of service attacks which prevent access or use of a website or take down communications or 911 systems. Cyber terrorism must be a consideration in planning, as government agencies are a target.

The goal must be directed to save lives, prevent injuries, and preserve property and to contain and mitigate the incident while protecting the environment. If persons are injured it becomes critical that emergency medical assistance arrive early and the injured are removed to the appropriate hospital quickly. A plan coordinating EMS resources along with law enforcement, fire service, public works, and other organizations must be used. The goal is to have the injured removed to a hospital no more than one hour from the time of injury. Rapid transport to the appropriate medical facility should ensure a high survival rate. The first hour following injury is called the "golden hour" in which survival rates are high if appropriate treatment is applied. Planning must address the law enforcement role in rapid access to the injured and their transport.

The first step in any crisis management planning is to identify the risk factors by examining prior emergencies within the jurisdiction and in contiguous areas to ascertain what incidents have occurred and may occur. A source of data which every political entity at the state, county, and local level can access is the Pre-Disaster Mitigation plan, which is available in the public record and provides information regarding natural disasters, threats, and vulnerabilities of the political subdivisions. These plans will identify many of the natural and technological threats, vulnerabilities, and mitigation strategies available. The plan should also list the critical infrastructure present. These plans present data derived from research and provide a starting point for data collection. With the types of incidents identified, examine the less probable scenarios and determine which need plans. Some agencies ignore the "low probability, high consequence incidents" and plan for the middle case. The plans could be scalable, allowing the same plans to be "scaled up" for more intense or widespread incidents. When examining the events, determine what actions in the past were successful and what actions needed improvement. Examine any unusual geographic, technological, or other issues that might affect the area, such as a nuclear power facility, a military base, an airport, an industry using toxic materials, pipelines, major transportation routes, dams or levees, nearby volcanos, and earthquake-prone areas. Review intelligence on threat groups who might target the area. Use the available intelligence resources, including other local, state, and federal resources. The state fusion center or joint terrorism task force may be a source of information. The agency should encourage officers to make Suspicious Activity Reports (SAR) of any occurrences, individuals, or events which attract their attention regarding terrorism or what appears to be organized criminal acts or groups. Groups or individuals may practice for attacks, conduct surveillance, or perform "dry runs" prior to the attack. Resource and information sharing along with mutual aid agreements in writing should be in place and play a part in an annual exercise.

When conducting a risk assessment, the probability of the incident occurring and its effects should be considered. Incidents with a significant probability of occurring must be addressed; however, unlikely events with potentially catastrophic outcomes should be considered. The events which might cause substantial loss of life, serious injuries, or catastrophic financial loss should take priority. The secondary priority would be the loss of critical infrastructure or personnel that would negatively impact the community. This may include public safety personnel; communications, healthcare, power, water, and sewer systems; natural gas infrastructure transportation facilities; and computer resources. The lower priority would be the loss of routine infrastructure or personnel, which might generate inconvenience but not significantly impair the public or the agency. Public safety agencies should have a minimum of three layers of backup on mission critical infrastructure such as power, environmental control, communications, fuel, and support for deployed personnel such as food, water, shelter, communications, transportation assets, expendable supplies, and restroom facilities. Interacting and networking with surrounding agencies may allow shared support during smaller or medium-intensity emergencies. Agencies should be prepared to be self-sufficient during widespread emergencies as others may have resources committed and be unable to provide mutual aid. Hurricanes of category three or higher may isolate any area and deny access to outside resources and may even impair communications of every type. In these circumstances the use of amateur radio systems and satellite telephones may be the only method to communicate outside the affected area.

A review of emergency operation plans of entities that provide critical infrastructure and support during emergencies with coordination is a crucial, mandatory factor. Agency mission-critical infrastructure, such as power, telephone service, radio, fuel, food, and water, along with other services, should have at least three levels of redundancy to assure that services can be delivered. The use of the Government Emergency Telecommunication System (GETS) to prioritize both cellular and landline telephone communications is imperative. This agency can prioritize reestablishment of landline communications for government agencies. Interagency communications are essential and must be functional under the heavy call load during a crisis. Additional radio groups, telephone lines, and staffing of communication centers will be needed and must be available rapidly. Physical security of critical facilities and infrastructure is required in some circumstances. This will consume a significant amount of law enforcement manpower.

Planning Checklist

- Identify potential targets and scenarios from intelligence sources
- Natural events and hazards can be identified from the local Pre-Disaster Mitigation plan
- Establish a chain of command and interagency agreements
- Determine the location of emergency operation centers and establish communication methods to be used with other agencies
- Obtain and deploy personnel as needed with alternate communication methods
- Conduct test exercises and review response plans
- Determine methods for organizing and providing shelters, evacuation, and emergency power, fuel, food, water, transportation, communications, and restroom facilities on- and off-site

- Develop plans for traffic control and crowd control
- Establish methods to control rumors and provide information to the media using direct contact, websites, and social media
- Establish a quiet area for isolation and decompression to facilitate a respite from the crisis for on-duty personnel
- Consider having Critical Incident Stress Debriefing/Management (CISD/CISM) trained mental health professionals available
- Develop plans to use spontaneous volunteers
- Initial efforts should be directed at identifying the magnitude and extent of the incident, and methods to contain and isolate the incident. This should be followed by identifying and deploying the needed assets to mitigate the incident. Prolonged incidents will require modification in the agency operational deployments. Shift changes and the use of non-field personnel for field assignments along with mutual aid must be incorporated into operations. Contingencies, many unplanned, will require innovative thinking coupled with expedient plans to be resolved. Some of these issues include:
  - Conflicting and contradictory information will occur initially with fragmented reports
  - 911 and agency communications will likely be overwhelmed
  - Initial responding units will likely only see portions of the event and may not comprehend the magnitude or extent of the event
  - Emergency vehicles and those fleeing the scene may clog roadways
  - Debris from storms or building collapse may impede access to urban areas
  - The injured may overwhelm on-scene EMS and local hospitals
  - A priority will be to maintain open routes to and from the scene
  - The first-arriving officers may be "overwhelmed" by the extent of the event
  - The initial "command and control" of the event will be fragmented
  - Several command posts may be established but will need to be consolidated
  - Cellular service may fail because of volume or loss of infrastructure
  - Resource acquisition and allocation will be critical in the first hours of the event
  - Strategic withdrawal may become necessary to concentrate forces with reinforcements, conduct accountability checks, and preserve assets

- A command-level officer should assume control of the incident on scene as soon as feasible
- An assessment of the needed resources should be conducted early, and those assets identified and mobilized
- Plans must address expedient resource acquisition outside normal methods
- Coordinate with other public safety agencies and other responding agencies to assure their operations are coordinated and used appropriately
- Conduct an intelligence assessment as needed
- Evaluate incoming information and adjust plans and operations as required
- Consider early information will be inadequate, flawed, fragmented, or contradictory
- Confirm responding personnel are properly equipped and using personal protective equipment (PPE) as needed
- Reevaluate the hazards and incident status as an ongoing process
- Consider Unified Command if multiple agencies or multiple jurisdictions are involved
- Control rumors and keep the media informed, use social media to update the public
- Use the incident command staff efficiently and delegate when feasible

The typical incident response scenario in chronological order is listed below. It confirms the major steps needed to mitigate a crisis. One needs to remember that some of the functions could be conducted in parallel.

- Determine the extent and intensity of the incident
- Determine methods to contain and isolate the event and the resources required to do so
- Request the resources needed
- Establish a command post
- Establish egress routes
- Establish unified command if needed
- Remember the tasks to mitigate the incident will be more difficult than they appear, consume more resources than anticipated, and take longer than estimated
- Establish the order of priority in an incident action plan (IAP)

- Establish backup plans and remain flexible if the first plan fails; be ready to use another plan, and if the situation becomes untenable, be prepared to retreat, evacuate, and fall back to rally points

The action steps include:

- Take control of the scene, if feasible
- Establish a command post
- Mobilize the needed resources
- Contain and isolate the incident
- Remove and treat the injured
- Establish egress and ingress routes
- Establish perimeters, inner and outer
- Develop a written IAP if needed
- Evacuate as needed
- Mitigate the incident
- Communicate with the media and public; use social media to disseminate timely information
- Preserve the crime scene

This appears straightforward, but upon application numerous contingencies will arise that no emergency plan can address. This requires a mentally agile command-grade officer who can think and make decisions in a time-limited manner within a stressful setting, while receiving contradictory and fragmented information. Cooperation and coordination with a diverse group of entities is required, and the lead agency or agency with legal responsibility may not be clear or present. However, law enforcement commanders should not be hesitant to step into this vacuum and take control until these issues are resolved.

A concern following incident mitigation is about crime scene issues if the incident involves or may involve a crime. Incidents which appear to be an unintentional event involving hazardous materials must be investigated to determine if criminal intent or criminal negligence played a role in the release. Remember that responders revert to training in a crisis, making realistic exercises a necessity.

Planning

To understand risks and probable crisis events one must determine what events might occur. The usual criminal acts are obvious, such as a hostage situation, barricaded shooter, active shooter, kidnapping, and so forth. However, what may not be obvious are the natural and technological events that may affect the jurisdiction. In lieu of conducting original research, much of this effort has been accomplished. Each level of government receiving federal funding of any type must complete and maintain a Pre-Disaster Mitigation (PDM) plan.

These plans are reviewed at the local, state, and federal level. Plans are mandated to be current and are periodically reviewed by Federal Emergency Management Agency (FEMA). Locate your jurisdiction's plan, locate your state's plan, and review them. Your local emergency management agency (EMA) director can be of assistance. Some agencies have discovered, following a disaster, that their plan was not current, or they had no plan, making them ineligible for financial disaster assistance. One law enforcement agency discovered its municipality's plan was not current when a traffic safety grant award was denied.

Most plans will have had substantial research regarding historical weather and natural events. Many plans will detail resources available, provide locations and types of critical infrastructure, and identify ongoing mitigation plans and projects, plus delineate previous events. Some plans will address the periodicity of natural events.

The area EMA director may be able to provide other information regarding technological hazards, such as hazardous materials in fixed facilities through Tier One and Tier Two Environmental Protection Agency (EPA) reporting and hazardous materials transportation studies. The law enforcement leader may want to attend Local Emergency Planning Committee (LEPC) meetings about "all hazards" or EPA Tier 3 reporting. The meetings and reports are valuable as they provide information regarding the threats from release and potential targets of theft or targets of terrorism. One need only examine the Bhopal, India, methyl isocyanate release or the Graniteville, South Carolina, chlorine release to understand the potential for disaster from a hazardous materials release, or to remember the 1937 New London School natural gas explosion, which killed almost 300 students and teachers.

The EPA Tier One and Two reports will assist in mapping the hazardous materials threat. Other considerations include dams, nuclear power facilities, natural gas storage facilities and chemical storage facilities, rivers with barge traffic, ports, pipelines, bridges, refineries, major highways, and railroads. These present a substantial hazardous materials release threat.

Terrorism threats may be obtained from local intelligence, federal agencies, the Joint Terrorism Task Force (JTTF) for the region, or state fusion center. However, a member of the agency may have to undergo a security background to gain access and even then, information sharing will be limited. Efforts should be made to identify any threat groups operating within the region, and any threat groups which have a substantial support within the region. Even if the threat group only has supporters, the supporters may be providing financial aid, safe houses, sites for training, or sites for storage of equipment or weapons. Some agencies consider outlaw motorcycle gangs and street gangs as a threat group. The threat posed should be evaluated, and maintaining intelligence on the activities of these groups is essential as they are a threat to law enforcement.

Agencies without an intelligence program should consider starting the program to track information, rate the reliability of information, convert the information to intelligence, and disseminate the intelligence. Care should be used to comply with applicable state and local requirements. Consideration of meeting federal requirements is also recommended if such is not mandated by law. Multiple safeguards must be in place to protect this encrypted database from penetration or compromise. Some agencies keep these records on isolated computers in a secure area not connected to a network, intranet, or Internet to ensure security of the database. Although extreme, storage of intelligence and confidential informant information in this manner or sophisticated encryption programs for security purposes is not unusual.

Mutual Aid Agreements and Memoranda of Understanding (MOU)

The probability of an event overwhelming local resources is high. The agency should establish workable, documented, and exercised mutual aid agreements. These should be crystalized in writing, reviewed by the legal advisor, and approved by the agency chief executive officer (CEO) and governing body. With these agreements several facets must be addressed.

- Confirm that the agreement or MOU conforms to local, state, and FEMA requirements
- The chain of command is specified
- The ability to purchase and financial accountability is addressed
- Which agency or agencies will bear costs and the manner of accountability
- The persons authorized to place the agreement in effect and to terminate the agreement during or following the crisis
- The logistics and resources to be provided by each agency
- Method of termination of the agreement or MOU during or following the event
- Post-crisis accounting and payment methods
- Method for resolving disputes during and following the crisis
- The agreement or MOU is reviewed annually and updated as needed

- The agreement or MOU is exercised as part of a drill and critiqued annually with some agencies practicing a tabletop exercise prior to the full-scale exercise
- Make certain the MOU is reviewed by the agency legal advisor

In many instances during and following a crisis, federal monies are available for salaries. Only the overtime worked because of the crisis is eligible for reimbursement. This means the agency must still meet the payroll during the crisis and be reimbursed for expenditures. A large-scale crisis may deplete the annual overtime budget in a short period. Agencies remote from New York City depleted overtime budgets following the 9/11 event or later with the anthrax attacks. Agencies with known threats such as floods, hurricanes, wildfires, and tornados should have sufficient historical perspective to allow planning for such events from a financial perspective.

However, fiscal constraints may not allow the agency to have a large financial overtime fund to draw from for a "potential crisis." Many local and state agencies operate at their legislatively mandated borrowing limits. A "rainy day" fund may not be feasible or, if present, may be raided for other non-emergency purposes. Cash flow during a crisis can be an issue. Some local entities depend upon tax revenue to fund day-to-day operations. During a crisis this tax revenue stream may not be available as the crisis disrupts commercial activity.

This may place a local government entity in a situation of no cash reserves, no revenue stream, and no borrowing capability. Thus, the ability to be eligible for and to receive federal monies is critical. The law enforcement leader should address the fiscal issues with the governing body's CEO and the chief financial officer (CFO) of the entity. Plans should be constructed to deal with any fiscal crisis created by a disaster. In many instances the fiscal impact of a disaster may be more long-lived and present a more substantial threat to the entity's existence than the disaster itself presented. Following hurricanes, many businesses fail because of these impacts.

Many states, regions, and localities will have mutual aid "systems" which may be funded at a federal, state, regional, or local level. Determine if participation in the system is available to your agency. Some CEOs are reluctant to participate or devote resources in terms of manpower to such systems. This can be a mistake, as participation may enable the agency to receive benefits in terms of training for those personnel participating during a crisis. Officers participating also have knowledge of how the system operates and the resources available, and will have direct contact with officials within the system. Strong consideration should be given to participating in such systems.

Stafford Act

Several acts govern the way money is spent. The Stafford Act, which is used in declared disasters, is somewhat complex. However, it may provide monies for overtime during a portion of the crisis, provide monies for emergency repairs of structures or infrastructure, pay for debris removal, and cover other facets of the crisis. The extent of a disaster, the dollar amount of damages, the geographical area affected, the population affected, and the ability of local and state assets to mitigate the disaster will determine whether a disaster is declared. Some areas may receive the full assistance of the Stafford Act and other funding, while areas not severely damaged may only receive monies during the first 72 hours of the disaster. Other areas, even though damaged, may receive no monies. The local or state EMA director may be able to better explain this complex act and the factors used to determine eligibility. Remember, even if approval is given for funds, months may pass before the monies arrive.

If a governmental entity is eligible to receive monies, in most instances the monies will be used to restore the damages to their pre-disaster state. Those agencies with projects identified in the Pre-disaster mitigation plan may receive monies to complete the projects if such would mitigate this type of event. This makes participation in the plan and identification of projects which may assist infrastructure in resisting disasters crucial.

Interactions with EMA and FEMA

During a crisis and following a crisis in the consequence phase of a disaster, law enforcement will have to interact with local, state EMA, and FEMA. The emergency management agency's mission is to provide coordination, access to resources, and expert assistance. Their mission is not to direct emergency operations. One important facet to remember is that EMA and FEMA operational philosophies are based upon the fire service model and tend to use fire service philosophy. This may conflict with some law enforcement philosophies. Law enforcement leaders should be prepared to be flexible and understand some law enforcement needs and philosophies may not be well understood by EMA and FEMA personnel. The National Incident Management System (NIMS) and Incident Command System (ICS) programs used are also fire service-based, but the law enforcement version, Law Enforcement Incident Management System (LIMS), does function well for routine crises. An important issue is not to force law enforcement operations into the fire service model. The fire service models usually use an "all or none" and central command control response, whereas law enforcement operations tend to be protocol driven and use officer discretion to direct actions. Use the parts of ICS that fit law enforcement needs and discard those parts of minimal value.

Another important aspect is record keeping. Expenditures prior to and in preparation for many events may be reimbursable if a disaster is declared. The same is true during and following the crisis. The problem for the law enforcement leader is one is never certain the crisis will be a declared disaster and the items purchased will be reimbursable in those events which are known to be imminent.

The law enforcement leader should meet and interact with the local EMA director before a crisis occurs. Knowledge of the personalities and competencies of the EMA director and staff are important for the law enforcement leader to understand. Many EMA directors and staff members will be fire service-based. This may present issues in understanding law enforcement operations during a crisis. A common issue of contention is scene control, evidence preservation, law enforcement intelligence, security of communications, and the imposition of a fire service-based bureaucracy on a law enforcement operation. Some state and federal bureaucracies stifle operations and are more concerned with chain of command and documentation than delivery of services. The issues seen following Katrina reflect the failure of some local officials and state officials to react appropriately, followed by the FEMA bureaucracy, which prevented resources from arriving in areas of need. When dealing with EMA and FEMA, the law enforcement leader should remember his or her agency's mission and that the role of EMA and FEMA is supportive, not directive. In other words, make decisions based upon law enforcement necessity, not to comply with a bureaucracy.

Record Keeping

A critical aspect of a crisis is record keeping. Law enforcement leaders should use available resources to track assets and personnel used during a crisis. This should include computer-aided dispatch; fleet records of vehicle usage, repairs, and fuel expenses, including vehicle make, model, asset number, and mileage or hours of operation; financial records of any purchases made; and overtime records of personnel costs incurred. These records will be crucial during a declared disaster in terms of documenting expenditures. Prior to a disaster a meeting with the local EMA director can better identify the data sets needed during a disaster.

Following a declared disaster some vehicle and equipment use expenses may be reimbursed. The reimbursement rates may be based upon hours of operation or mileage. This makes tracking vehicle and equipment operation hours or mileage important. FEMA uses a standard reimbursement scheme based upon the type equipment and hours operated or type of vehicle and the mileage driven.

Some supplies and equipment bought during the event may be reimbursable. The key is to keep good records and be able to justify any purchases as disaster related.

Continuity of Operations

Each agency must have a plan for continuity of operations in austere conditions. In many instances, agencies following Hurricane Katrina found themselves isolated for many days. Further, resources needed were slow in coming. Most agencies use a 72-hour autonomous operational period. This was woefully inadequate in a Katrina-type event. In the recent tornado outbreak in the Southeast, some rural agencies found themselves isolated for days with no communications and with little outside assistance. The agency must have a workable chain of command even if the CEO is absent. The plan must allow the ranking officer to unilaterally declare an emergency and function as the agency CEO until relieved by a higher-ranking officer. Agencies must plan for emergency power, an alternate dispatch and operations center, provisions for fuel and vehicle repair, and a method to communicate when conventional methods are not available, such as satellite telephones or amateur radio. If displaced the agency may have to establish a temporary operational location. The feeding of staff, providing sleeping facilities, and even providing restroom facilities are issues in small-scale intense events or large-scale events such as wildfires or hurricanes.

Some agencies have found that establishing law enforcement shelters for law enforcement families and pets assures the officers their family is safe and protected. During the officer's down time, he or she can visit the family. This has improved officer response and continued performance. Most agencies report a good response during a disaster but following the disaster the CEO should prepare for the distasteful task of dealing with those who failed to report to duty. Most disciplinary actions for failure to report have been upheld by the courts. Each agency should have a clear policy on reporting during an emergency to allow necessary personal actions but mandating reporting for duty within a specified time. The law enforcement leader should have discussed this issue during the construction and implementation of the policy with the governing body, personnel board or director, and the agency staff.

Past events should be reviewed, and the necessary equipment, supplies, consumables, and expendables should be considered. Because of ammunition shortages experienced by many police agencies for a variety of factors, some agencies began stockpiling to have at least two years of ammunition for qualification stored. Some agencies who only kept enough ammunition for annual firearms qualifications found themselves backordered for a year and had to delay firearms qualifications. External events remote to the agency can affect the availability of resources.

Many agencies have experienced substantial vehicle problems during a crisis with lack of fuel and vehicle tires. Agencies faced with civil unrest, hurricanes, and tornados report that tire damage because of debris or sabotage disabled many vehicles. The availability of full-sized spare tires and multiple spares is essential. Some agencies have agreements with a mobile tire changing or repair service for emergency assistance.

A review of past events can provide insight into the necessity of keeping specific supplies and other materials which may be needed on hand. Another logistical issue is purchasing and tracking of purchases. Keeping a vendor list in which the agency can charge items is essential, as is tracking the purchases. Some smaller agencies have issued credit cards to supervisors for emergency use. The problem is the loss of power may render credit card use impossible.

One small agency solved its fuel problem with a public-private partnership. The local fuel vendor bore the costs of establishing emergency power circuits for gasoline and diesel pumps. The local police agency purchased a generator transportable to the site. This facilitated the fuel vendor providing fuel for the law enforcement agency during a power failure.

NIMS and LIMS

The National Incident Management System (NIMS) mandates many tasks be completed. This process also divides emergency support functions into several categories. It mandates incident management (using the Incident Command System) training for responders with specialized training for supervisors, leaders, and elected officials.

The position of the person will determine the training needed, but as a rule responders will need the ICS-100 and ICS-200 level courses. In some instances, these can be completed online. Supervisors will need the ICS-300, ICS-700, and ICS-800 level courses. Upper-level supervisors and leaders will need the ICS-400 level classes. The ICS-300 and ICS-400 level classes require small group dynamics with classroom training. Select a group certified to teach the ICS-

300 and ICS-400 level classes who have personnel with a law enforcement background. Several entities teaching these classes have adapted the fire service-based ICS classes into a Law Enforcement Incident Management System (LIMS), which uses the essentials of ICS and IMS but with a law enforcement operation thrust. These classes reflect the standards in use by many agencies and are important for law enforcement leaders and responders to understand how the fire service-based ICS and NIMS works.

NIMS requires resources within the agency be typed and inventoried. Definitions as to what requirements must be met to consider the resource for outside use are available under the auspices of NIMS. What one agency considers a tactical team may not be considered such by another agency. NIMS establishes standards for equipment, units, teams, and personnel. This standard allows a leader to know what terminology to use to request a specific resource and know what he or she should receive via the request.

Law enforcement tends to consider NIMS, ICS, and IMS simply a command system which manages emergencies. NIMS is far more complex. Each agency is mandated by presidential directive to comply with NIMS and use ICS. Annual reports are required to establish compliance with the mandate through FEMA's NIMSCAST. Your EMA director may assist you in this somewhat complicated process.

The problem with NIMS, IMS, or ICS arises when this fire service philosophy, which mandates a narrow span of control, suppresses autonomy, uses unsecure radio traffic and plain language with no brevity phrases, and uses a centralized control, conflicts with law enforcement, which operates in an entirely different manner. Autonomy is encouraged and is essential in most operations, and law enforcement encourages large spans of control, uses coded language and brevity phrases on secure radio groups, and has operational security with security of communications as an issue. Law enforcement uses an intelligence function and is constrained by law as to how and when some operations can be conducted and what information can be gathered, stored, and disseminated. For instance, law enforcement in most instances will need a search warrant, or consent, to investigate a crime scene in a private residence, whereas the fire service is not required to obtain such to conduct a fire investigation. The fire service is driven by eliminating risk prior and during operations, whereas law enforcement is forced to accept substantial risk in many operations. The only risk mitigation available to law enforcement may be limited to the way the operation is conducted or which tactics are used.

IMS and ICS were developed to handle specific events which are predictable in terms of hazard, response requirements, and types of events. Law enforcement has a much broader array of events, which have a multitude of factors and intensity levels. Law enforcement responses are further complicated by the consideration of use of force and other legal constraints. IMS and ICS works well on the routine incidents with known issues and known hazards but fails in more complex law enforcement-type incidents unless modified.

IMS and ICS may not be useful in intense or widespread events in which multiple incidents are in progress (swarm attacks or Mumbai-type events) when the command is flooded with reports of events with conflicting information and resources are limited. ICS would call this an Area Command, but in many instances law enforcement will not be able to communicate to a central command. What occurs is small unit tactics using whatever immediate resources are available while the upper-level command attempts to make sense of the events and procures the appropriate resources. In an active school shooting, the event is over in minutes, followed, usually, by the suicide of the shooter; however, in a terrorist-type event, the event will proceed until the terrorists are neutralized or expend their ammunition. IMS and ICS are not well configured or flexible enough to deal with rapidly evolving events in which responders must use independent action to resolve or contain the event. In this circumstance small unit tactics used by the military better fit the needs of officers. These tactics use available resources guided by on-scene supervisors with independent action by individual officers following general guidance issued by the ranking officer. Little communication may take place once the officers are deployed, as it may not be feasible. The military practices these tactics, and those used by the Marines are especially applicable to these circumstances. ICS is woefully inadequate and even a hindrance in this type of event.

Differences in philosophy in ICS can be seen at a motor vehicle crash. The fire service may see a motor vehicle crash (MVC) as a severe risk to its personnel from moving traffic and attempt to stop traffic. Law enforcement realizes that some risk is inherent to traffic operations at an MVC but can reduce risks by using visibility vests and slowing traffic, and law enforcement is more concerned with the public risk caused by a traffic backup with resultant rear-end collisions and injuries to civilians. Blocking traffic will needlessly endanger the public. Conflict arises in such circumstances when fire equipment is used to block lanes or impede traffic flow. What the fire service seems to ignore is the substantial risk for upstream traffic crashes and the hazard posed to the public, which is equipped poorly to deal with such hazards.

One sees accounts in which the law enforcement responders take police action to force compliance of fire service or EMS responders regarding placement of vehicles or obstructing traffic at crash scenes. Fire and EMS personnel see an MVC as an event in which they must gain access to victims and treat injuries and in which they must eliminate any traffic flow risks to themselves. This is typical of the "all or nothing" response procedures used by the fire service as opposed to the protocol-driven law enforcement procedures that balance safety with the risk presented. They have little regard for evidence preservation, and most are not cognizant that an MVC is treated as a crime scene by law enforcement. Law enforcement is concerned with evidence preservation and expediting traffic flow to prevent upstream traffic crashes and to protect the public. This is also seen at hazardous materials incidents or clandestine laboratories involving law enforcement where a crime is suspected or must be ruled out. An example of the "all or nothing" fire service rationale would be fire service personnel operating in level A protection while law enforcement is working alongside the same personnel in level B or level C protection in their risk-based protocols.

Granted, the access to victims and treatment of the victims is a priority; however, these tasks can be accomplished with minor modifications to assist in evidence preservation. Fire service personnel can be protected from traffic in most instances without closing a roadway. Many of the conflicts on scene can be resolved prior to the event with memoranda of understanding (MOU). The MOU can explain the relationships on scene. In most circumstances law enforcement can enforce its will upon other responders as they are ceded the authority to regulate traffic crash scenes or potential crime scenes. This may result in alienation and negative media coverage should a conflict arise between responders. Resolution of operational issues should be handled prior to their arising on scene.

Should law enforcement be the incident commander or incident manager of MVCs? In most circumstances the answer is yes. However, this does not mean that law enforcement should direct other responders in how their mission is accomplished unless the law enforcement officer (LEO) serving as the incident commander is an expert in the area. What the incident commander should do is arrive at an agreement as to what evidence needs protecting or what constraints are placed upon other responders regarding their mission, how access to scene will be controlled, apparatus and vehicle placement, and traffic flow. The scene of an emergency is not the place to engage in a power struggle for scene control, have an argument about which agency is in charge, or have a shouting match over the issue. Some agencies have had responders leave scenes when their agency was denied control of scene. This type of conflict should be resolved via MOU prior to the event rather than on scene.

In tactical situations the protection of non-tactical EMS and fire service personnel are a priority. They must be excluded from the outer perimeter, which is not optimal, simply to protect them. Most police leaders do not want untrained and ill-equipped EMS or fire service personnel within the outer perimeter as personnel to guide and protect them must be assigned. This detracts from resources available for the mission. Untrained EMS and fire service personnel at a tactical emergency are liability. At the same time their services are usually needed.

The optimal solution is for law enforcement to provide its own inner perimeter EMS personnel. Many agencies use law enforcement officers trained as paramedics or EMTs as tactical EMS providers using programs such as TacMed Essentials. However, when that is not feasible, be aware that training exists for EMS and fire service personnel to become proficient in operating in the tactical setting. The ultimate solution is to achieve a working relationship and establish procedures prior to the event using MOU. Most law enforcement leaders want to be able to operate with their own personnel trained as tactical medical providers to afford autonomy and security of the operation. Law enforcement screening is more intense than that employed by the EMS and fire service. Several law enforcement agencies have been embarrassed to find EMS or fire service personnel assigned to their tactical medical team are convicted felons or had prior drug arrests.

Simulated officer rescue. Photograph by Dr. John Wipfler.

What Is IMS?

The Incident Management System (IMS) accomplishes several roles and is useful in routine crises.

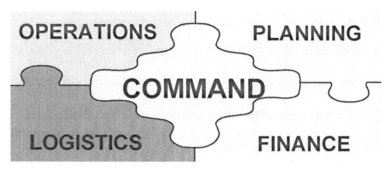

What is IMS?

A Management System for Large and Small Incidents—the system is modular and expandable, meaning it can be used for small or large events.

IMS is Based on Five Basic Functions

- Planning
- Finance
- Logistics
- Safety
- **Intelligence** (this is added for law enforcement)

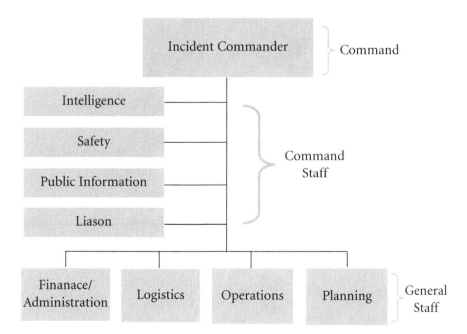

Why Use IMS?

- Responder Safety: IMS provides a standardized pattern for response and ensures responder safety with span of control and upwards and downwards communication (some which may be detrimental to law enforcement)
- Establish Strategy: IMS allows a strategy to be formed and operates by management by objectives, and in large or intense events, the generation of an Incident Action Plan (IAP)
- Effective Use of Resources: IMS centralizes resource control, making certain the resources are sent to where they are most needed
- Tactical Coordination: IMS provides a clear chain of command
- Establish Roles and Responsibilities: IMS provides a clear role and responsibility for each function
- Applicable across Jurisdictions and Functions: the process is standard
- IMS is flexible and scalable
- IMS represents organizational "best practices"

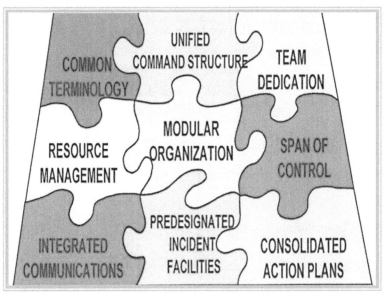

The components of IMS.

Problems with IMS for Law Enforcement

- Fire Service Philosophy: IMS uses a fire service philosophy which may not present the best options for the law enforcement approach.
- Rigid Structure: Although expandable, IMS is not flexible in many aspects, as IMS was designed for incidents related to the fire service which are routine and have known hazards and risks.
- Central Control: IMS uses centralized control, whereas many law enforcement operations will need to be semi-autonomous and, in many situations, autonomous from a central control once mission parameters are established and assets dispatched.
- Narrow Span of Control: In many law enforcement operations a span of control of one supervisor for 30 officers is not uncommon. The fire service and IMS recommends a much narrower span of control, one supervisor for two to seven personnel, which fails to take into the account the need for autonomy in most law enforcement operations.
- No Autonomy of Personnel: IMS suppresses autonomy and is dependent upon narrow spans of control and a central control philosophy. One must ask for permission to act prior to acting. This is not amenable in many law enforcement operations where officers report after they have acted. Law enforcement rewards autonomy and independence.
- No Independent Actions: IMS attempts to prevent independent action called "freelancing," while many law enforcement operations will need officers to act independent of central control. In almost every instance the officer must act without consulting a supervisor.
- Ask before You Act: IMS pushes the concept of "ask before you act." In law enforcement operations the reporting in most instances is "after the fact."
- Personnel Tend to Be "Specialists": In the fire service many personnel are specialists, as opposed to law enforcement officers who tend to be generalists, especially in small agencies. This means the officer may have a broader area of knowledge, responsibilities, and skills than those specialized with a narrow scope of duties and responsibilities as in the fire service.

Law Enforcement Operations with IMS

- Large spans of control are required
- Law enforcement does not need a rigid framework to operate
- Law enforcement encourages autonomy and rewards independence

- Law enforcement encourages independent action
- Law enforcement acts and reports afterwards
- Law enforcement uses small unit tactics using resources at hand and local guidance in events such as a "swarm attack" or in situations where communications are limited
- Central control is "after the fact" reporting in many law enforcement actions
- Remember IMS is a "guide" and should be adapted for law enforcement use, which may include modifications, such as larger spans of control, discarding unneeded staff and operational positions, a loose central control, use of code and signals as needed, and small unit tactics

The law enforcement version of IMS should be used at every incident conducive to making use of the IMS routine. The key is to modify the system to fit the needs of the agency while discarding the unneeded components or concepts.

In the IMS structure, the command staff consists of intelligence, safety, liaison, and the public information officer (PIO) reporting to the incident commander (IC). These individuals are charged with the safe and efficient operation of the incident.

Intelligence provides information regarding the event and persons involved in the event. This may include criminal histories, social and educational histories, medical histories of suspects or victims during a hostage situation, intentions of a person or a group, and the capabilities of a person or group. Intelligence may provide data regarding the scene, structures, instruments or devices involved, mobility of suspects, terrain, weather, or other factors affecting the event. Intelligence serves as a resource regarding information relating to the event. Intelligence officers may interview families, consult outside agencies and intelligence databases, obtain medical information from medical providers, consult with subject matter experts, liaise with hostage negotiators, and use national databases to obtain relevant information regarding persons, places, events, or objects.

Safety provides an independent oversight of the plans and operations to assure that the risks are acceptable and no intrinsically unsafe acts occur. In some law enforcement operations, the safety concept is organic within each operational unit and is called the "One Person Rule." This allows each operational group or section to establish safety rules which are not to be violated. "The Rule" allows any member of the operational section or group to question a plan or operation or to halt the operation should he or she observe a substantial safety issue. This is designed around the concept used by commercial airline flight crews in which anyone of any rank can question the safety of an act or operation and if need be halt the operation. The IC may assign a specific individual responsibility for this oversight. Scouts or observers may be recruited to assist the safety officer and to provide feedback to the IC.

Liaison provides interrelationships with other agencies operating at the incident or serving as resources. This may include other governmental entities such as law enforcement, fire service, and EMS; public works or private industry; and non-governmental responders such as the American Red Cross or Salvation Army. This position provides coordination and information flow to and from these entities.

The public information officer (PIO) provides information to the media, handles media inquiries, and keeps agency social media sites updated. This is a critical position in intense events or large-scale events which may require public actions. The public may need to avoid a specific area because of traffic issues, shelter in place because of armed individuals, or evacuate an area. The PIO is the link between the IC and media, and through social media, the public.

The operational-level general staff includes finance/administration, logistics, operations, and planning categories. Finance and administration handle the details of how and where to purchase, track overtime, and provide guidance regarding administrative rules and budgets. In many instances this function, especially in smaller events, may be combined with logistics. In large-scale or intense events, the CFO of the agency may play this role.

Logistics is responsible for the acquisition of resources. This may be through purchase, rental, or mutual aid. This section is also responsible for establishing staging areas for other agencies, acquiring vehicles, fuel, potable water, food, and medical assistance, along with warehousing equipment and supplies, plus moving these items to the areas of need. Logistics will also handle donations and coordinate volunteers. Spontaneous volunteers must be handled and can overwhelm a scene if not placed to work in non-hazardous roles in accordance to agency policy.

Planning is the section which determines the objectives and specific needs for the next operational cycle. Operational cycles are 12 hours usually but may be shorter in intense events. Operational cycles are usually based around "day" or "night." Planning determines the personnel, equipment, and expendable needs for each operational cycle. In smaller events this role may be undertaken by the IC or combined with logistics.

Operations are the active components of the IMS which seeks to resolve the issues by direct action. This may include several subsections such as a traffic control, perimeter, negotiations, search teams, bomb squad, entry team, arrest team, clandestine laboratory team, air operations, and tactical. They may be divided by function, geography, agency, or locale. The function and naming should follow local procedures. However, NIMS does resource typing, and when feasible follow the NIMS terminology for naming.

What Does IMS Do?

IMS takes accepted business practices and applies them to emergency response. The IMS organizational structure and the tasks performed by the IMS staff are comparable to the organizational structure and tasks performed by business managers. Just as businesses use these practices to improve their efficiency and effectiveness, response agencies can use IMS to improve the efficiency and effectiveness of their joint response efforts when an incident occurs.

IMS is recognized as the foundation for an effective, "all-risk" emergency response and recovery capability. It involves:

- Management by Objectives: as determined by the IC. These may be very specific, such as the neutralization of a specific threat, or general, such as rerouting traffic from an incident site or evacuating a specific area.
- Delegation: of specific functions to others, such as safety, logistics, liaison, intelligence, and operations. The level of delegation will be general in most events with the specific section chief expected to accomplish the objectives provided by the IC within a time parameter.
- Empowerment: provides specific tasks and parameters to those involved in the form of objectives. The methods of implementation of the objectives in the Incident Action Plan (IAP) are a function of the operations section chief. Just as other section chiefs operate in a semi-autonomous manner once assigned objectives by the IC.

Effective Incident Management

Requires:

- Establishing Objectives: the IC must determine what the objectives are in terms of priority.
- Setting Priorities: the more common immediate objective is protection of life. This may mean that a "quick response team" or "hasty team" makes entry to neutralize an active shooter, while the IC de-

velops a plan to rescue those wounded. In some instances, these teams might be the first-arriving officer engaging the active shooter. The priorities are protection of life, incident stabilization, protection of property, and protection of the environment.

- Assigning Resources: the IC will need to determine what additional resources are needed and start the process of obtaining them. When feasible this should be delegated to the logistics section chief in large incidents.
- Priorities

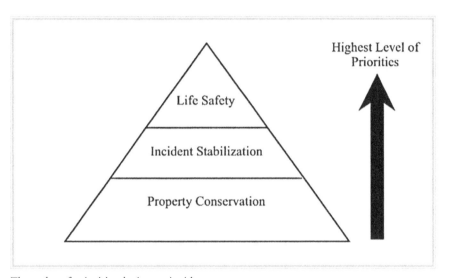

The order of priorities during an incident.

- ○ Life Safety: protection of citizens, protection of responders, and protection of offenders. One important issue to remember is the rescue of the dead is futile. The impulse for many law enforcement personnel is to enter the "kill zone" to effect rescue without taking time to determine the hazards and if the downed person is alive. In TacMed Essentials the algorithm is to wait at least 30 seconds before attempting rescue if you witness the person go down. This time is used to seek hard cover, assess the nature of the threat, determine the threat location, and formulate a rescue plan. If one is entering a scene in which persons are down from gunfire, one should first seek hard cover and perform an assessment prior to acting. Rushing in will likely result in more

Simulated downed officer in need of rescue. Photograph by Dr. John Wipfler.

casualties. If individuals are down from reasons other than gun-fire, one must consider the agent which might be present, ranging from sarin nerve gas, to toxic industrial chemicals such as chlorine or anhydrous ammonia, to more conventional carbon monoxide. Personal Protective Equipment (PPE) is required to enter such a scene.

○ Incident Resolution: the incident should be stabilized and an incident action plan formulated for resolution of the law enforcement phase of the event. The initial plan may be to neutralize an active shooter, but to stabilize the event law enforcement will need to eliminate the possibility of other shooters and begin evacuation of those injured. This requires interfacing with fire rescue as the elimination of the threat of other shooters may run in parallel to rescues from secured areas. The IC may also have to deal with many uninjured persons who may need rescue and are potential witnesses. The need for investigative efforts to locate witnesses may have to be delayed in the initial phases of the event. The other aspect is those injured or uninjured individuals present may be offenders who have tried to blend with victims and bystanders. This is substantial concern following a bombing or active shooter in swarm attacks.

○ Property and Environment Conservation: the lower priorities but still a substantial concern is the need to stop damage to property, return the property to owner for remediation, and prevent damage to the environment. The IC may have to make difficult decisions. For instance, a barn is located with almost 100 pounds of deteriorating nitroglycerin-based dynamite stored in the barn's loft. The IC must decide if he or she will put bomb technicians at risk to preserve property when substantial life risk exists. In this circumstance the protection of responder safety takes precedent over the protection of property. The IC may elect to destroy the dynamite in place by burning it and in the process destroying the barn.

Legal Aspects of IMS

- Homeland Security Presidential Directive 5: NIMS
- Department of Homeland Security: National Response Plan
- OSHA: 29 CFR 1910.120
- EPA: 40 CFR 311
- Some local or state laws may require IMS to be used
- Executive directives from CEO of organization or directive from CEO of governing body may mandate the use of IMS

A legal basis exists for using IMS. Federal laws require its use for persons responding to hazardous materials incidents. The Superfund Amendments and Reauthorization Act of 1986 (SARA), established federal regulations for handling hazardous materials and directed the Occupational Safety and Health Administration (OSHA) to establish rules for operations at hazardous materials incidents.

OSHA rule 1910.120, effective March 6, 1990, requires that organizations that handle hazardous materials use ICS/IMS. The regulation states:

> The Incident Command System shall be established by those employers for the incidents that will be under their control and shall be interfaced with the other organizations or agencies who may respond to such an incident.

Non-OSHA states are required by the Environmental Protection Agency to use IMS at hazardous materials incidents. Although law enforcement is not the lead agency in most hazardous materials events, with the exception of clandestine drug laboratories, they may be supporting such an event with perimeter control and evacuations and should follow the IMS precepts adapted to law enforcement use.

Concepts and Principles of IMS

IMS should include:

Common Terminology: When multiple agencies are involved who do not use the same terminology, the NIMS typing terminology and plain language radio traffic should be used. However, when a single agency is involved or agencies using a common code or signal system, plain language is not needed and is not recommended.

Modular Organization: The modular organization using the incident commander (IC), command staff including safety officer, liaison, public information officer (PIO), and intelligence, along with sections for finance/administration, logistics, planning, and operations should be used. This allows for expansion or contraction of the IC structure during the lifespan of the event. This structure should be familiar to the personnel involved.

Integrated Communications: Common radio groups should be designated and used by the IC. The IC may assign these groups. In some events in which unified command is operating with agencies with diverse radio systems, it may be required that a representative for each agency with a portable radio be available to the command post to transmit information or receive information. Although cumbersome this is not an uncommon impediment experienced during a multi-agency response.

A Unified Command Structure: This is essential when the event involves multiple and diverse agencies. The agency missions will be different, as will priorities. The IC should be designated by prior MOU, or the agency which has a legal role, such as law enforcement during a criminal act or what is believed to be a criminal act. However, the lead agency may change several times during an event. For instance, in a school shooting the initial reacting agency is the school, which hands off IC to law enforcement, which serves as the IC until the shooter is neutralized. The lead agency would become fire rescue and EMS to aid the injured. Law enforcement would assume the lead following evacuation of the injured for the crime scene processing. Eventually the school officials would assume the lead as remediation of the facility and counseling of the students and staff begins. Although law enforcement remains the IC, the focus of the mission and objectives, along with lead agency, may change several times during an event.

Consolidated Action Plans: IMS allows consolidation of the action plan plus input from all stakeholders. This is important as actions must be coordinated and resources used efficiently.

A Manageable Span of Control: Although law enforcement operates with much larger spans of control, this still needs to be a manageable number of personnel. An important facet is making certain responders can communicate and receive direction from the IC and can pass information back to the IC. This allows the IC to maintain situational awareness.

Designated Incident Facilities: The IC will designate the location of the command post, triage areas, staging areas, rehabilitation areas, and the like. This should be communicated to responders.

Comprehensive Resource Management: IMS facilitates comprehensive management of resources directed from the command post. Duplication of resources, duplication of requests, and scattering of scarce resources through the event is eliminated with logistics controlled from a single section. The IC can apply the resources to the locations needed and where the resources will be more effective.

This section provides the foundation for IMS. Remember that the IMS principles have been tested and proven by business and industry and by response agencies.

Common terminology is essential in any emergency response management system with multiple agencies not using common terminology but is not necessary for single-agency operations.

- Major organizational functions and units are named
- In multiple incidents occur, each incident is named
- Common names from NIMS resource typing are used for personnel, equipment, and facilities
- Clear text is used in radio transmissions when common terminology is not shared between agencies (no "ten codes" and no signals at events with multiple agencies, but agencies with the same codes and signals may use them)
- IMS is used during single-agency events but the agency may continue to use its signals or codes. In events with multiples agencies using the same radio signals and codes, plain text is not necessary. In fact,

Who is in charge? This is a photograph of a motor vehicle crash following pursuit by police of robbery suspects. The crash caused power lines to fall to the ground. A multifaceted problem existed with possibly armed suspects, a vehicle leaking oil and gasoline, and downed power lines impeding access to the vehicle. The key is law enforcement is in charge until the suspects are no longer a threat, then fire and EMS take over to extricate the patients and provide hazard control. Photograph by Jim Smith.

plain text uses more airtime than signals and codes and if not required, should not be used. One study showed that plain language consumed more than three times the airtime as coded signals or brevity phrases

Single Command

- No overlap of jurisdictional boundaries exists
- A single IC is designated by the agency with the management responsibility or most assets committed. Remember, if the event is a crime or suspected crime, law enforcement should serve as the IC.
- Unity of Command: a single IC or unified command is functional
- Span of Control: remains manageable but may be very large in some law enforcement operations, such as traffic or perimeter control
- Division of Labor: various tasks are assigned to the functional sections
- Accountability: based upon assignment and tasks, each responder is accountable to one supervisor for his or her tasks

Unified Command

- *The incident is within a single jurisdiction with multiple agencies*
- *The incident is multijurisdictional*
- *Individuals representing different agencies or jurisdictions share command responsibility*

Most incidents involve a primary response agency with responsibility for the incident. Unified command can be used for a collaborative approach to solve the problems created by an incident. Roles played by agencies responding under a unified command must be identified before the incident. These decisions should be crystallized in MOU.

Unified command is used when the incident is within a single jurisdiction, but more than one agency shares management responsibility. An example would be severe weather in which law enforcement is evacuating victims and controlling traffic, while fire rescue and EMS are assisting those injured, DOT is clearing roads, Red Cross is opening and staffing shelters, and the Salvation Army is feeding public safety responders. Shared command and a Unified Command would be indicated as the missions will overlap. Assisting agencies (such as Red Cross, Salvation Army, public works, or utilities) are not part of the unified command but may be represented at the command post or emergency operations center (EOC). Unified command is also used when the incident is multijurisdictional in nature, or when more than one individual, designated by his or her jurisdiction or agency, shares management responsibility.

The involved agencies contribute to the command process by:

- Determining goals and objectives
- Planning jointly for tactical activities
- Conducting integrated tactical operations
- Maximizing the use of assigned resources
- Example: A hazardous materials spill in which more than one agency has responsibility for the event, including a private industry, private hazardous materials contractor, and local fire, EMS, and law enforcement, with state environmental management officials, local contractors delivering supplies such as diking materials and other supplies.

The lead agency may change as the event evolves. This means the objectives and mission may change to meet events as they occur.

The critical need at any emergency is for responders to communicate, coordinate, and cooperate. During a crisis is not the time to meet counterparts in other agencies. Previous training and experience should be considered when

Command post. A command post does not need an elaborate vehicle or facility as here from left to right EMS Chief, Mayor, State Representative, Police Chief, and Fire Chief, manage a large scale short-lived hazardous material incident. The incident required evacuations including children from a school. Photograph by Sharon Lee.

the CEO selects a person to serve in a unified command setting. The staffing patterns and structure of a unified command should be established prior to the event. This is the reason for crystallizing MOU. Differences, agendas, and agency missions should be established prior to the event.

Unified Command Concept

The concept of unified command means the involved agencies contribute to the command process by:

- Determining objectives and issues which need resolution
- Planning jointly for mitigation and tactical activities
- Conducting coordinated mitigation and tactical operations
- Maximizing the use of available resources

A unified command structure should consist of one command-level official from each jurisdiction or representatives of the involved departments within a single political entity. This need not be the CEO, but in many instances the CEO will serve in this capacity.

Selection of participants to work a unified command structure depends on the location and type of event. Previous training or experience of the individuals should be considered in functioning as a group, such as in an exercise, and may be a deciding factor in the selection.

Regardless of whether single or unified command is used, government entities must determine prior to the event which agency or agencies will assume the lead during a variety of incidents. Further, the agencies need to determine how the transition from one lead to another will occur. This is of concern when private or non-governmental entities might be involved in unified command. This occurs when the event involves an industry or business which has a substantial operation affected by the event. This may be a chemical facility, refinery, storage facility, hazardous materials site, or other industry.

An important consideration is what law enforcement's role is in your area's EMA Emergency Operations Plan (EOP). Are the law enforcement responsibilities shared with other agencies at the local, county, state, regional, or federal level? The involved communities should have specified which agency would assume the command function in the EOP.

Implementing the incident action plan under unified command is the responsibility of the operations section chief. He or she would represent the agency with the most substantial assets deployed or the agency with jurisdiction of the type of event or location of the event.

Area Command

Public health emergencies are an example of where Area Command is used. Other examples include the use of a biological agent (such as the anthrax attack), a SARs outbreak, civil unrest (e.g., the 1992 Los Angeles riots), intense criminal events with mobile active shooters (e.g., the North Hollywood Bank of America branch shootout), or similar events require an area command.

Example: Officers are down at two locations, both involving a large riot. Tactical assets are needed to rescue the officers. The law enforcement area commander will decide what assets are sent to each event. The area commander determines what resources are used when multiple requests are made, and resources have competing requests which must be prioritized. The area commander makes the decision about which request receives the resource based on information provided by the on-scene incident commanders. This may also be a situation in which the on-scene commander elects to use the resources at hand to complete the mission rather than depending upon external resources.

Police officers confront disorderly persons during a riot. Photograph by Dr. John Wipfler.

Developing and Implementing the Plan

An immediate priority during the initial phases of an incident is to develop an incident action plan to stabilize the event and mitigate hazards. The plan should have specific and measurable objectives. The initial plan may be a "stop gap" plan to mitigate an immediate set of hazards or problems. The final incident stabilization plan and mitigation plan may take time. In many instances, such as with an active shooter, the first on-scene officer engages the shooter while a quick response team composed of on-scene diverse resources may be sent to engage the shooter if the initial effort fails in an attempt to neutralize or isolate the shooter. Measurable goals may be as simple as to isolate a shooter, evacuate an area, secure a perimeter, open arterial routes for emergency vehicles, or provide a safe evacuation corridor.

- To identify and take appropriate actions during the stabilization phase of the incident is a priority. The immediate goal is to determine what is occurring, determine what assets are needed to mitigate the situation and request them, use a quick response team if needed and isolate any dangerous individuals, gain control of the situation, establish an inner perimeter, evacuate as needed, establish an outer perimeter, control traffic and crowds, establish resource staging areas, and deploy the assets as they arrive.

- Remember that many of these steps will run in parallel.
- Designate Functions which Are Not Critical: use your command presence to direct and control, to request assets, and to communicate with the public through social media and the media.
- Resist the Urge to Join the Chaos: many CEOs and command-level officers will want to join or direct the tactical operations; however, this urge should be resisted, and the CEO's or command-level officer's presence should be used as a decision maker, to obtain assets, to make policy-related decisions, and to deal with other decision makers, and when feasible, communicate with the media as a recognizable "figurehead."
- Obtain Needed Resources: these may be from within the responding agency, via mutual aid, or requested from the emergency operations center (EOC), EMA, or federal law enforcement agencies. The critical aspect is knowing what resources are available and their location, capabilities, and response time.
- Develop a Plan: the plan must be in measurable and specific objectives. The plan may address critical issues initially. Remember the plan will change as resources change. Develop a second plan for the long term if the event is intense or has the potential for extended operations. Always have a fallback plan if your position becomes untenable. Designate rally points which are remote to the site.
- Execute the Plan: this should be the operations section chief's job, not the IC or CEO's job.
- Evaluate the Results: this should be performed continually and the plan adjusted as needed.

Size Up

1. Size up or assess the situation — the questions to ask include:
   - How bad is the situation?
   - Am I safe where I am located?
   - What immediate resources do I need?
   - Do I need a quick response team to intercede now? Do I have the resources for a quick response team? What briefing, and objectives, should I provide the quick response team?
   - Can I isolate the incident quickly?
   - Where will I establish a command post?

- Where will I establish staging areas?
- Where will I establish safe triage areas for the injured and safe evacuation corridors if needed?

2. Identify contingencies
   - What is going wrong now?
   - What is going wrong in the future?
   - What can go wrong?
   - How far can the bullets, hazardous material, explosion blast wave, or bomb fragments travel? Am I under glass if a bullet or explosion hazards exists (falling glass is deadly)? Do I need Command Post security? What about secondary devices if an explosion is involved?
   - What resources are not available?
   - Remember "Murphy"
   - Are terrain, wind direction, and weather important? Weather conditions and wind direction can be critical for hazardous materials events and air operations. If so, obtain a forecast and current conditions from the nearest National Weather Service Office. Consider an onsite weather station (most hazardous materials units will have one).

3. Determine objectives
   - What needs to be done now and within the next few minutes?
   - What are the critical tasks which need to be accomplished?
   - Base the objectives around the available resources.
   - The plan may need to have several phases such as immediate needs, initial stabilization efforts, and intermediate and final stabilization interventions. The plan needs to be flexible and easily changed, as the plan may be altered as additional information is developed or resources become available. Remember to have the intelligence officer provide input on the known human threat factors.

4. Identify needed resources: most will be obvious. Ask for what you believe is required but do not hesitate to request more than appears to be needed, as the incoming assets can be cancelled should they not be needed. Remember obtaining assets takes time as do responding assets.

5. Build a plan and a structure: build a plan and build an operational structure. Select who will be the command staff and section chiefs.

6. Act: as soon as feasible take action, especially if immediate mitigation is needed by a quick response team or first-arriving officer in the case of an active shooter, immediate evacuations, or rescues.

Size up reports should include:

1. The unit making the report and location: "One Adam 12 at Cottonwood School's main entrance with shots fired and students leaving the building."
2. A description of the situation: specify what is happening or believed to be happening. "One Adam 12, students report a suspect, male white, with green shirt with a long gun firing shots in the front hallway … unknown if anyone is down … making entry to conduct assessment and confirm situation."
3. Obvious conditions: emphasize any hazards or problems noted. "One Adam 12, have made entry, I have three students down in the front hallway who appear deceased, I hear shots fired in the east hallway but have no visual on the shooter, need units for a QRT, need a supervisor, tactical team, and need EMS."
4. Initial actions taken: advise what actions were taken, which might include establishing a perimeter, immediate evacuations, rescue of persons, engaging an active shooter. "One Adam 12, I have a visual on the shooter, armed with a long gun, wearing a vest that has wires, is holding a female student hostage, male white wearing a green shirt and white shorts, suspect does not have a visual on me … unable to take a shot because of hostage … have units responding enter the front hallway … bring a patrol rifle … come to the first intersection and meet me."
5. Safety concerns: ongoing issues which present a hazard to responders. This may include areas which are subject to gunfire, structural collapse, IEDs, hazardous materials present, vapor or gas plume, fires, or other hazards. "One Adam 12, the suspect is stationary but holding a female hostage in a white shirt and blue jeans … I have students down in the east and west hallways with unknown status.… estimate eight to 10 students down, advise EMS the number of patients … still unable to engage suspect because of hostage, have responding officers come to my location with a patrol rifle … request the bomb squad as the suspect appears to be wearing a vest with wires attached to it … students advise no other shooters and I do not hear any other gunshots and have not seen any additional armed personnel."
6. Identification and location of Command Post: specify where the command post is located. "One L 20 is on scene at Cottonwood School and establishing command post at the front of the school on the south side of the building … sending One Adam 14, 17, 2K80, and One L 90 to assist One Adam 12, One Adam 14 has a scoped patrol rifle and has authority to engage the suspect … if unable to engage the suspect isolate

the suspect ... One Adam 12 direct the units to points they can isolate the suspect's movement ... One Adam 21 will be entering with EMS to ascertain the condition of the three students down in the main hallway ... One Adam 24 will be directing students, faculty, and staff to the playground area and protecting them."

7. Request resources: if resources that will be required are known (tactical team, EMS, hazardous materials unit, bomb squad), request them immediately. "One L 20 requesting a tactical alert, clear this radio group, declaring a mass casualty event with an active shooter, notify EMS ... need SWAT, bomb squad, air support, intelligence, command staff, command post vehicle, a dozen RAs ... send all available units in this sector to the command post in front of Cottonwood School ... One L 20 will be Cottonwood Command, One Adam 12 will be Entry Team, One Adam 21 will be EMS cover, One Adam 24 will be evacuation ... the staging area will be the church parking lot on the south side of the school."

8. As the units arrive they will be assigned to various sectors which may include command post, safety, intelligence, liaison, or sections such as logistics (handing staging), finance-administration, planning, or operations. Operations may include QRT, entry team, tactical medics, EMS cover, inner perimeter, precision marksmen, surveillance, outer perimeter, traffic control, command post security, crowd control, evacuation, and related functions.

Contingencies

"Murphy's Laws" apply to incident management:

- You will miss the obvious.
- Nothing is easy as it looks.
- Everything takes longer than you think it will.
- No one understands what you say on the radio.
- Everyone talks on the radio at the same time or uses the wrong radio group.
- The vital equipment you need is unserviceable.
- If anything can go wrong, it will, at the worst possible time.
- The emergency plan does not address this contingency.
- The person you need with a skill is not available.
- If you think about a mitigation strategy, you should have performed it 20 minutes ago.
- Murphy was an optimist.

Define the Objectives

Objectives are:

- Measurable
- Used to monitor incident progress and establish priorities
- Based on size up and contingencies: What do you want to do? How do you want to do it?
- Neutralize the shooter, contain the shooter, rescue downed persons, keep the crowd out, re-route traffic, transport the injured, preserve the crime scene, locate and isolate witnesses, prepare for shift change

Resources

- What resources are needed? Manpower, specialty teams, heavy equipment?
- Are they available locally? If not, where can they be obtained?
- Where does one obtain the resources? Agency resource list, mutual aid agreements, MOU, EOC, EMA, state-level agencies, or federal agencies
- How long will it take the resources to arrive? If feasible know this prior to asking for the asset.
- What other agencies or specialty teams are needed? SWAT, tactical medics, bomb squad, search and rescue (SAR), swift water rescue, air assets, public works, utilities, department of transportation (DOT), disaster medical assistance team (DMAT), disaster mortuary team (DMORT), hazardous materials team, federal agencies?
- Special requirements? Radiation health personnel, chemical biological specialists, clandestine drug laboratory responders, domestic civil support teams, DMORT
- Can you operate with another plan? Does a better way to achieve the mission and objectives exist? Be open to suggestions and avoid "group think," where everyone agrees with any plan without considering potential issues, or taking the path of least resistance.
- Quick Response Team: Is one needed? Events with active shooters, hostage situations, or in other events that potentially require immediate action prior to a tactical team deployment, the first-arriving officer may enter to engage the shooter, or the IC may elect to deploy a quick response team (QRT) for immediate intervention as soon as

it can be established. This team is composed of on-scene responders (sometimes called a hasty team) using equipment immediately available. The mission is to neutralize a threat, contain a threat, or isolate a threat until tactical assets arrive. The decision to employ a quick response team is risk prone (so is the first-arriving officer attempting to engage a shooter), but in a situation in which a life or lives is/are at risk and rapid intervention stands a reasonable chance of succeeding, the first-arriving officer may enter and engage the shooter or the IC may employ a QRT. Most teams are composed of patrol officers as first responders to a scene. These teams are ad hoc and directed by whoever the IC appoints. In some circumstances the members may be from several agencies. The issue is they have not worked or trained together and may not be familiar with agency policies or with other members of the team. Nonetheless, with an active shooter this may be the best immediate alternative to neutralize or isolate the shooter if the first-arriving officer has failed or requires support.

Incident Action Plan

- Responsibilities: this not only establishes the person and agency in charge, but who will be responsible for the many facets of the operation.
- Chain of Command: the plan should designate the chain of command, especially if the chain of command deviates from the standard ICS format.
- Coordination: radio groups, hand signals, audible evacuation signals, radio check-in times, and personnel accountability should be established.
- During chaos at an intense incident, resist the urge to join the fray: many CEOs and command staff members will want to engage in tactical operations, or fulfill the role as the operations section chief. This should be avoided as a CEO or command staff-level individual is more valuable as an asset to coordinate, command, and obtain resources especially when dealing with other decision makers.
- Take the Needed Steps to Obtain Resources: this may be as simple as a telephone or radio call, or may involve a complicated approval process, or could involve the purchase or rental of equipment.
- Execute the Plan: place the plan in action but continually reassess the progress while modifying the plan to meet contingencies.

- Consider a Two-Phase Plan: in many circumstances the initial plan is constructed in a hasty manner, and as the initial plan is implemented, a second more developed plan considering arriving assets may be developed, but have a fallback plan and rallying points should the situation become untenable.

Possible actions for incident stabilization:

- Establish command
- Contain the event and establish a QRT as needed
- Isolate the area and establish perimeters
- Obtain resources
- Setting up a staging area
- Stop the threat
- Assist the injured
- Remember to have a plan, a backup plan, and a fallback plan with rally points should the situation become untenable and evacuation is required.

EOC and Command Post Operations

Many CEOs will not want to be "stuck" in an EOC but would prefer to be in the field at the scene of the crisis. This has benefits and detriments. If the CEO has a trusted subordinate to staff the EOC and act on his or her behalf, the CEO can operate in the field or at the scene of the event. However, the CEO, unless he or she is acting as the operations chief or IC, must resist the temptation to engage in issuing orders to those personnel involved. Many CEOs want to serve as both the incident commander and as the operations chief along with the role as a decision maker. This causes the CEO to lose focus on the event and his or her situational awareness. Unless the event is isolated and small scale, the CEO should resist the temptation to serve in multiple roles.

The CEO's role at an event in which he or she is in the command post will vary. Many will want to serve as the incident commander but such, especially in a large-scale event, may not be advisable. The CEO may be better served to place himself or herself in the role of a decision maker and allow a trusted subordinate to serve in the role of incident commander. This allows the CEO to focus upon the strategic issues, policy issues, and resources while leaving the tactical-level operations to other qualified personnel. This also frees the CEO to assist with public relations and the media. The public will expect to see the CEO at some point and may feel reassured if he or she can provide information and advice regarding the event. This is especially important in situations in which evacuations are required.

In many emergencies, especially those of a large scale or those which are resource intense, the CEO may be better served to interact with other decision makers in obtaining resources, making fiscal-related decisions, solving issues at the agency level, and interacting with other decision makers such as appointed and elected officials. The role of CEO is decision making at the agency level or strategic level regarding policy and public relations. Tactical decision making is the role of line supervisory personnel serving as the IC or operations chief. However, the CEO should provide guidance and direction regarding the "envelope" of operations allowable.

Interagency Operations with Local, Regional, and State Agencies

When using outside agencies for assistance, one consideration is the designation of the incident commander and using unified command. In many instances leaders from a smaller agency may be intimidated by larger agencies. The local leader should not relinquish command unless the outside resources will have more assets committed than the local agency. However, this does not mean the local leader should direct outside agencies. He or she should specify the mission for the outside agency and allow that agency direct control of its operations within parameters set by the requesting agency. The local leader should consult and involve outside agencies in a unified command structure.

The diversity of agencies involved in a unified command structure in small-scale intense events is surprising. The usual responders, law enforcement, fire service, and EMS, are expected. However, other responders who may be needed include animal control, department of public works, department of transportation, public health department, and non-governmental agencies such as Salvation Army and Red Cross, along with state- and federal-level responders. If a private industry is involved, one may see their CEO or facility manager serving within the unified command. This is common in events involving hazardous materials in which a private contractor may be used for the mitigation of the event and remediation of the site.

In some instances, the need for unified command will have law enforcement in a secondary role. Examples include large fires in which law enforcement controls a perimeter, controls crowds, assists with evacuation, and keeps traffic flowing. This is more of a supportive role to the fire service. Issues may develop when an event has components requiring fire service, EMS, and law enforcement. A common problem will be a barricaded person with a firearm in which individuals are down within sight of the shooter, and a fire involving the structure or adjacent structure is present. EMS and the fire service missions will mandate they attempt some form of rescue and fire suppression. Law enforcement will need to control the scene and remain in incident command but will need to work with fire and EMS to facilitate the needed efforts to accomplish those missions in a risk tolerable manner.

This may involve law enforcement tactical assets removing victims to hard cover for care by law enforcement tactical medical providers (best case scenario), or for the victims to be moved to locations in which non-tactical medical providers can render care. The fire service may have to fight fires in the "hot zone" defensively with remote appliances or unmanned elevated master streams.

The urge to rush into a scene and perform rescue of downed persons and fight fires must be resisted in potential tactical situations. Public safety personnel entering the kill zone provides additional targets. One should remember the secondary bomb attack in the Sandy Springs, Georgia, abortion clinic bombing, in which responders were lured into the scene by the first bomb detonated by Eric Robert Rudolph, to be targeted by a second device. Rudolph eventually killed a police officer in Birmingham, Alabama, by using similar tactics with a remote radio detonating device to trigger a large dynamite bomb near the entry of an abortion clinic. Rudolph detonated the device, concealed in a potted plant, as the officer approached and investigated the suspicious object. The blast did considerable damage to the clinic and injured a nurse entering the clinic. Some scenes involving fires have been used to lure fire service, EMS, and law enforcement personnel into the "kill zone." This tactic has become common for those targeting the government, as law enforcement and fire service personnel are the more visible representatives of government.

State and federal agencies may desire to assume the role of incident commander but the guiding caveat for the local leader remains he or she is responsible for the community and local operations. When these state and federal assets leave, the local officials will have to face the positive or negative outcomes with local constituents. However, in some events, such as a terrorist attack, the FBI is the lead agency by law. This should not exclude the local law enforcement leader from playing a role in a unified command setting.

Some local leaders have demonstrated their ire at state and federal responders by removing local assets from the incident and leaving the scene. In a recent weather-related disaster in Alabama, a police chief physically ejected representatives from a federal agency attempting to direct operations of the local agency. The local law enforcement leader should strike a balance between autonomy and ceding incident command to an outside agency. The key is to work cooperatively while maintaining input into the decision-making process. One should remember that when the event is over, the outside agencies will leave, and the law enforcement leader must answer to the citizens and elected officials of the community for the actions taken.

Interfacing with Non-Governmental Agencies and Volunteers

Although most law enforcement leaders tend to consider the non-governmental entities as "nice to haves," they play substantial roles in emergencies. The Red Cross can provide shelters for evacuees while the Salvation Army may provide meals on site to emergency responders as part of their many support functions.

Each locale will have a variety of these agencies with varying capabilities. Those with national affiliations such as the Red Cross and Salvation Army can be expected to meet certain standards. Others should be vetted. The coordination point for many of these agencies will be the local EMA office that may be able to provide a list of these agencies and their capabilities.

Some religious groups also provide these services on a local, regional, or national level. Check with local church leaders and determine if any of the churches provide such services. Some may even have their responders trained to the CERT level. A good project for social and civic clubs along with local churches is to form a Community Emergency Response Team (CERT). If the members can commit to the training and the entity purchase the emergency equipment needed (modest costs), these groups can prove to be valuable in emergencies such as severe weather, earthquake, or other widespread disasters. Other agencies may engage in specialized endeavors such as animal rescue by the Humane Society United States and Society for the Prevention of Cruelty to Animals. These agencies are well recognized have substantial experience in operating in crisis settings and are usually self-supporting.

Many response groups will have to have a disaster site cleared of hazards to operate, but those with the CERT program can operate in an autonomous manner with minor to moderate hazards present. This frees local responders for more important tasks rather than "baby sitting" non-trained volunteer groups trying to help.

In natural disasters some individuals will volunteer spontaneously to assist. In some circumstances they can provide valuable assistance until trained assets arrive. However, they sometimes present a problem for on-scene responders and can become injured themselves or find themselves in need of rescue. As soon as feasible if volunteers are present and might prove helpful, they should be assigned low-risk jobs according to agency policy. Some agencies use them to direct traffic in staging areas, unload and distribute food and water, or other non-hazardous or minimal-risk jobs. They may, operative word "**may**," be of some assistance early in the event. They should be thanked and relieved as soon as formal resources and personnel are present. One consideration is the liability of the agency for injury to the volunteer or damage to the volunteer's property used in the crisis. The agency CEO should have a policy regarding use of spontaneous volunteers, as many people will respond and want to help.

The trained volunteers with recognized groups are valuable assets. Many of the ham radio groups (amateur radio), search and rescue (SAR), mounted posse, water search and recovery units, and even dive teams are trained volunteers. Learn the units in your region and their reputation prior to using them. Some states have well-organized and well-trained volunteer self-defense forces which can provide valuable services during a natural disaster. The EMA director and other law enforcement agencies will be a good source of information. A MOU should be established specifying the call-out method to be used, the resources available, how quickly the resources can be deployed, how any costs incurred will be paid, and the method of insuring the volunteers and their equipment. As noted earlier, the MOU should be approved by your legal adviser.

Avoiding Too Many Layers of Bureaucracy during a Crisis

One of the benefits of IMS is the modular nature of the system. However, it does introduce unneeded layers of supervision in some circumstances. Some middle-level managers or even upper-level managers will attempt to insert themselves into the chain of command. In ideal situations the line supervisor should have direct access to the incident commander who has direct access of the CEO, or the IC is acting on behalf of the CEO. No more than two layers of supervision should exist between a line supervisor and the CEO or person acting on behalf of the CEO. In many instances the IC is acting on behalf of the CEO, which is the optimal setting. One of the fundamental problems with most bureaucracies is the multiple layers of supervision which must approve decisions. This impedes the flow of critical decisions and is a primary cause of communication problems and with feedback. The fewer layers the better. The ideal circumstance is the line worker is never more than two layers away from the CEO or a person acting on behalf of the CEO.

Examples of the multiple layers of decision makers and unnecessary bureaucracy can be seen during the response to Katrina. Some responders reported that they had more than 15 layers of supervision which had to approve their actions. With many layers of supervision, the cycle of approval is too long, the chances of garbled communications and misunderstood messages is high, and the lack of understanding by remote managers will be an issue.

The ability to act on behalf of the CEO must be pushed to the lowest feasible level. In most events the IC should have the authority to act unilaterally for the CEO until the CEO can take charge as the IC after arriving on scene and receiving a briefing or arriving at the EOC. During a crisis the agency must remain agile and return requests for decisions rapidly. In many events the CEO must be willing to cede decision-making authority regarding non-policy matters to IC.

Preparing for Your Next Crisis

The preparation for the next crisis should occur when the present crisis ends. As soon as feasible conduct the post-incident critique. However, prior to doing so, check with your legal advisor and determine if the resulting documents will be discoverable. If so, the critique may have to be altered for legal purposes, and some agencies, because of the discoverable nature of such reports, do not conduct post-incident critiques unless they are a legal work product in preparation for a lawsuit, to prevent their discovery.

The personnel who participated in the incident should have an opportunity to have input into the critique. Some agencies conduct round table discussions while others collect a check sheet with narrative. The number of responders participating may drive the method. The easier of the processes is to develop a checklist with narrative, which can be emailed, completed, and returned via email, or alternatively handwritten.

This allows the information to be collated, summarized, and evaluated. The evaluations should be used to determine what procedures or policies might need altering and any issues such as needed equipment or training are addressed. Some agencies make certain each responder receives a summary of the critique and proposed changes. This allows the employees who participated in the event to comment on the proposed changes.

Time is crucial in obtaining the input from the responders, developing the critique, and determining what changes are needed. In many instances, during the immediate post-event emotions, elected officials and the public will be amenable to making the needed changes to prevent a similar event, mitigate a similar event, purchase needed equipment, or conduct needed training. Act promptly to obtain the needed changes or items. The caveat is elected officials and the public will have a short memory with good outcomes but a long memory for outcomes which were not believed to be acceptable.

The law enforcement leader should have known already what areas of his or her agency were weak or in need of training or equipment and use this post-incident "emotional period" to his or her advantage. If one has a plan already assembled, with modification the plan can be quickly presented to the governing body for approval and funding.

Emergency Planning Recommendations

The recent severe weather in the eastern and southeastern US underscores the need for the ability to rapidly respond with adequate resources to mitigate the damage created by natural events such as hurricanes, floods, wildfires, and tornados. Each agency must also address the need to respond to terrorist events, technological failures such as extensive power failure, nuclear emergencies, conflagration, hazardous materials events, civil disorder, or riots.

Some of the lessons learned from recent severe weather carry over into emergency planning.

- Review emergency plans and after-action reports with "lesson learned" objectives in mind. Revise the plans to reduce bureaucracy and fund the needed changes. Do not allow problems to repeat themselves.
- When feasible, emphasize mitigation of hazards or issues rather than reactions to them.
- Remove bureaucracy from emergency operations by compressing the levels of management. Establish what emergency powers local officials have to maintain order during emergencies. This should include such curfew, closing of businesses, evacuations, and related acts.
- Use the time preceding known events such as hurricanes and floods to perform evacuations, staging of assets, and emergency response resources.
- Determine what assets are in place to communicate with the public during an emergency. This may include portable independently powered public safety and broadcast radio, portable cellular sites, satellite telephones, social media, and portable telephone switches.
- Pre-plan and establish secure evacuation centers as needed.
- Pre-plan with EMS, public health officials, and hospitals a response to a biological attack or natural disease outbreak requiring

quarantine. This could be influenza, SARS, smallpox, zoonotic diseases, or other communicable diseases.

- Pre-plan with non-governmental organizations that provide services such as the Salvation Army, Red Cross, religious organizations, and fraternal organizations.
- Pre-plan for the use of spontaneous volunteers and Community Emergency Response Teams (CERT) using volunteers based around fraternal and religious organizations.
- Emphasize self-sufficiency of the public with 72-hour kits.

Lessons Learned from Others

Failure to learn from mistakes of others and from prior events can doom one to failure with current incidents. An example is the lack of changes in the firefighting, rescue/ EMS, and law enforcement procedures from events preceding the "7/7" bombings in the UK. The King's Cross Fire in 1987 in the subway system had demonstrated that limited communications were available within the system tunnels, lack of coordination between agencies, and deficiencies in rescue capability. The ability to communicate hampered the response dramatically. These same problems were present in the "7/7" bombings of the London subway system some 20 years later with no remediation taken.

Similar issues can be seen with the lack of prior planning and communications issues with the 9/11 attacks. The World Trade Center was a prime target, as evidenced by its first bombing attack. Public safety failed to change communication plans following the initial attack and failed to recognize that follow-up attacks were imminent.

The designers of the World Trade Center considered an aircraft collision with the structures as one of the possible disaster scenarios and constructed the towers to resist them. Tom Clancy wrote a scenario in which an aircraft fully loaded with fuel and at high speed was used to destroy the nation's capitol building several years prior to the World Trade Center attack. This bestselling novel certainly was read by public safety planners and terrorists alike. If the designers of the World Trade Center and a popular novelist could see this scenario occurring, why does it appear that public safety leaders failed to grasp the potential even following a prior bombing attack? September 11th is a study, as was Pearl Harbor, in failing to conceptualize that such an event could occur and failing to prepare for it.

Chapter 2

Identification of Threats and Vulnerability

Threat Identification

Each community will have a series of threats which may be manmade or natural. The vulnerabilities will vary, with some common to most communities. The natural threats will likely be addressed in the appropriate Pre-Disaster Mitigation Plan. Pay close attention to the periodicity of events. Although this does not guarantee the event will follow a pattern, it does allow the planning cycle for the events to occur. Some natural events may have warning prior to occurrence, such as a hurricane, some floods, a tsunami, and even tornadoes. However, this warning cycle may be short and for some events, such as earthquake, flash flooding, or volcanic eruptions, little or no warning may be present.

Law enforcement leaders should pay special attention to communities with special natural hazards that pose a substantial risk to life. Those living in the shadow of a volcano, in a tsunami-susceptible area, or in earthquake-prone areas should prepare for these events even though they may appear unlikely. Volcanic lahars and mudflows present a dramatic risk to life and some warning may exist. This means a prompt notification system and exercised evacuation plans must exist. The same is true of a tsunami as only minutes from the warning to arrival may exist.

Law enforcement leaders may not be responsible directly for the plans, warning system, or exercises, but they will likely play a role in the mass notification system and evacuations. Special attention should be paid to making certain those law enforcement families and pets in the danger area are familiar with the warning system, have a family plan to evacuate, and have exercised the family plan. Mass notification systems using cellular telephone, social media, and other commercial communication systems may be overloaded or non-functional during a crisis. Secondary methods or ensuring the primary system is functional in a variety of settings is critical.

Technological Hazards

Most communities will have technological hazards, which may be a passive hazard such as power failure, or an active hazard such as a hazardous materials release. Attention should be paid to businesses and industry which may have hazardous materials. These may pose a release hazard, a fire or explosion hazard, or the hazardous materials may be a theft target. Even rural areas have substantial risks in these areas, with costly restricted pesticides a theft or terrorist target; theft of anhydrous ammonia for the manufacture of methamphetamine can be an issue (albeit less an issue now that the "shake and bake" method of manufacturing has supplanted it and imported methamphetamine has dropped in price); there may be fires or releases of these agents as well.

Hospitals can be an issue with nuclear medicine and oncology facilities. These may possess substantial quantities of radioactive material, which is a hazardous material issue or a theft target for a terrorist. Even more exotic hazards may be an issue as patients with radioactive seed implants have been known to leave the facility with the implants in place. These individuals emit enough radiation to be a hazard to others, plus the implants may detach and present an environmental radiation hazard. Law enforcement has been called to prevent the patient from leaving or to return the patient to a radiation-protected setting in the hospital. The responding officer is faced with a person emitting radiation who may refuse to return. One must confirm through public health officials the person does in fact pose a radiation danger prior to using force to place the patient in the hospital. In some cases, a court order is required to do so. The officer is faced with a minimal risk of radiation exposure, but nonetheless the risk does exist. Although an unusual event, this demonstrates the difficulty the issue of hazardous materials may pose for the law enforcement leader.

The law enforcement leader should participate in the local emergency planning committee (LEPC) conducted by the emergency management agency (EMA). This allows some knowledge of local industry and business which may possess hazardous materials, have hazardous processes, or have items which a theft prone or attractive to terrorists for theft or disruption.

Many communities have converted this hazardous materials committee to an "all hazards" committee. This also allows networking of the stakeholders in the area.

Transportation of hazardous materials is another issue. Hazardous materials transit major highways and interstates, are transported by barge or ships on rivers and by sea, and are transported by pipeline and by air. Most EMA offices will have conducted a hazardous materials study, which addresses fixed facilities and transportation hazards. This study is well worth reading.

Other sources of danger include water purification and sewage treatment facilities which may use chlorine in gas form or other toxic industrial chemicals. Many highway departments and construction firms use a portable radiation source (neutron emitter) which is used to test the density of asphalt and soil. This radiation source is a terrorist target as it could be used with an explosive to create a dirty bomb. Even medical facilities such as a dentist office are theft-prone for nitrous oxide used to obtain a "high."

Threat Groups

Every agency has threat groups operating within its region. Many areas are unaware of the existence of the groups. Agencies participating in a regional intelligence program, or with a state fusion center, or participating in a JTTF, should be aware of the existing threat groups. However, the caveat is to remember that intelligence begins with the local agencies. Several of the terrorist plots disrupted in the US have occurred because of the actions of local agencies or the intelligence provided by local agencies. If one's agency is not participating in any of these groups, one should attempt to locate one in the region or state, and determine what programs are available. Some state fusion centers appoint liaison officers within local agencies to represent an area or region. This allows sharing of non-classified but law enforcement-sensitive material.

Some terrorist groups, self-radicalized individuals, prefer rural areas for safe houses, training, logistic storage locations, and meetings. Because one's agency is rural or small does not mean threat groups are not operating in your area. Open-source information has demonstrated that the observational skills of officers may be the key to detecting a threat group. Rural officers in one jurisdiction noted increased firearms training, which led to the detection of a threat group. A routine traffic stop piqued an officer's attention, and he thought he had detected a cigarette smuggling operation. What he discovered was an international threat group operating in the US and financing its operations with cigarette sales.

Lone Wolves

Lone wolves are self-radicalized individuals who assemble a plan and conduct an operation with little or no external support. Examples include George Metesky, the "Mad Bomber" of New York City; Theodore J. Kaczynski, the Unabomber; Eric Robert Rudolph, the Olympic Park Bomber; Timothy McVeigh, the Oklahoma City Bomber; James Eagan Holmes, the shooter in the Aurora, Colorado, theater attack; and Stephen Paddock, the Las Vegas shooter. These individuals leave little signature prior to the event. The typical domestic or international terrorist group has substantial infrastructure and support operations which may be detectable. One or two individuals, if well-funded, can execute an operation which is very difficult to detect prior to its execution.

George Metesky, the "Mad Bomber" of New York City, constructed more than 30 bombs and detonated more than 20 of them, injuring more than a dozen people. He targeted theaters, telephone booths, libraries, train stations, and other structures. He was angry with Consolidated Edison over a workplace injury. He conducted a 16-year bombing spree before he was caught. Metesky had little signature, and if he had not written threat letters, he likely would not have been caught. Letters he wrote to Consolidated Edison about his injury were matched to threat letters he sent during the bombing campaign.

Ted Kaczynski, the Unabomber, conducted a bombing campaign lasting 18 years with 16 known bombs. His bombs killed three and injured more than a dozen. He had little signature, as he lived isolated in Montana, traveled by bus (paying cash), and handmade his bombs, leaving no traceable retail-sold materials behind. The bombs were hand delivered or sent via US Mail. His detection was from letters he wrote to a newspaper taking credit for the bombings and demanding his manifesto be published. When the manifesto was published, a relative recognized the document and notified law enforcement.

These two individuals with minimal external support and little money conducted well-organized terror campaigns that killed several and maimed dozens. The entire resources of law enforcement agencies nationwide failed to detect them for more than a dozen years. The lone wolf, because of these factors, may not be detectible until an operation is underway or completed, as evidenced in the Oklahoma City Bombing.

Most terrorist groups have a large support base that generates money, transmits orders, and trains, hides, and provides logistical support to a small number of leaders and a small operations group. Even though many groups use sophisticated concealment techniques, diversions, and cut outs, and have multiple and parallel groups, detection of these activities is likely. Detection may indicate the presence but may not reveal the intentions of the group. Therefore, information gathering and an intelligence program on a local level is important, as is the transmission of the information to a central state-level fusion center.

Some groups, less organized right-wing groups for instance, may use a visible leader who engages in no illegal activities but serves as a figurehead for the loosely organized group. Using legitimate communications channels, such as radio, television, Internet sites, social media, and shortwave radio, the leader emphasizes that direct action is needed. The leader is careful to use language that does not implicate himself or herself in illegal activities but requests the followers to act. This is not illegal when executed properly and allows the leader to be insulated against legal action. This is called "leaderless resistance." *The Turner Diaries*, which inspired Timothy McVey, is a printed form of leaderless resistance. The leaderless resistance concept was conceived during the 1960s Cold War era when the USSR was believed to be about to conquer the US. This technique was to be used to counter the occupation of the US by forces from the USSR.

Another issue is those who might be mentally disturbed. These individuals may have a different type of motivation. The motivation may be a result of delusions or other beliefs existing within his or her thought process. In some circumstances these factors may not be easily visible. A person being mentally disturbed does not infer a lack of intelligence, motivation, and drive to accomplish a task known only to the person. This is not to imply that every person engaged in active aggressive behavior is mentally disturbed but says that some may not have discernible motives and that the actions may not appear logical to outside observers. Those with a history of mental health issues may not be considered a threat as their actions may be viewed as non-threatening and simply part of their delusions or fantasy world. What is of interest is that data published by the FBI indicates those with mental health issues tend to have a higher casualty rate when compared to other active shooters. This could be a result of the loss of inhibitions as part of the mental health issue.

Critical Infrastructure

Depending on the view of the individual classifying critical infrastructure, a variety of facilities, highways and bridges, utilities, government entities, medical facilities, and others can be classified as critical to the needs of the community. From the law enforcement perspective, critical infrastructure includes police facilities, vehicles, fuel, power, jail, and needed support such as water, food, medical support, and bathroom facilities. The loss of power, water, or sewage service to a jail renders it unusable, just as an outbreak of a dangerous communicable disease such as SARS would render the facility unusable.

Obvious critical infrastructure includes highways, transportation facilities, fuel storage and pipelines, power generation and transmission facilities, hospitals, water treatment and sewage facilities, telephone and Internet services, radio transmission facilities, utility control systems such as SCADA, emergency shelters, and facilities providing food and groceries, medical facilities, and others. In some instances, the retail outlets for some vendors may be critical infrastructure, as they deliver vital materials such as fuel, food, and emergency supplies to the public during a crisis.

Most pre-disaster mitigation plans can provide a list of the identified critical infrastructure. In some plans the locations of the infrastructure are also provided. The plan may also provide a restoration priority list of services such as power and telephone services.

Local Critical Infrastructure versus Strategic Infrastructure

The law enforcement leader should be aware of any strategic infrastructure which may be of national importance. This may be a symbolic structure such the Statute of Liberty, or a functional structure such as a nuclear weapons storage facility or nuclear power facility. A location with national strategic importance is far more likely a target than one with only local significance. These should be identified and their protection and associated threat intelligence reviewed. Plans should be developed to prevent, respond to, and mitigate such events involving these sites.

Hackers and IT Issues

Agencies of any size experience a threat from hackers. Any computers connected to the Internet are subject to intrusion. Websites can be defaced, or a denial of service attack is possible, as is the introduction of ransomware, theft of data, or introduction of viruses. Law enforcement agencies are complacent about Internet and computer security. A knowledgeable IT staff is important in this role, and smaller agencies may need to seek an outside consultant. However, if an outside consultant is used make certain to vet his or her background.

Intrusion into an agency computer could compromise confidential information about cases, reveal the identity of confidential informants, and provide demographic data, home addresses, emails, and telephone numbers of employees. The intrusion might encrypt data, making is useless to the agency. The only certain method to prevent hacking or intrusion is to not connect the computer with sensitive data to a network or the Internet. Some agencies have adopted this practice to protect confidential informant information, personnel records, and active criminal case information.

Another substantial issue is the storage of backup data offsite. Many agencies do not back up their data or if the data is backed up, the backed-up data is stored onsite. The proper method is to back the data up onto a physical media, store it in a secure location offsite, use a secure cloud storage facility, and encrypt the data using a robust encryption program. Another alternative is to use a commercial service to store the data. If a commercial service is used one must assure that the data is well protected and encrypted. The problem with cloud use is that if a natural event or technological event occurs which causes a loss of Internet connectivity, the data in the cloud may not be accessible. Many commercial concerns, particularly non-chain businesses, fail following the loss of customer data or operational data because of fire, flood, or hurricanes. Some data from FEMA indicates that as many as a third of local businesses fail following a hurricane for financial and operational issues.

Some agencies use encryption algorithms to protect data so that if the data is stolen, decryption is difficult. If an encryption program is used, a robust program recommended by an IT expert should be chosen.

Another issue is the security of laptop computers in patrol cars or used offsite by investigators. These computers should be password protected and data encrypted. Another tactic used by some agencies is to have locking laptop mounts in the patrol cars as a theft deterrent.

The law enforcement leader should identify a member of the agency with forensic IT training or obtain forensic IT training for an investigator to serve as a resource. Computer-related crimes are common. An investigator without enough training is at a disadvantage in obtaining information from social networks, personal computers, or smart phones. In some instances, crucial evidence may be stored on a game console or cloud account. The appropriate software and hardware are required to obtain such evidentiary information following the obtaining of a search warrant.

Another serious security deficiency present in most communities is the lack of protection of supervisory control and data acquisition systems or SCADA. These system through telephone or radio control many essential utility functions such as water pumps, levels in water tanks, sewage pumps and systems, electrical switching, and building environmental controls. Many of these systems do not use encryption and can be hacked easily. One law enforcement leader was amazed to find his community had an open-radio SCADA system with no encryption. These systems controlled the city's water system, sewage system, and electrical system, servicing a population of more than 125,000 over a 90+ square mile area.

Lessons Learned from Others

One agency found their website had been defaced. The hacker had placed obscene photographs on the website and redirected those clicking on links on the site to report crimes to pornographic sites. While the law enforcement leaders directed the IT staff to address the hacking, the hacked site was a distractor. The hacker had successfully penetrated the agency's personnel files and downloaded many of the police officer's personnel files. This breach was not discovered until days later when the IT staff had an opportunity to track the hacker's movements within the agency system. The agency leader immediately contracted with a credit monitoring service to monitor those officers' credit ratings. Those with compromised files were advised immediately. After the fact the agency enhanced its protection for its website, personnel files, and criminal records.

One metropolitan police chief found himself confronted with a frantic utility services director. The utility services director indicated he just fired an employee who had access to the SCADA control systems citywide. The utility services director said the employee had threatened to shut down electrical, water, and sewage services throughout the city. The skeptical police chief soon discovered the employee could in fact follow through with his threats. The police chief suggested the utility services director change the SCADA system passwords but discovered the older system was not protected by passwords, but one only had to know the radio frequencies and the appropriate tone codes to manipulate the system. The police chief approached the former employee and explained to him in a forceful manner the significance of the threat and the criminal penalties for making such a threat or carrying out such a threat. The city replaced the aging SCADA system over the next several weeks to one which was encrypted and used a robust security system to protect it. The employee had been terminated for making death threats to the utility services director and bringing a firearm to work with him. This same employee later made threats to kill the municipality's mayor and threatened to carry out a school shooting. This resulted in the former employee's prosecution for making a terrorist threat. Some dismissed the threats as the individual appeared to have mental health issues. However, a review of data involving mass murder and shootings with multiple victims reveals those with mental health issues are common perpetrators, and these individuals tend to have a higher number of victims when compared with other shooters. Mental health issues do not guarantee action by a person, and these same issues do not prevent the person from acting on his or her threats. Such individuals should be the target of "red flag" laws if such laws exist within the jurisdiction to remove firearms from their possession.

Chapter 3

Situational Awareness

Situational awareness is practiced by most law enforcement officers. They scan for threats and to maintain an awareness of their surroundings. This hyper-vigilance is ingrained and is a sought-after skill. In the day-to-day setting use of this skill is a practical and tactical skill. However, what officers may not be aware of is they are likely practicing this skill at not only the tactical level, but also at the strategic level.

For instance, the mayor and police chief advise the media they are concerned with the influx of methamphetamine manufacturers. Officers seeing the media reports determine a strategic shift in the focus of the agency is coming and officers start learning about methamphetamine manufacturing, trafficking, and sales. The officers took a strategic change and implemented the needed tactical-level changes to already be focusing on the issue prior to the memorandum announcing the change in the focus of operations. The officers were following strategic intelligence within the agency and converting it to activities at the tactical level. This is an essential skill as strategic intelligence may not appear to affect events locally, but this intelligence can be useful for determining trends, discovering intentions of threat groups, and identifying targets and tactics used by threat groups.

Information versus Intelligence

Officers and agencies gather large amounts of information. However, until the information is synthesized into an actionable product, it remains information. Information can be gathered from a number of sources. An individual, preferably trained as an analyst, must examine the information and literally put the "pieces of the puzzle together." This may involve using computer programs to search for associates, performing link analysis or geographical analysis, or simply remembering odd facts which can link disparate pieces of data. The final product which is actionable information is called intelligence. Line officers perform this task at the tactical level daily. They place disparate pieces of information together to link individuals to criminal acts, such as by matching a BOLO to a vehicle, object, or person they observe.

Intelligence can assist in identifying vulnerabilities. Intelligence can assist in identifying criminals, criminal groups, persons of interest, and threat groups. Current intelligence can provide actionable material which may allow law enforcement to thwart crimes, plans of threat groups, or even a lone wolf.

Intelligence sources vary, but the more common one is open-source materials. These are materials within the public venue. Media reports can provide support to situational awareness; letters to the editor may assist in identifying persons of interest in regard to issues that affect a locale. Other sources include social media. A good analyst can link individuals through social media sites. Some individuals are foolish enough to comment upon criminal acts on their site, and some are stupid enough to display stolen items or even post videos of the crime itself. Photographs of individuals are obtained easily, and some may include metadata that can be used to provide a location via GPS coordinates contained in the photograph. These can be helpful during an investigation.

Some threat groups use the Internet, Internet sites, and social media to spread their views. Once again this provides the philosophy of the group and photographs of its members in some instances, and the photographs may provide locations through metadata. In several circumstances, photograph GPS metadata has located "secret" threat group firing ranges, "club houses" or "safe houses," and member residences. Even if metadata is not available and identities are obscured, the quality of firearms, perhaps vehicles, and even the style of camouflage or uniform may be revealed in the photographs. Social media is an excellent open source of information. With this in mind the agency should have a strict policy about what social media sites are used and what can be posted regarding the officer's employment, as criminals and threat groups can use the same process against agencies.

Covert sources include a variety of sources of information. One common source for criminal matters is an informant. The informant may be a criminal "working off" an offense for officers, a good citizen informant who has no personal interest in the individuals or event, a co-conspirator who "chickens out," or perhaps one of the better informants, a "mad girlfriend or spouse." These individuals can provide information of varying quality which must be corroborated through other means. One area which is not tracked in many cases is the anonymous citizen complaint or tip. They can provide valuable information and should be tracked.

No matter how insignificant the complaint or tip, it should be recorded and sent to the intelligence analyst. In many instances the analyst in smaller agencies may be an investigator assigned the duties as an added additional duty. In very small agencies, the CEO may be the investigator and analyst. A good example of a seemingly trivial complaint is an elderly woman repeatedly complained about a gunshots fired in the woods behind her residence. She kept telling officers responding to the complaint that "people were shooting machine guns." Officers discounted the information as the "little old lady" was a constant complainer until a threat group was identified as using a nearby residence. Her complaints allowed officers to locate the training area of the threat group. Officers were able to covertly observe the threat group's training and firearms proficiency. The observations allowed officers to detect illegal firearms (short-barreled shotguns and rifles converted to automatic), obtain a search warrant for the group's "safe house," and make arrests for firearms violations.

Closed-record checks can include offense reports, arrest reports, field interview cards, suspicious activity reports, and calls for service. These provide valuable data that may link suspects to other persons, locales, vehicles, or criminal acts. Although such data availability varies by locale, officers in Alabama have the ability to search statewide arrest reports, offense reports, vehicle data, correction systems data, the driver's license database with photographs, statewide driving and criminal history, traffic citation data, and criminal court cases. This tool allows any officer to search these databases from his or her patrol car. When used by an analyst this becomes a very powerful research tool.

Undercover operations are more resource intensive but can produce substantial information, as can physical surveillance. Both require a significant belief that an illegal operation is underway, and the commitment of resources may be substantial. Many smaller agencies will not have the resources for such operations. Electronic intelligence and wiretapping requires court orders and resources not found in smaller agencies. These sources of information are reserved for larger criminal operations and suspected terrorist groups.

Strategic Intelligence

Prior to 9/11, federal strategic intelligence sharing was rare. Joint terrorism task forces existed in only large agencies and little information was forthcoming. With the intelligence failures pre-9/11, the sharing of law enforcement sensitive

(LES), restricted distribution, and for official use only (FOUO) intelligence is now widespread. The average law enforcement leader is deluged with strategic intelligence if he or she is a member of Law Enforcement Online (LEO with access to FBI LES), regional information sharing systems, state-level fusion centers, Homeland Security Information Network (HSIN), InfraGard (for private sector and utilities), TRIPWIRE (for bombing prevention), Bomb Arson Tracking System (for data from the Bomb Data Center), and others. The law enforcement leader should spend several hours a week reviewing strategic intelligence. This helps the leader to see trends, prepare for potential events, see responses from other agencies, and foresee his or her agency's needs. This intelligence may also tie together trends in events the agency is seeing to an ongoing investigation or alert the law enforcement leader to what his or her officers need to be looking for in terms of tactical intelligence.

Tactical Intelligence

Tactical intelligence is information that may result from strategic intelligence in terms of what an officer should be looking for regarding behavior or trends, but this information is useful at the street level or local level. Examples of tactical information include areas in which crime occurs, those involved in local crimes or regional crimes, local crime trends, law enforcement techniques that are successful, and other useful information for the locale. What is important is the information gleaned should be sent upwards. Many smaller agencies do not have analysts, but all states have fusion centers. The role of an analyst in smaller agencies is played by investigators or the CEO.

These individuals should be seeing strategic intelligence and tactical intelligence. Criminal trends and terrorism are detected in this manner. The assembly of what appears to be random data may be sufficient to detect a pattern or trend in criminal activities.

Tactical intelligence is gathered in a variety of methods. An analyst should be examining arrest reports, offense reports, field contact cards, traffic citations, and calls for service. Online forums also present a fertile source of information as do social media.

To perform risk assessment one must know what threats exist. The threat may be natural or manmade. The key is to identify the threats that affect the agency, area, or event. The threat must be quantified in terms of severity and likelihood that the threat will be affecting the operation, agency, event, or locale. This is the first step in determining what risks are present and to what extent they may affect an event, locale, or agency, plus the likelihood must be considered. Some threats will be remote, provide minimal risks, and are unlikely, while others will be likely, local, and present a substantial effect should they occur.

Vulnerabilities

These are weaknesses which affect the health, safety, and wellbeing of persons and assets. These weaknesses can be exploited to kill or injure persons, disrupt an event or system, deny access to an asset, of damage or destroy the asset. These may range from a lack of training, inadequate equipment, lack of personnel, and lack of planning or threat assessment, to poor protective intelligence, poor operating procedures, or poor physical security.

One can also associate vulnerabilities to a specific function or part of physical security, such as the lack of perimeter fencing or poor protective intelligence. In some circumstances vulnerabilities may not be detected by those planning an event or developing plans, therefore, this makes flexible plans a necessity. The law enforcement leader must be agile mentally and be able to adapt to a dynamic situation for which no formal plan exists.

Effects

The effects are the results that can be expected should the vulnerability be exploited. These may range from inconvenience to a loss of life. The typical terrorism effect will be to generate fear through substantial media coverage of the loss of life and substantial destruction of a physical asset. Criminals will want to be able to obtain something of value which can be converted to currency. This includes information or physical objects. One must couple the likelihood of the worst case outcome with the probability of the effect occurring should the vulnerability be exploited. The lack of a perimeter fence as cited earlier might in a minimal event simply inconvenience security personnel with people in the wrong area, or the lack of perimeter fencing might allow a criminal to steal valuable assets, damage or destroy assets, or to attack a principal.

$$\text{Risk} = \text{Threat} \times \text{Vulnerability} \times \text{Effect}$$

The formula used to quantify the risk is the threat multiplied with vulnerability and effect. One can see that high numbers (meaning a substantial threat, risk, or serious damage, injury, death) will provide a larger number. The higher the number the more substantial the risk, but reducing any one category to a one or reducing the three categories modestly brings the risk number down significantly. Many of the measurements will be of a subjective and qualitative nature rather than an exact measurement. This data should be used as a guide and not seen as an absolute.

People are the more important asset to be protected from injury regardless of how the injury is inflicted. This may include natural events such as severe weather, earthquake, flood, or lightning strike, or may include manmade events such as robbery, assault, collapse of a structure because of faulty construction, release of a hazardous material, or terrorist attack. The effects include injury, loss of life, and permanent impairment.

Information can be the target of an attack. This may be a denial of service attack in which a resource is flooded with requests and is unable to be utilized, or this could be the theft of information, the physical disruption of fiber optic cable carrying information, or the destruction of equipment such as radios which transmit or receive information. The more common attack will be a denial of service or "hacking" in which information compromised. The defenses against such an attack require a knowledgeable IT staff with physical and electronic firewalls. One technique used with success is social engineering, in which through phishing a user reveals his or her account and password.

In other circumstances by using public information a hacker may be able to construct a user name and password. Many individuals use a password with some form of their name and a common date such as a date of birth. This may enable a hacker to use combinations to break a simple password. A pass phrase is recommended such that the person constructs a logical sentence and uses the first letter of each word in the sentence along with a series of numbers and special characters. "I enjoy the opera on Wednesday afternoons in March" would be IetooWaiM coupled with a series of numbers and special characters, making the password more secure.

Equipment may be attacked directly through sabotage or indirectly, such as by disrupting a power supply. This may cause the inability to operate equipment, which might be a radio transmitter, a fiber optic hub, a gasoline pump, or powered gate. Taking the attack to the extreme, a SCADA system could be compromised and the water supply to a city disrupted or power to a city disrupted.

Facilities can be damaged by illegal entry in which damage is done or by non-violent means through denial of use. A common tactic used by some environmental activists is to handcuff or chain themselves together using metal or PVC pipe to cover their hands making it difficult for police to remove the locking systems. The courts have been mixed in terms of the allowable force which can be used to cause the protesters to release themselves. Reasonable efforts should be made to avoid using force to make protesters to release themselves. One court ruled that the application of oleoresin capsicum (OC or pepper spray) using swabs was excessive force but in another federal circuit, after officers had tried several methods to remove sleeping dragons (a protestor maneuver that links protesters together in ways that are difficult to break), the use of OC was affirmed as reasonable. If one views the circumstances of the 2011 UC Davis event in which officers used OC against peaceful protesters not allowing officers to leave, while the crowd presented a substantial threat, the officers involved were disciplined or terminated. This puts officers in a tenuous position in which they will be second guessed regarding the use of OC against those resisting arrest in a peaceful manner.

Social impacts from disruption or attacks may include fear. Terrorists have used attacks and threats to prevent voters from going to polling places and voting or to prevent attendance of other social functions. The IRA was adept in targeting theaters for bombings, while the Mad Bomber kept New Yorkers on edge for years with his bombs in a variety of locations. The Unabomber used his campaign of terror against universities and businesses involved in technology for more than a dozen years. A good example of fear is the panic purchasing of gasoline following the 9/11 attacks. The attacks had absolutely no influence on the supply of fuel, yet out of fear, many areas of the country experienced gasoline shortages because of panic buying. Similar fears following the US Mail anthrax attacks in which many citizens were fearful of any white powdery substances. Law enforcement was deluged with calls about white powder for months in which few if any were credible. Even today many citizens are fearful of any white powdery substance in an unusual location.

Common Threats

Criminal action whether internal or external to an event should be a consideration. Many criminal acts can be deterred by visible security and access control. The more common issues will be theft, burglary, and robbery.

Protesters will be a consideration in some events. Developing intelligence to determine what events might be a target of protests is important. This means one must have knowledge of the area threat groups and maintain situational awareness of events which might attract outside threat groups.

Terrorism should be a consideration for any large contingent of people. Terrorism has shifted from symbolic targets to softer targets. Numerous deaths and injuries will generate the headlines need to induce fear. Therefore, this should be a consideration at any event. In most cases the risk will be minimal, but the potential should not be discounted.

Severe weather such as a tornado or severe thunderstorm present obvious hazards, but other less obvious threats are heat and high humidity. Heat exhaustion and heat stroke are substantial risks to a large group of individuals exposed at an event with high temperatures and high humidity. One must have the ability to shelter or evacuate those exposed to lightning, tornadic winds, hail, or other phenomena such as flash floods. However, one must also be prepared to provide cooling locations, hydration locations, and medical personnel when individuals will be exposed to high temperatures and high humidity.

Technical failures can include systems which may support communications, power, computer systems, access to the Internet, HVAC in structures, or failure of portions of a structure. An overlooked issue for any event is the survey of the physical structure by a qualified individual to not only ascertain if the structure can accommodate the number of persons in terms of life, health, and safety codes, but also assure the weight and movement of persons will be supported by the structure. Collapses of structures because of loading is not an uncommon event.

Unplanned events include emergencies which are by their nature unforeseen. These events are troublesome as an incident manager has had little preparation regarding the event and the factors surrounding it. This requires "catch up" planning and response. A phenomenon which is affecting public safety is the use of social media to rally persons to a location. This may result in a flash mob. Some events even have live video fed to the Internet with multiple viewers. The intelligence function within the Law Enforcement Incident Management System should make an effort to monitor blogs and social media sites to determine what information is posted or if live video feeds are occurring.

Unprepared personnel can cause an issue. Personnel without sufficient training are a liability. They may place themselves at risk and even require rescue. The key for the incident manager is to know the capabilities and training level of the personnel involved and not commit those with inadequate training.

Measurements can be made qualitatively with the factors assessed subjectively and verbally, or a quantitative assessment may be used with specific factors assigned a numeric value. The preferred method is to qualitatively assess an incident; however, this may not be feasible during an event. Those events with lead time allowing planning should have qualitative assessment performed.

Qualitative Assessment

Critical: a substantial risk to this incident
High: the danger is known to exist

Medium: a potential danger exists

Low: not a credible danger

Vulnerabilities

Critical: no countermeasures in place; this vulnerability can be exploited

High: some countermeasures are in place, but they may not be adequate

Medium: countermeasures are in place, but some vulnerability remains

Low: effective countermeasures have reduced the ability to use the vulnerability

$$Risk = Threat \times Vulnerability \times Effect$$

Risk Calculation

Value and Rank	Threat	Vulnerabilities	Effect
4. Critical	Confirmed Threat	Ineffective Countermeasures	Catastrophic, loss of life, disruption of operations
3. High	Credible Threat	Some Effective Countermeasures	Serious Injuries and disruption of operations
2. Medium	Potential Threat	Very Effective Countermeasures	Moderate Injuries or disruption of operations
1. Low	Low Credibility	Multiple Layers of Countermeasures	Minimal effects

Risk Levels

Value	Level	Caveats
36–64	Extreme	All factors are high and at least one critical factor
24–35	High	Two or more factors high and none low
16–23	Moderate	No more than two factors high
8–15	Low	All factors moderate to low
1–7	Minimal	No high or critical factors present

Managing Risk

In some incidents the risk can be managed by countermeasures or elimination of the threat factor. Several actions are available to the incident manager.

Possible actions serving as countermeasures:

If an event, cancel it
Prevent or deter threats
Establish safety procedures
Additional training and equipment
Redundant systems

Chapter 4

Resources

In some instances, if countermeasures are not enough or attainable with the resources available and the targeted incident is an event, consider cancelling the event. Other factors may be to institute countermeasures such as fencing to deter illegal entry or theft. Plan and train personnel to counter specific threats such as crowd control while using technology and equipment to defeat threats. This may be in the form of PPE or additional operational equipment such as closed-circuit video surveillance, magnetometers, etc. Critical systems can have redundant features such as generator power for offsite power failures. The final mitigation strategy is the use of adequate resources to respond to a crisis should one occur. The downside to this type of countermeasure is that it presumes other countermeasures have failed and the incident has occurred, requiring outside resources to mitigate the effects rather than to prevent the failure. Prevention is the obvious mitigation tactic of choice.

Potential Threats

Terrorism should be a consideration in all events and incidents; however, most planned events will have minimal chances of attack by terrorists, but this does not prevent a self-radicalized person or a person with a perceived grievance from attacking. This does not rule out a local person with mental health issues who might cause an incident or attack an event. The potential for terrorism, no matter how unlikely, must be considered at any incident and during any planned event.

Active shooters or an attack by a person using other weapons (such as knives, IEDs, incendiary devices, or vehicles, which is called active aggressive behavior) present a threat to any gathering of people. The vulnerability reduction from an active shooter or active aggressive behavior occurs in concentric circles of protection. The outer layer is protective intelligence whereby organizations and law enforcement track threat groups and behavior consistent with that of active shooters and active aggressive behavior. The problem herein is that some persons and groups exhibit the behaviors which indicate they may become a threat and may even make a threat, but do not follow through with the threat. Another issue is in many instances those with mental health problems may exhibit normal behavior if they take prescribed medications. Upon stopping the medications, the original mental health issue returns with the associated abnormal behavior. With budget constraints, many of those institutionalized persons with mental health issues are returned to their previous environment where they do not take their medications and many act out. However, some are identified and stopped. The second layer of protection is the physical security of a facility or venue. These facilities or venues with high risk, such as a densely occupied stadium, should have enough staff in place to perform magnetometer screening and screening of hand-carried items. Events should have threat assessment performed and the likely threats prepared for in terms of mitigating the threat. Screening and magnetometers may eliminate many edged weapons and firearms but are not capable of detecting non-metallic edged weapons, incendiaries, or IEDs. Hand search of carried items may reduce these threats at a fixed venue. The next layer is response. Those occupying a venue or facility should be trained to respond to an active shooter or active aggressive behavior by fleeing the location, hiding in secure locations, or as a last resort, fighting with the actor. Law enforcement response and mitigation efforts to aid the injured are the final layer. Unless law enforcement is physically present, the likelihood is the actor will have completed his or her mission and committed suicide. Terrorists and committed actors will continue their shooting or violent spree until ammunition is expended or the actor is neutralized. The means an organized and prompt response by law enforcement is needed along with EMS to attend the injured. In many instances, especially in rural jurisdictions, the first (and sometimes only officer available) must locate, isolate, and engage the shooter or other person engaged in aggressive behavior.

Improvised explosive devices (IEDs) are a threat in any setting. In many instances this will be a criminal act rather than an act of terrorism. Common uses of IEDs include revenge attacks, vandalism, as a distraction while another crime occurs, experimentation by juveniles, and terrorism. The usual screening methods of persons with a magnetometer and bag screenings will likely defeat many of the more common IEDs. However, a sophisticated device may be concealed in several parcels or upon the bodies of several persons, and more rarely, within the body of person. These may defeat common detection methods.

IEDs may be concealed within a vehicle or the vehicle used to transport the embedded IED (vehicle-borne IED or VBIED) with the vehicle used to penetrate barriers. The other factor may be a person-borne IED (PBIED) or suicide bomber. Remember, if one concentrates persons outside a venue to be screened, these are an inviting target for an IED. The use of the IED may be to attract media attention and instill terror in those present. Even a bomb threat or threat of an active shooter can disrupt an event and attract media attention.

Protestors can be an issue within themselves, with an incident, or at an event. The key is intelligence. One should have some foresight of events which may attract protestors or at least be familiar with the protest group and the tactics used. A protective intelligence failure can be critical and law enforcement assets overwhelmed if proper preparation is not made for known events. Most protest groups will be peaceful, but some engage in violent tactics designed to destroy property and injure law enforcement. Some common tactics include the protestors wearing protective equipment such as helmets, body armor, and air-purifying respirators to defeat tear gas and OC (pepper spray) and using impact tools. Some use thrown objects and incendiaries against law enforcement. Some protest groups video record the event and a few bring lawyers with them to observe the protest to intimidate law enforcement.

Crowds are a substantial issue at any incident or event. The potential for mob violence or stampedes is always an issue of concern, as is the attack of the crowd using firearms, IEDs, incendiaries, edged weapons, or vehicles. However, the crowd demographic may predict the issues. With events serving alcohol the demographic will make a difference. One would expect little threat from a crowd at the opera serving "fine wine and cheese" as opposed to a rock concert serving beer. The function of law enforcement at the "wine tasting" opera event would be to protect the patrons from external threats, whereas beer-imbibing rock fans with festival seating would present a substantial threat to themselves and law enforcement. Crowd composition matters in terms of the predicted behavior and services needed to support an event or incident.

Severe weather is an issue in many incidents and events. The weather may present problems, and weather continues to be a major threat in outdoor events. In some incidents and events, the threat of lightning, high winds, heavy rain, or temperature extremes will adversely affect operating conditions. The provision for cooling and hydration stations in warm, humid climates is essential, as are restroom facilities, which are sometimes a neglected consideration. Further, one must anticipate what one will do if severe weather is imminent or occurs. Where are shelters and are they adequate? Some weather-related phenomena can be predicted, such as approaching storms, hurricanes, and even tornadoes, while others may happen with minimal warning, such as a "pop up" thunderstorm or "bolt out of the blue" lightning strike. When feasible, the incident manager should check the weather forecast. Many National Weather Service Offices will provide detailed short-term forecasts for incidents or events. For a long-lived incident such as a state fair or multiday festival in which weather is a critical factor, some weather service offices may deploy a team to the site.

Hazardous materials events can cause issues which may involve evacuations, large numbers of persons injured and contaminated, road closures, and other operational issues. The role of law enforcement is supportive in most cases unless the event involves an act of terrorism or suspected crime. Anhydrous ammonia theft for manufacturing methamphetamine has led to substantial releases, but as the methods of manufacture of methamphetamine have changed, this type incident is no longer common. Hazardous materials may be located within a fixed facility or transported via pipeline, rail, air, or roadway. Most EMA offices will have a hazardous materials transportation study which details the type and quantities of hazardous materials along with fixed sites with hazardous materials as required by the Superfund Amendments and Reauthorization Act (SARA).

System failure or communications failure present substantial risks that these failures may impede the ability of law enforcement to accomplish their mission. Even the loss of Internet connectivity may downgrade the ability of agencies to control an incident or protect a venue. Some states have placed the driver's license, crime reporting modules, uniform traffic citations, and motor vehicle crash reporting modules online such that Internet connectivity is required to use these databases and to generate any of these completed forms. Younger officers who never had to handwrite reports or traffic citations and use voice communications to obtain data may find these procedures cumbersome and slow.

Unprepared personnel are a common issue. Personnel may be assigned positions for which they have had little training and no experience. While law enforcement personnel are generalists, they may have little training or experience with physical security and screening of items or people. They may also view this as a job beneath their qualifications and in doing so not apply enough attention to the task.

Sustained power failure is an issue which can be crippling. Many emergencies will involve power failure, and events with large crowds can be especially adversely affected. Buildings without emergency power to supply the high volume air conditioning (HVAC) become uninhabitable quickly. Traffic lights do not work, one cannot pump gasoline, purchases cannot be made with credit cards, water pressure drops, sewage begins to back up, cellular telephones fail, and other essential systems fail. One must carefully examine what systems are critical and make certain these systems have a power supply. Especially critical will be radio communications, as commercial services should not be relied upon. Facilities must be available to recharge portable radios, pump gasoline for vehicles, and run the HVAC of essential structures such as the communications center and jail.

Isolation or loss of outside support is one of the more common scenarios following a large-scale disaster such as Hurricane Katrina, western US wildfires, or flooding. Agencies and individual officers must have a continuity of operations plan for agency and employees' families. One issue is to provide a dedicated shelter for public safety families and their pets. This facilitates officers knowing their families are safe and allows them to concentrate on the mission.

Managing Vulnerabilities

Some of the tactics which are useful in reducing vulnerabilities include:

- Increase training and equipment for those responsible for the event or operation
- Increase external resources such as mutual aid units
- Establish backup systems for critical systems such as power, surveillance, intrusion detection systems, lighting, and communications
- Establish special units with needed resources, which might include units to respond to civil disturbances, tactical events, or mass casualty events
- Acquire additional technology and support to replace personnel or improve their capabilities with communications, mobile computing, or enhanced surveillance

Mitigating Impact

This can include a variety of tactics including response and coordination of the incident.

- Operational security is critical during every phase but is of concern during a response. The use of encrypted radios and code is recommended.

- Onsite EMS and fire services can reduce the response time and enhance familiarity of the venue for these responders.
- Interoperability of communications is critical. Responders should be able to communicate on scene with each other and a unified command is recommended.
- The public information function is important. This should be staffed by a person with enough training and background to be able to provide intelligent and accurate information in a timely manner to the media and through social media.
- External resources should have been addressed in the IAP and exercises, if feasible, prior to the event.
- Evacuation plans are essential and will vary by type. One type of evacuation will be needed for severe weather versus others for fires or a bomb threat. Even something as mundane as wind direction may be a critical factor in evacuations if a hazardous material might be involved.

Specialized Equipment and Scene Control

Scene assessment may require specialized equipment such as thermal imagers, low-light optics, canines, robots, bomb suits, air-purifying respirators (APRs), self-contained breathing apparatus (SCBA), chemical protective clothing, or overhead surveillance by aircraft or drone. Knowing the locations and acquisition method for this specialized equipment and personnel and knowing one might require it prior to its need is essential.

Scene control will involve more than stringing yellow police tape around the venue. Scene control will include limiting egress and ingress to the site, managing traffic related to the event, segregating those injured or contaminated, and keeping arterial access routes open. A necessity will be tangible perimeters, which may consist of police line tape, barricades, or personnel.

Access points will need to be established. Based upon the type of event, credentialing may be needed to assure only authorized personnel are allowed on site. Staging areas will need to be secure and when feasible siting near an access point is needed. The access points will need to transition from secure to non-secure areas using tangible barriers and personnel as needed.

The use of layered security is important. This should include an inner perimeter and at least an outer perimeter. Some agencies prefer functional areas such as staging and triage areas inside the outer perimeter; however, depending upon the assets available to guard them, these areas may have to be established independently and secured separately. An important consideration is the type of event. Those involving hazardous materials, gunfire, or explosions will likely have very large outer perimeters. The larger the perimeter, the more porous and less secure the perimeter becomes.

Scene security is important, and officers should not only face inward, they should also be conducting counter surveillance outward. This is to detect secondary devices, individuals involved in swarm attacks targeting on-scene responders, or those with an abnormal interest in the operations. Some agencies video record crowds to locate potential suspects, especially at fires. If credentialing is required, officers should scrutinize those onsite and those attempting to enter to determine whether they are wearing valid credentials.

Infrastructure protection on scene will include not only the physical site but also the command post and the essential infrastructure of the response, which may include specialty vehicles and equipment. Personnel should be assigned to guard these locations to prevent attack, tampering, or theft. This might also include generators supplying power and the HVAC system. The HVAC system may be especially vulnerable. In several incidents, including a shopping mall and a college dormitory facility, the introduction of tear gas or oleoresin capsicum (OC or pepper spray) has resulted in multiple casualties and evacuation of the affected facilities. Although these substances are not likely to cause death or injury directly, stampedes from them have caused multiple fatalities, those with respiratory compromise from asthma and chronic obstructive pulmonary diseases will be adversely affected, and deaths have occurred in these circumstances from the medical conditions following exposure to tear gas or OC.

Crowd control will be an issue at many events and incidents. Crowd dynamics will vary based upon the crowd size, the crowd composition, the crowd purpose, and the event purpose. Crowds attending a venue are more likely to have less "mob like" behavior and more of a "stampede type" behavior. Exceptions will include crowds with access to alcohol or those attending some sports matches, such as soccer games. These crowds may have spontaneous fights or mob behavior and can be hostile to other parties and law enforcement. One issue is that the use of OC in crowds may cause a stampede, injuring many individuals in the crowd.

Flash mobs can be a spontaneous mob gathering at an incident or attracted to law enforcement operations. Some flash mobs are mobilized via social media, telephone or email trees, or by word of mouth. This has become an issue with some groups, such as sovereign citizens and left-wing radical groups, who may be hostile to law enforcement. Their use of "telephone trees" and social media are cause for concern. This type gathering is a common tactic used by sovereign citizens and anarchists to intimidate and hinder law enforcement operations.

Tactics used by law enforcement may vary based upon the intent or actions of the crowd, the size of the crowd, its location, and the available resources. In some cases, establishing containment of the crowd may be necessary, or, if outnumbered, a strategic withdrawal may be needed. The key is to maintain officer safety, balancing the need for law enforcement action versus the threat posed to officers.

Operational impacts of special events and incidents will vary but usually include delays in answering routine calls for service, disruption of response to minor incidents, consumption of overtime monies, and loss of surge capacity. Extended operations may preclude maintenance of equipment and accelerate equipment failure, while the loss of down time for officers may increase stress levels and decrease performance abilities. The agency should address the maximum number of hours allowable to work, the use of overtime, and the use of reserve or mutual aid personnel to minimize these effects. Some agencies limit work hours to no more than 12 hours in a 24-hour period for planned events and no more than 16 hours for unplanned events. However, this may not be feasible when contingencies occur. Some law enforcement personnel have worked many hours beyond these limits with little or no rest. The issue of performance degradation and vigilance fatigue becomes a considerable issue in such circumstances. The likelihood for injury and negative performance become more common when insufficient rest and sleep ensue in such events.

Lessons Learned

During one hurricane, an agency deployed its full 160 personnel at the peak of the storm. The resulting issue was how to transition from a full deployment to a 50% deployment once the hurricane's major impacts passed, as officers had been on duty a minimum of 24 hours with some going 36 hours without rest or sleep (the agency worked 12-hour shifts). This was unplanned for in procedures and not addressed. The command staff struggled and eventually decided to send those personnel with the longest period of service home for 12 hours. Public safety families and pets were safely sheltered in public safety-only shelters. Officers secured their families and pets and returned home. The issue then became that many officers started repairs and dealt with contingencies at home rather than resting or sleeping. Many were unable to return to duty even following 12 hours off duty. This led to a shortage of personnel on duty, but those on duty facing more than 24 continuous duty had to be released. Many encountered contingencies at their homes and were in a similar condition as those first released, with an even larger number of personnel not returning to duty. The agency managed to continue to provide an adequate service but at the expense of fatigued personnel and the loss of efficiency. No injuries or negative outcomes were attributed to the failure of the agency's hurricane response plan, but many officers were very unhappy and expressed their concern with how the plan was executed. The agency decided that future deployments would be limited to 16 hours with a mandatory eight hours off duty. Procedures were put into place to have external contractors, at the expense of the agency, to respond and secure officer's residences to perform emergency roof and window repairs. This afforded the agency an assurance that it would have sufficient personnel to staff its needs.

During an airshow at a regional airport a pop-up thunderstorm caused a substantial threat as inadequate shelter was available when the thunderstorm approached. The show organizers only had about 15 minutes of warning before the storm began to produce quarter-sized hail. No plan was in place to shelter the crowd. Many attendees sought shelter under the wings of parked aircraft, violated restricted areas, and some sheltered in nearby hangers hastily opened. Many minor injuries were caused by crowd movement knocking attendees down, strikes by hailstones, and even individuals striking propellers and antennas of the parked aircraft in their haste to seek shelter. The publicity of the incident led to the cancellation of this and future air shows at this venue.

Chapter 5

Terrorism

Terrorism in many cases is defined from the perspective of the observer. Many who call themselves "freedom fighters" are defined as terrorists by other segments of a society. A common definition of terrorism is the use of unlawful violence to effect social or political change. One can use this broad definition to include organized crime, outlaw motorcycle gangs, and street gangs. In countries such as Mexico, narcotics traffickers and organizations use tactics to induce terror in the society and do meet the definition of terrorists as given above. A term used occasionally is "narco-terrorism."

Some organizations have used the term "hate group" to address groups which may only be a proto-terrorist group. This term can accurately describe many groups which espouse hatred toward an ethnic group, culture, sexual orientation, or lifestyle. In some instances, the hate group "hates" anyone not a member of the group. Others use the term "threat group," which provides a more generic representation of the group.

Does it matter if the shooter is a terrorist or "crazy" when officers respond to an active shooter? The answer the public provides is "no," however, to law enforcement the difference may be substantial. A mentally disturbed person may conduct a well-planned assault and kill many people; however, this is usually an individual, not a group, and the resources involved will be minimal. The shooter will likely commit suicide but in a few cases may respond to negotiations.

Terrorism-related active shooters are likely part of a parallel or swarm attack and will be armed with substantial long guns, be well trained, and possibly have explosives such as hand grenades or pipe bombs. Terrorists will attempt to kill as many individuals as possible and will have to be neutralized by law enforcement. They are not likely to negotiate, as the dogma of the terrorist group will prohibit it. In this case, law enforcement must take immediate steps to intervene.

In most hostage situations the event is a crime "gone wrong" and not a planned event. The hostage-takers will negotiate. Terrorists have the event well planned and intend to kill many individuals, including law enforcement. This means an assault to neutralize the terrorists is a first resort rather than a last resort, as is used in traditional hostage situations. The terrorists intend to die fighting.

Single and Multiple Focus Groups

Terrorists come with many motivations. A few groups are single focus or have a philosophy which provides a narrow interest. Examples include animal welfare, anti-war, anti-abortion, and some environmental groups. Groups such as sovereign citizens are anti-government but tend to accept anyone as a member, while other terrorist or hate groups only allow persons with certain ethnic or racial characteristics to join. Sovereign citizens have a focus which is anti-government and do not accept the US government as legitimate.

More common are the multiple focus groups. These groups tend to have a broader spectrum of interests. Some anti-abortion groups are also anti-government, as the government sanctions abortion, while the same group also opposes LGBTQ rights. They see the government as approving, as some locales allow same-sex marriages. Others dislike anyone who is not from a specific racial or ethnic group, oppose immigration, are anti-government, and may even support a narrow religious focus.

In the past many groups could be defined by the group's philosophy and area of interest. However, with the advent of the Internet, recruitment, propaganda, and funding have become easier, allowing many terrorist groups to diversify in several areas of interest. This is true of domestic groups, especially right-wing groups, which have been anti-government and demonstrate hatred for those of varying ethnic and racial groups. They have added opposition to some religious groups and even oppose those of some political parties.

The use of the Internet has allowed organizations to become decentralized and operate without formal structures. "Leaderless resistance" is a useful concept in which leaders of the hate group or terrorist organization can exhort members to take direct action in speeches and programs carefully crafted to avoid any suggestion of illegality.

Devoted followers may act upon the instruction by attacking the identified enemies of the group. This allows the leadership plausible deniability and does not cost the leadership resources or money. The group can covertly take responsibility for the actions and use the publicity to spur other followers to act. Amorphous groups such as Anonymous have used these tactics with substantial success.

Soft Targets

The switch in targets from symbolic targets using explosives to attacking poorly defended targets with firearms, vehicles, and explosives is now common. The attack of students in schools and private citizens in hotels and shopping malls has become an issue as they present poorly protected target-rich environments, since the target is people, not infrastructure. Killing to invoke terror is the object of terrorists, while others may be killing to gain attention. An example would be the attempted assassination of President Reagan, in which John Hinckley Jr. attempted to attract the attention of media star Jodie Foster by shooting the President.

Response to Active Shooters

Active shooters have been an issue for law enforcement for many years, but the media attention, especially in school shootings, has made the public aware of the events. Deaths in schools from criminal actions were notable in the 1920s–1930s, with the 1927 Bath, Michigan, school bombing killing more than 40 and the school explosion in New London, Texas, in 1937 killing almost 300. Charles Whitman, the Austin, Texas, tower shooter, killed 14 and wounded dozens in 1966. In 1984 James Huberty killed more than 20 in a McDonald's restaurant in California and wounded almost as many. Contemporary shootings at Columbine, Colorado, Connecticut, and Florida underscore the issue that a single person, usually mentally disturbed, can kill dozens prior to police intervention or the shooter committing suicide. In fact, many active shooters commit suicide prior to police confrontation. These events are over in minutes and the actions taken onsite by potential victims during the event determine, in many incidents, how many are injured or killed.

Law enforcement must train to respond to such attacks to neutralize an active shooter, but if officers are faced with trained terrorists seeking a "soft target," conventional tactics may not be adequate. A siege such as the Beslan school siege (in Russia in 2004) is likely to end with many fatalities. The mentally disturbed person will likely self-destruct, but terrorists will attempt to gain media attention with a dramatic event that ends only when they are neutralized. The shooting of hostages in public view may be a tactic used. If the event presents as a terrorist event, the tactic should be containment followed by an assault as soon as feasible.

EMS Issues

In a multiple-casualty situation EMS assets may be overwhelmed. The law enforcement agency must be prepared for improvised EMS tactics. Initially officers will ignore the injured to assure the shooter or shooters are neutralized. However, once this task is completed the officers may be faced with dozens of injured persons. Immediate intervention with tactical medical training may literally save lives. This is now becoming a follow-up action by some agencies in that officers may distribute bleeding control kits (plastic bags containing visual and written instructions with non-sterile gauze and elastic-type tape to control external bleeding) to those victims conscious and make emergency intervention once the law enforcement mission is complete, while awaiting EMS resources. A necessity for the officer's own protection is a basic knowledge of tactical medicine. Courses such as the four-hour Downed Operator Casualty Care Course offered by TacMed Essentials are critical. Additional training for EMTs and paramedics is also available and recommended, such as the 40-hour TacMed Essentials program. Tactical teams and special operations groups should have an officer trained as an EMT or preferably a paramedic with the additional formal tactical medicine skills as an organic member. A less optimal solution is to use EMS providers with tactical medicine training.

Response to Bombings

Bombings are rare but present unique issues for officers responding. A bomb is an inexpensive and easily manufactured device to target a specific person, symbolic target, infrastructure, or group of persons. The usual tactic is to injure many persons to garner media attention or complete the desires of the bomber to destroy a target for personal reasons.

One consideration the responding officers must consider is whether the bomb is a distraction for a conventional crime such as a robbery. A common bank robbery tactic is to call in a bomb threat to a school and while officers are engaged in a search or perhaps an evacuation, a bank is robbed.

Another consideration is whether the bomb threat is a ruse to create an evacuation to allow shooters to ambush those leaving a protected building. This tactic was used by the juvenile school shooters in Jonesboro, Arkansas, who pulled a fire alarm in the school and shot students and teachers as they evacuated the school.

- Is the explosion designed to have public safety responders on scene as targets?
- Are secondary devices present? Observe the area and consider vehicle-borne improvised explosive devices (VBIEDs) or pre-placed improvised explosive devices (IEDs), and check nearby vehicles for their status, as being stolen, having mismatched tags, or being a rental vehicle should be suspect.
- Will the bomber engage responders with rifle fire?
- Is a person-borne improvised explosive device (PBIED) worn by an onlooker, or person injured, to target responders with a suicide bomb?
- Is this the start of parallel or swarm attacks?
- Is the target infrastructure designed to amplify other attacks? If the target attacked removes substantial abilities to operate, such as by loss of power, water, communications, or transportation, other attacks may be imminent.
- Always have officers facing outward and providing security for responders, including protecting the law enforcement command post and vehicles.
- Treat explosions as a criminal or terrorist act until proven otherwise.

Response to Suicide Bombings

Suicide bombings, better described as a person-borne improvised explosive device (PBIED), are not common in the US but have occurred and have been attempted. Some of these attempts have occurred in a school setting with bombers using common metallic pipe bombs or other expedient IEDs. The more common filler in a pipe bomb is smokeless powder, but with TATP and related explosives becoming common, one must consider that this very unstable explosive may be the filler. This makes shooting a potential PBIED likely to cause detonation. The current procedure with many agencies is to target areas outside where the PBEID may be carried. This may leave an officer in a situation in which he or she must make a head shot with a handgun. With skill levels among many officers mediocre and the distance needed to be maintained to prevent injury from an explosion, this tactic becomes problematic.

Targets sought by suicide bombers will likely be a densely populated locale. One must consider suicide bombings as the opening for parallel or swarm attacks. Responders are at risk for secondary devices or worse, secondary PBIEDs.

Most suicide bombers will not be compliant to officer commands. If a suspect approaches an officer and states he or she is wearing a PBIED, the officer should take defensive maneuvers and take cover. The suspect should not be allowed to approach or leave, and some agencies allow officers to engage a suspect with gunfire under these circumstances. Agency policies should dictate the engagement rules, but the suspect should not be engaged with gunfire in areas in which the shot may strike the device when feasible. A strike by a bullet may detonate the IED. However, should a potential suicide bomber be compliant to officer commands, the officer should have the suspect undress while the officer remains in a position of cover while observing the suspect. Removal of clothing should reveal a PBIED present unless the device is secreted in the rectum. The officer should not approach the suspect even if no device is visible but should have the suspect prone out on the ground and await bomb technicians. Using binoculars to examine the suspect is recommended and officers should pay attention to the rectal area for protruding wires with a switch. Approach is usually undertaken by a bomb squad or tactical robot to minimize danger to law enforcement personnel.

Person Borne Improvised Explosive Device. This is a re-creation of a PBIED. Photograph by Jim Smith.

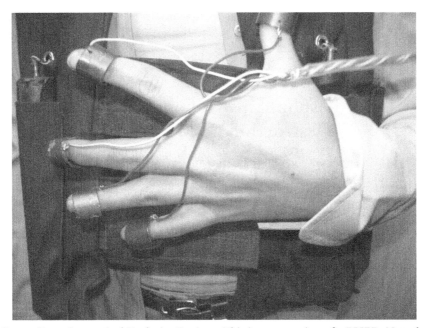

Person Borne Improvised Explosive Device—This is a re-creation of a PBIED. Note the electrical wires and contacts on the fingers. Bringing the contacts on the fingers together detonates the device. Photograph by Jim Smith.

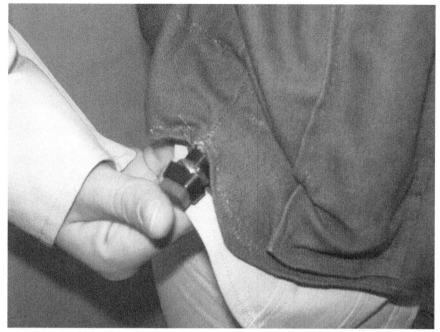

Person Borne Improvised Explosive Device—This is a re-creation of a PBIED. Note the push button switch to detonate the device. Note what is not seen in the photograph is a booby trap switch which when the vest is removed detonates the device. Photograph by Jim Smith.

Response to Weapons of Mass Destruction (WMD) Events

WMD events may include the deployment of explosives, chemical agents, biological agents, or radiological devices. The use of nuclear weapons is outside the scope of this text.

Chemical weapons are the second easiest agent to use in the WMD arena. Mass assaults with firearms are the easiest terrorist attack; bombs and chemical agents would be the methods of choice in terms of ease. Toxic industrial chemicals, stolen without substantial difficulty, can be used with devastating effects. Little or no security exists for anhydrous ammonia or chlorine gases. These agents can affect a large area downwind from the release point. Even OC released into a confined space or outdoors in densely populated area such as an outdoor fair or football stadium can cause a panic stampede with deaths and injuries. The use of OC in crowded nightclubs has resulted in injuries and fatalities from the stampede on several occasions. Pesticides, especially restricted organophosphates, can be used as expedient nerve agents or toxic agents. The synthesis of nerve agents is difficult, making the theft of pesticides a simpler solution. Pesticides could be dispersed as liquids, powders, or from the air, providing multiple options of delivery. Other chemicals such as cyanide could be dispersed as a gas or on a small scale used to contaminate a water supply such as a water cooler. The issue with cyanide is that high concentration in the gas form is needed to cause injury, making its use indoors preferable. The amount of cyanide to contaminate a public water supply is substantial, making this threat somewhat less feasible. However, the terror value of a threat to contaminate a public water supply coupled with the theft of cyanide could provide an ideal terrorist tool to frighten the public.

Radiological Events

These events involve the use of radioactive material. Many might suspect radioactive material is guarded closely. This is not the case in many settings. As many as 1,000 radioactive sources are reporting missing in the US annually. Some sources, such as those used to measure soil density, are stored inside a structure protected only by a padlock or simply locked in a toolbox on the back of a truck. Sources are also available in industrial and medical settings. Although these sources may be alarmed, they are not likely guarded by armed personnel.

Radioactive materials may be dispersed in a variety of methods, which may include explosives such as a dirty bomb, in powder form dumped into a ventilation system, or introduced into a water system. The key is these present an ideal terror weapon in that any radiation-related event will induce substantial public fear, the cost of decontamination will be high, and the areas contaminated will be closed and access denied for long periods. These are weapons with a substantial economic impact with few short-term hazards.

Dirty Bombs

A dirty bomb can be used for terrorism in several scenarios with the more common one a Radiological Dispersion Device (RDD). This usually a bomb designed to disperse radioactive materials through an explosion. Other means include spilling the radioactive material into a ventilation system or placing the material in an envelope or package and mailing it to the target. These events create terror out of proportion to their destructive nature, can produce a denial of use, and may cause long-range health problems.

The usual source of radioactive materials will be a stolen radiography source. However, other sources exist, such as shipments of radioactive material, radioactive medical implants, and radioactive material waste shipments. Radiography sources are used to generate gamma rays or neutron radiation to sterilize items, for other medical purposes, and for industrial purposes such as checking for fractures of pipe or measuring density in soil, concrete, or asphalt. The sources may not be alarmed and are usually stored in an isolated area, making them theft prone. Hospitals, state highway departments, and some large industry use these sources, and if the source container integrity is violated, a serious contamination hazard will exist. When responding to unexplained explosions, suspicious powders received in the mail, or suspicious items, the responders should consider and determine if radioactive material is involved. Most bomb squads carry radiation detection equipment; some fire department hazardous materials units may have radiation detection gear. Most local EMA and state radiation control agencies will have radiation detection equipment.

The scenario likely to involve radioactive material is the explosive dispersal of the material. Radioactive material survives the explosion's thermal event and shock wave. The thermal plume will effectively disperse the radioactive material in the immediate area and downwind. The explosion will distract responders and may divert their attention sufficiently to not consider an RDD. Common radioactive sources contain cobalt-60, cesium-137, americium-241, or iridium-192.

Threats to deploy an RDD do occur. If credible this threat should be treated seriously and federal assistance sought. Sophisticated search assets and response assets may be deployed to locate the radioactive material or respond to such an event. A credible threat coupled with the loss or theft of a radioactive source should be considered a crisis.

An RDD will provide threats from the normal explosive and fragment hazards along with radioactive material. The RDD will not likely contain a substantial amount of radioactive material, but an explosion will distribute it over a large area. Explosions produce a plume from hot gases which entrain radioactive particles and disperse them over wide areas. An RDD with a substantial amount of radioactive material could contaminate a several square mile area depending upon weather conditions and winds. For this reason, an upwind approach to an explosion site is needed. Surveys with a radiation detection instrument should be considered, and when feasible responders should wear radiation pagers set to alarm if radiation is detected. In such an event outside resources from the state and federal levels will be needed. This will include state radiological health, the FBI, and the Department of Energy. The problem of radioactive contamination will not go away like some hazardous materials but will remain continuous until mitigated.

Additional threats may include not only the radiation issue, but also that many radioactive materials are heavy metals and toxic. The radioactive materials involved may be biologically active and bioconcentrate in organs if ingested or inhaled.

The more immediate issue is determining that a radioactive material has been used. The only method available is with radiation detection instruments. Once it is detected, the responders will be compelled to don respiratory protection and protective clothing with radiation dosimeters. The levels of exposure and doses to responding personnel need to be determined. Sophisticated isotopic analysis can provide the nature of the threat and even the isotope present.

With radioactive materials and radiation, the same provisions used to protect from bombs through time, distance, and shielding apply. Responders should spend minimal time within the radiation area and maintain a maximum distance feasible from the site while keeping any available solid objects between oneself and the radiation source.

The North American Emergency Response Guide (NAERG) recommends a minimal isolation area of 25–50 meters (80 to 160 feet) in every direction and to remain upwind of any radioactive material incident. If responders suspect explosives are involved, a retreat upwind to at least 1,500 feet is recommended.

One clue that radioactive material could be involved is shielding. Massive shields of lead are used to reduce gamma radiation and a device may be shielded to protect those transporting or emplacing the object. Shielding may also be used to prevent detection of the RDD with a radiation detection device. Some radioactive material may have packaging with the yellow and magenta propeller-shaped warning of radiation. The bomb squad will be a valuable asset in these situations.

Decontamination efforts may consist of doffing clothing and taking a shower. However, when available, hazardous materials technicians and health physics technicians should direct decontamination. Personnel operating in contaminated areas should wear appropriate protective clothing, dosimeters, and respiratory protection. This may be as simple at Tyvek coveralls and a N99 mask or may require chemical-protective clothing with air-purifying respirators (APRs) or self-contained breathing apparatus (SCBA). The type of radioactive material present along with the levels of contamination will dictate the type of personal protective equipment (PPE) required. When feasible, responders need to wear dosimeters and in high radiation areas exposure times may be limited with resultant stay times limited. Strict standards exist for radiation dose levels responders are allowed to receive during emergency operations. This is the reason health physicists and radiation protection personnel need to be involved in formulating operations.

However, in many circumstances the advice and guidance from experts may be an "after the fact" event unless a high index of suspicion is used in events that could present a radiation hazard or involve radioactive contamination. Responders should avoid eating or drinking if radioactive material is a possibility to reduce the body burden from ingesting contaminated items.

Biological Agents

The role of law enforcement in a biological attack may be varied. Law enforcement resources will be used to investigate the manner in which the agent was delivered and the person or group involved. Officers can expect to be involved in the epidemiological aspects of the investigation to determine the spread of the disease. This assists in tracking those called the index patient or patients to whom the initial exposure occurred, or a fixed locale may be the source of the contamination.

In some circumstances the outbreak may be determined as an intentional act or a natural occurrence. This is true in many agents which may have natural sources, such as the plague (*Yersinia pestis*) which occurs in the southwestern US. However, multiple cases of the plague in the northeastern US where the disease is not endemic would argue for an intentional attack. The US anthrax attacks took several days before the disparate locations were linked and investigations determined this was an intentional act, not a natural outbreak. Anthrax is a naturally occurring bacterium and is endemic to portions of the US.

Complicating the issues is the latent period between exposure and clinical signs or symptoms. Exposure to biological agents has a "lag time" of hours to days before the person infected exhibits any signs or symptoms. This may make tracking their movements to ascertain where the exposure occurred difficult. If the person is infectious, tracking his or her movements and contacts may become important in reducing the spread of the disease if human-to-human transmissible.

Many biological agents producing disease will present with "flu-like illnesses" in patients. If the agent is dispersed during influenza season, the differentiation of influenza and another disease may be difficult initially.

Law enforcement may have problems with staffing if officers are exposed to biological agents and must be quarantined. If the agent is transmissible human-to-human, protection of law enforcement personnel will become a priority. Some persons or areas may be quarantined. Law enforcement will be expected to staff the quarantine areas, retaining persons within the zone.

The issue of the person or persons authorized to declare quarantine and what authority does law enforcement have to enforce quarantine is important. In some states the department of public health may declare quarantine or restrict travel, while in other states the governor must make a declaration of a state of emergency. A few states allow political subdivisions to declare quarantines or travel restrictions. A review of the applicable laws is important. In most instances the declaration of quarantine for natural incidents has not been performed in many years. In one state, the mayor of a city declared a quarantine against smallpox in 1910 to prevent linemen erecting telegraph lines from entering the city who were believed to be infected with smallpox. Further, the funding process to quarantine individuals or locales should be known. The laws in some states place the cost of quarantine on the state or political subdivision declaring the quarantine.

Some jurisdictions allow broad powers to public health investigators and law enforcement during a public health crisis. Some public health officials may be able to seize items and order the quarantine of an area or persons or even an entire community. Many of the laws are old, and some remain unchanged from the early 1900s.

In the case of human-to-human transmission, the typical PPE will likely be nitrile gloves, protective clothing, and a N99 filter mask. Supplies of these items may be depleted quickly. A serious issue may occur with staffing, as some officers may exhibit an irrational fear of disease and fail to report for duty or shirk official responsibilities. Other issues will be the necessity of protecting healthcare facilities. If the Strategic National Stockpile of medical equipment and drugs is activated, law enforcement will be required to protect the site where the equipment is stored and distributed. If drugs such as antibiotics are distributed or persons vaccinated, law enforcement will be required to protect these sites. Disorder and perhaps rioting or looting should be anticipated. This may further drain resources attempting to mitigate these issues.

In some cases, officers may be required to ingest antibiotics or other drugs or be vaccinated for prophylactic reasons. Perhaps the "unknown" aspect of dealing with a biological incident will keep some officers from reporting for duty along with those who are ill. Staffing will be an issue. Data from the CDC suggests that up to one-third of those not ill may fail to report to work because of fear of exposure to the disease or the need to care for ill family members. A similar issue will occur with medical personnel. Familiarity with local public health authorities is a necessity. A public health exercise for an outbreak is an important tool to acquaint law enforcement with public health procedures and provide reassurance through education to those in law enforcement.

Response to Suspected Chemical, Radiological, or Biological Weapons

What formerly was a theoretical problem has become a problem for many jurisdictions at least as a hoax. The probability of a person using a lethal chemical, radiological, or biological agent is very low, but law enforcement must treat any device as live.

The more common scenario occurs when a suspect package or letter is received, and the addressee opens the item to find a powder. The letter may warn the powder is anthrax, ricin, abrin, poison, or some other agent such as radioactive material. The suspect package may be used as an extortion device or to rob a bank. An unusual scenario is the use of a suspected biological or chemical agent in the ventilation system of a structure. This type of attack has been used frequently and, in some instances, unintentionally, when OC spray is used within the structure. The HVAC system acquires the agent and distributes it widely. The concern regarding the dispersal of OC or tear gas agents is the initial symptoms are like that of nerve agents (eye pain, shortness of breath, and rhinorrhea, which is nasal secretions). Officers encountering multiple people with similar symptoms such as short of breath, eye pain, and nasal secretions should consider that the exposure may be to a nerve agent or other toxic agent. The law enforcement officer should not enter the area, especially if people are down. In most events the type of agent will not be known during the initial phase of the crisis. Those in the area in which the agent is dispersed will likely be contaminated and contact with them should be avoided to prevent cross-contamination. Another sign of nerve agent deployment is persons down and seizing. Most officers will not have appropriate respiratory protection or chemical suits, although some agencies cross use the PPE for clandestine laboratories for such events (if the items are rated for such use). Even though remaining upwind and outside a scene is contrary to the law enforcement rescue mentality, in these circumstances one is likely to become a victim if one enters the scene.

In the past some of those exposed to what was labeled anthrax, abrin, or ricin were decontaminated rigorously and administered antibiotics prior to testing of the suspect substance. The process should be a procedure developed in concert with your local public health authorities, hazardous materials responders, and bomb squad. The local FBI office can provide access to a special agent bomb technician and WMD coordinator knowledgeable regarding WMD. FBI-certified bomb squads have personnel trained in responding to these types of events.

Usually removal of clothing will eliminate a large amount of the contaminants. If followed by a soap and water shower with special attention washing hair, this will likely be the extent of decontamination needed. Many states have public health laboratories equipped to rapidly assay and determine if a biological agent is involved. Field tests are also useful and may provide a presumptive identification pending more sophisticated procedures. Onsite testing may involve determining if the material is radioactive or some other toxic material. Organophosphate insecticides, phosphorus-based insecticides, and similar toxic substances can be used in lieu of a biological agent. However, field tests are notorious for false positives.

Notify the FBI of any suspected biological, chemical, or radiological weapons as they have primary federal jurisdiction in the use of WMD. The federal resources may be able to help identify the substance. Other agencies which might be able to assist include a hazardous materials response unit, national guard civil support teams, and emergency management.

The more common issue with a suspect device is the exposure of several people through handling. The area involved will need to be isolated until the substance can be analyzed. Some biological toxins, such as ricin and abrin, are very toxic, with no antidote, making caution with unknown powders or liquids essential. Cyanide compounds have been found in the possession of several threat groups; however, high levels of cyanide gas are required to incapacitate or kill when compared with nerve agents. A potential source of substitute nerve agents is the agricultural organophosphate insecticides. These could be obtained through theft or other illegal acquisition.

Emergency management through SARA tracks the location of many hazardous materials. The theft of dangerous materials should alert law enforcement to the possibility of use as a weapon. One agency worked a case in which a small amount, two pounds, of sodium cyanide was stolen. The theft was followed by a threat to contaminate the city's water supply. Water board and public health officials concluded that tons of cyanide would be needed to contaminate the water supply and the threat might be credible but could not be executed with the small amount of cyanide stolen. What was discovered during the investigation that only a few cyanide antidote kits were available. What concerned investigators was the potential use of the cyanide to contaminate a small water source, such as water cooler, or food items in a public setting such as a salad bar. The area public safety agencies, public health, and hospitals were alerted regarding the threat. The suspect was arrested and the cyanide recovered prior to its use.

Antidotes for cyanide and nerve agents exist in the form of kits, and EMS providers in the hospital and field setting are familiar with them. However, many EMS providers will have only small quantities of these items, and they are likely for self-use. Some law enforcement agencies at risk for exposure to nerve agents have trained officers and issued DuoDote® kits. The issuance may be limited to specialty units such as tactical or bomb squad units. Law enforcement must coordinate with hazardous material teams to determine how decontamination will occur and to which hospital the injured will be transported. If officers must be decontaminated, how will firearms and radio equipment be secured? Prior coordination and procedures crystallized in writing through memoranda of understanding are essential. Otherwise officers potentially contaminated will not relinquish firearms or other equipment without a procedure to secure them. If the event is a criminal act, which one must presume such in many cases, law enforcement may be the incident commander with fire and EMS providing support. In many instances the preservation of a crime scene will be difficult because of potential contamination and the ensuing chaos of such an event.

Since OC spray has become available to the public several incidents have occurred in which the OC was released in an enclosed structure. The results of these releases range from multiple deaths from a stampede, to hospital treatment of several persons for exacerbating respiratory conditions such as asthma, to denial of use of the facility. OC spray used by security officers at a Chicago nightclub resulted in a stampede with multiple fatalities. A prank in a Florida mall in which juveniles sprayed several cans of OC into the HVAC return duct resulted in more than 30 people requiring on-scene medical treatment and several requiring medical treatment in an emergency room setting because of exacerbation of pre-existing respiratory problems. An incident in Alabama in which a tear gas grenade was discharged in university dormitory resulted in several people requiring medical treatment at a hospital, including one of the responding officers who assisted in evacuation. The elderly or those with preexisting conditions such as asthma or COPD may have a substantial reaction and suffer respiratory compromise from exposure to OC or tear gas. These individuals are likely to need decontamination and transport to a medical facility.

An uncommon threat will be to discharge a radiological device. The device would likely be constructed in concert with an explosive to assure dispersal of the radioactive material. A crude method of dispersal would be to crush the radioactive material into a powder form and mail it in envelope or disperse by a non-explosive means such as a blower.

The likely source of the radioactive material would be the theft of a radiographic source or medical isotopes. Most radiographic sources are not well protected against theft. This will be long-lived isotopes such as cobalt-60 or cesium-137 and present a serious radiation hazard if removed from their storage container. Medical isotopes, even though short-lived, can present a hazard as many are biologically active. If absorbed or ingested may bio-concentrate in a specific organ-system, such as the thyroid or liver, causing damage.

If a radiographic source is stolen, this should be viewed with concern as it may be used as a small radiological dispersion device. The local and state emergency management agency or state radiation safety agency can provide a list of facilities that store radioactive materials. One should note that several of these sources are "lost" or otherwise not accounted for each year. Bomb squads, fire department hazardous materials teams, and emergency management have radiation detection equipment. Most bomb squads wear radiation detection devices and are familiar with their use.

An out-of-the-ordinary attack which has been attempted by several threat groups is the employment of toxic gases such as carbon monoxide, chlorine, or anhydrous ammonia into occupied structures. Modern well-sealed structures attacked with a sufficient supply of carbon monoxide, chlorine, or anhydrous ammonia could potentially be lethal and at least deny use of the structure. Officers should be suspicious of gas cylinders in proximity to a ventilation system.

Suggested Protocol for a Suspect Chemical, Radiological or Biological Device

- Officer should be suspicious of reports of mass illness in public locations, government facilities, or public gatherings. These may be hysterical reactions to a smell or to others becoming ill.
- The officer should suspect a chemical attack if unusual symptoms are reported such as visual difficulty, difficulty breathing, collapse, or seizures.
- Officers should not enter the affected area if persons are down, experiencing seizures, or experiencing respiratory difficulty, as the officer may become a casualty.
- Avoid contact with those potentially contaminated.
- Stay upwind and uphill if feasible.
- Have those mobile walk out of the danger area and upwind.
- In circumstances in which no one is exhibiting any symptoms, the officer should isolate any suspect devices or packages present by evacuating away from the device in an upwind and uphill direction if feasible.
- Determine who and what might be contaminated and isolate the areas.
- Control the spread of contamination if feasible by segregating those contaminated away from those not contaminated.
- Make certain hazardous materials personnel, EMS, and the bomb squad are dispatched.
- Establish unified command and develop an incident action plan.

The threat of chemical, radiological, and biological agents must be reacted to in a manner to assure adequate response should the event involve a weapon of mass destruction. These reactions will expend substantial amounts of manpower and other resources, with the device likely a hoax. However, these serve as an opportunity to refine plans and train for the inevitable live event. One agency faced an industrial event (no hazardous materials were in use or stored on site) in which more than 100 employees were ill, complaining of headache and nausea with vomiting. Upon arrival the employees had self-evacuated. The employees were distraught but did not appear to be seriously ill. Fire department hazardous materials personnel along with bomb technicians in PPE investigated the site. What was discovered was a melted fluorescent light ballast, which generated a strong and disagreeable odor and caused one employee to vomit. What followed was a cascade of similar symptoms involving almost every employee working. More than 30 persons were transported for medical evaluation at a local hospital, and none were found to have any injury. Several months later a similar event occurred at a warehouse; once again no hazardous materials were stored or in use at the facility, from which more than 30 employees had self-evacuated. The employees were complaining of headache, disorientation, nausea, vomiting, and irregular pulse. These employees looked as if they were seriously ill. Once again fire department hazardous materials personnel and bomb technicians in PPE investigated and found elevated levels of carbon monoxide. Investigation revealed that a malfunctioning fork lift using propane was the origin of the carbon monoxide. Every employee had to be transported to a local hospital. Several required hyperbaric oxygen treatment and every employee had elevated carboxyhemoglobin levels.

Parallel and Swarm Attacks

A terrorist tactic which has been used with success is to attack multiple venues and even use secondary attackers to attack the responders. In these circumstances the first responders are overwhelmed and facing a well-armed and well-trained adversary willing to die.

Conventional tactics used by response teams may not be effective simply because of logistics. Most response teams do not train to protect themselves from attacks outside the inner perimeter. Staging areas and command posts will be likely targets. The original incident will likely involve a soft target with a high density of people. Hotels, hospitals, transportation facilities, government buildings, and police stations have been attacked with success.

The attacks will be intense, and the first-in responders will likely become casualties. Command and control along with communications will likely be fragmented and may fail. Responders involved in these events will have to use small unit tactics and, if communications are lost, coordinate their own operation. Many agencies will face the issue of patrol responders with limited weapons as some agencies still do not arm their officers with patrol rifles. Ammunition will become an issue. Few officers carry sufficient ammunition to engage in a firefight with a well-armed adversary. One state police agency equipped its officers with semiautomatic patrol rifles but only provided two magazines of 30 rounds. Most officers will have only three or four pistol magazines. The necessity of the officer carrying a "bail out bag" with additional ammunition and supplies has become common. Many officers carry charged rifle and pistol magazines in a "bail out bag" along with "battle dressings" and tourniquets.

A common finding in this type of attack is officers run out of ammunition. The ongoing intense and widespread nature of the attacks makes resupply problematic. Agencies should provide officers with a "bail out bag" with sufficient magazines for pistol and patrol rifle, along with a tactical medical kit. Some agencies equip officers with four 30-round magazines and four additional pistol magazines. One rural agency which usually has one officer working equips officers with both an AR-15 configuration rifle and a 7.62mm, M14 configuration with a four-power scope, along with a semiautomatic shotgun along with a TASER and pump-action bean bag shotgun. The agency also issues 33-round 9mm Glock pistol magazines for the officer's "bail out bags." A substantial quantify of ammunition in magazines for each weapon is carried in a transportable bag. The rationale is the single officer, if engaged, will need close, medium, and longer-range weapons. This allows some self-sufficiency in these events while awaiting outside backup and occurred following a bank robbery in which the robbers were better armed than the solo officer responding. Another agency issued patrol rifles in AR-15 configuration following the robbery and hostage taking at a restaurant in which the robbers using AR-15-type rifles kept officers at bay with semiautomatic gunfire while they completed the robbery and successfully eluded officers armed with shotguns. The officers now carry patrol rifles in addition to their issued shotguns.

Scene Access and Scene Control Issues

In many instances, scene control will be difficult at the typical chaotic event. Issues of evacuating civilians and the injured and protecting other responders will consume substantial resources. The on-scene commander must not only assist these responders and protect them, he or she must also protect staging areas and the command post.

One terrorist tactic which is of concern is the use of pre-placed IEDs, PBIEDs, or VBIEDs transported by cloned emergency vehicles. Another issue is the potential for penetration of the command post, staging area, or perimeters by terrorists dressed as responders. They may be able to use firearms or PBIEDs to disrupt operations and kill responders.

Go/No-Go Indicators

One substantial issue will be environments officers are not equipped to enter. Caution should be used if reports indicate or if officers observe multiple persons down from other than gunfire or complaining of breathing difficulty or medical problems. The officer should approach from upwind and uphill and avoiding smoke, mists, or vapors if feasible. If the officer encounters multiple individuals with medical problems such as shortness of breath, nasal secretions, eye pain, or dimness of vision, the officer should avoid contact with the individuals and retreat. These are sufficient indicators of a chemical attack to warrant withdrawal from the affected area. The problem is the initial symptoms of a nerve agent attack are very similar to OC spray. The difference will be that with a nerve agent attack, many of those exposed should be incapacitated or down, whereas, OC will cause most to flee but is not likely to cause incapacitation or collapse. Officers should not enter explosion areas unless doing so to save lives. Those believed to be dead on any explosion or WMD scene should be left in place.

Lessons Learned from Others

Issues which have affected the ability to respond to a swarm attack have been the failure of police commanders to recognize the scope and intensity of the attacks and the loss of communications from the personnel engaged in the attacks. The large numbers of casualties among officers and civilians will overwhelm EMS and hospital resources. Officers may become demoralized with the injury and death of colleagues and be faced by a well-armed adversary with better weapons and training. In the US most agencies are accustomed to dealing with single events of minor to moderate intensity. Likely limited tactical resources are available, and the deployment of these resources takes time. The swarm attack occurs in multiple locations, is intense, and uses tactics to keep the attackers mobile, and responders are deliberately targeted. The appropriate response is not law enforcement-based but should be based around small unit tactics in use by Marines. Agencies must prepare officers to operate in an autonomous manner with minimal guidance and no logistical support in this setting. The attacks in Mumbai demonstrated the lack of preparation of law enforcement, who faced a better-trained and better-armed terrorist. The officers, some equipped with revolvers and very limited ammunition, faced a terrorist equipped with military rifles, IEDs, and hand grenades along with sophisticated training in the use of these weapons. Officers in the Boston Marathon bombings, during the capture phase, faced well-armed and well-trained suspects armed with firearms and hand-thrown IEDs. Officers in the North Hollywood (1997) shootout and the Norco, California (1980), bank robberies faced criminals who possessed superior weapons and even body armor. Remember in the Norco bank robbery, rifle fire and shotgun-launched grenades destroyed numerous patrol cars, injured many officers (and killed one deputy sheriff), and even shot down a police helicopter. Both of these robberies occurred in California, yet in the 17 years following the Norco bank robbery, officers in North Hollywood were armed substantially in the same manner (albeit revolvers had been replaced with semiautomatic pistols), that is, with shotguns rather than patrol rifles. During the Norco robbery, while in pursuit of the suspects, officers had to commandeer a rifle, as did the officers in the North Hollywood bank robbery. This allowed the robbers in both incidents to hold police at a disadvantage and escape temporarily. They were only killed, killed themselves, or were captured following confrontation by heavily armed police tactical personnel after the robbers became separated during their escape attempts in both incidents. No longer can law enforcement presume that they will be as well armed as adversaries and better trained than their adversaries. This lesson one would have thought would have been well learned by law enforcement with the numerous incidents such as Norco and North Hollywood, yet many agencies still fail to issue patrol rifles and adequate ammunition and train officers in small unit tactics. Law enforcement is like any other bureaucracy, slow to change, and the bureaucratic inertia along with the philosophy, "this is how we have always done it," prevents change in tactics and equipment in a positive and progressive manner.

Demilitarized hand grenades recovered by the author. These hand grenades had been converted to live grenades. Photograph by Jim Smith.

Chapter 6

Natural Disasters

Natural disaster tends to be periodic and may affect an area on almost a regular basis. As the events which are probable are identified, a plan should be developed for response to the event. Further, plans for continuity of operations are essential as the event may affect agency infrastructure and personnel.

Common issues with any natural disaster will be loss of power, loss of access, loss of communications, and loss of logistical support. Most agencies are well prepared to operate for short periods, 72 hours or fewer, without external logistics. Hurricane Katina and the recent tornados in the southeastern US have demonstrated that the ability to operate in a self-sufficient mode may need to be seven to 10 days. Some agencies have moved their independent operation level to 21 to 30 days considering these events.

This means the agency must have enough consumables, including fuel, food, water, bathroom facilities, rest areas for eating and sleeping with environmental control, communications facilities, generators, and vehicle repair capabilities for the period. The more easily forgotten aspect is maintaining vehicles. The debris from many events will cause tire failure, and the normal vendors supplying such services and tires may not be available. Those agencies depending upon external vendors for fuel may find the lack of power prevents pumping fuel. Those agencies supplying their own fuel should have generator power available to pump the fuel. One uses external vendors for fuel, but during hurricane season the agency orders large tanks on skids with electric and hand pumps. These tanks are used to support the agency fleet during hurricane season with the fuel vendor replenishing them weekly. During a recent hurricane officers had to hand pump fuel when electrical power failed, but police vehicles remained operational.

Tornado

Tornados are a frequent event in many parts of the US. Key to preparing for a tornado is notification. The National Weather Service (NWS) has several methods used to notify agencies of an impending storm. Weather radios with an alert feature are used commonly, plus the NWS uses a program of text messaging and emails to public safety agencies. The National Warning System (NAWAS) is also used as a communications tool, and many NWS offices also have push-to-talk commercial radio service available to public safety agencies. The difference between a tornado watch and tornado warning is essential, as one allows preparation while the warning mandates immediate action to seek shelter. Officers should be directed procedurally on how to react to a tornado situation. In some instances, escape of the path can be accomplished by driving at right angles away from the projected path of the tornado. In other circumstances it may be necessary to seek shelter away from a vehicle if fleeing is not an option. A strong concrete and steel structure will serve as the better shelter. Flying glass and other debris is a tremendous hazard during a tornado.

Upon notification of a tornado watch the agency should alert field personnel and when feasible deploy officers trained as storm spotters. These officers can provide a first-hand observation of the weather conditions and may spot EF0 or EF1 tornados not easily seen by weather radar. Generator power and a tornado-resistant communication center with multiple methods of communicating are essential. Loss of commercial power is common during a tornado. Access issues will be a problem, as trees and debris will clog roads. Tire damage and multiple flat tires on emergency vehicles are common following a tornado because of windblown debris on the roadway. Mass casualties are not uncommon, and officers may find themselves as the only medical responder available. This makes the availability of trauma kits in patrol vehicles essential. Expedient transport of the injured to undamaged medical facilities may have to be undertaken by law enforcement if EMS assets are overwhelmed.

Some agencies have experienced the loss of the agency building or communications center during a severe weather event. Plans should address an alternative public safety answering point (PSAP) and communications site and communication methods should this occur. Failure of commercial telephone, cellular, and radio service is common. Those agencies with agency owned and operated communications systems may see damage to towers or transmitter sites. Multiple paths of communication should be planned to prevent loss of the PSAP and communications center and a redundant method of communicating with field personnel should be available. If the event is widespread, external responding agencies may be delayed. Some agencies in tornado and hurricane-prone areas have purchased chain saws and trained officers to use them. These can be used to clear access to agency facilities and roadways. Officers using chain saws must have appropriate training along with hand, eye, head, and leg protection.

Hurricanes, Floods, Earthquakes, and Wildfires

Hurricanes and floods provide substantial warning prior to affecting an area, allowing the agency to conduct preparations. Earthquakes and wildfires occur without warning. The loss of agency infrastructure and of utility infrastructure may make some areas untenable. The agency should have a plan to fully evacuate in cases of floods, wildfires, and hurricanes but also may consider leaving some responders on site in rated self-sufficient storm shelters in the event of a hurricane. These personnel can emerge following the hurricane and begin preliminary damage assessment and, in some instances, begin clearing access paths for external resources.

The primary killer in hurricanes is flooding. Access following the hurricane or flood may be via small boat. Some agencies have distant inland rallying points in which agency vehicles and equipment is moved to avoiding floods, hurricanes, and wildfires. With appropriate equipment to clear roads, debris, and trees, a column of relief vehicles, heavy equipment, and personnel can reenter the affected area. Offsite communications and remote PSAPs outside the affected area are another consideration. Although expensive, these can serve the agency until onsite facilities can be restored. Using the Government Emergency Telecommunications Service GETS), establishment of landlines to serve PSAPs can be provided the needed priority with telephone and cellular vendors.

Area security to prevent looting will be an issue. Many sightseers and spontaneous volunteers will appear. The agency must be ready to divert these individuals out of the dangerous areas and if feasible use those willing to volunteer. A badging or ID system must be put in place to identify returning residents and response entities such as local CERT or other non-governmental service agencies. One community asset may be the local CERT. Some religious and fraternal organizations can aid in these circumstances. The plan should address what agencies are available, the services provided, and a method of contact. The agencies should be vetted prior to use to determine they have adequate training and equipment and a history of acceptable performance.

The agency will need a plan and perhaps the assets in place to provide shelter food, water, bathroom, shower, and sleeping facilities following some of these events, as agency assets may be damaged or overwhelmed. With local infrastructure damaged, this may be problematic. The military 1033 Program is a good source of equipment of this nature. The need for rescue may be the priority following an earthquake, and earthquakes are notorious for damaging utility and communications infrastructure. The need for heavy equipment will have to be met. Prior arrangements and written agreements with local vendors, government public works, and state-level entities possessing this type of equipment will need to be secured prior to the need. The types of equipment and availability of organic operators with the equipment will need to be addressed.

Lessons Learned from Others

The "take home" lesson learned from many of these events is that planning is crucial, as is self-sufficiency. Agencies should review carefully what resources will be needed and for how long the agency should remain self-sufficient. The agency can then match available funding to acquire those assets deemed critical as monies become available. These assets are useful in day-to-day operations and small-scale emergencies. The key is to use the equipment and assets to ensure familiarity and reduce "shelf-life loss" through non-use of assets.

During a recent tornado in the Southeast, the EF3 tornado destroyed the commercial "push to talk" service used by the law enforcement agency. The agency was able to switch back to the less functional but still usable UHF radio system. The cellular towers in this city were overloaded, and those officers without wireless priority access through the Government Emergency Telecommunications System (GETS) could not communicate via cellular telephones. However, text messages still were able to be transmitted. Participating in the GETS wireless priority access system can facilitate cellular and landline communications during a crisis when telephone switches are overloaded.

One agency in the Southern US had no plan for blizzards but experienced a blizzard, which rendered roads impassable with several inches of snow, downed trees, and downed power lines. The loss of power during this cold weather and high winds made many facilities without emergency power unlivable and required evacuations. Facilities with emergency power learned that most of the generator systems were not able to handle HVAC systems, therefore environmental and temperature control within the structures was not possible. The incident manager (law enforcement served as the lead agency) for this event was initially concerned that no plans existed for such since this was the only blizzard experienced in this locale in its recorded history. However, upon reflection, the common issues of impassible roads, no power, downed trees, evacuations, and needing shelters for those displaced sounded familiar. What the incident manager decided is that the agency's hurricane plan was a good fit and the hurricane plan was used during the blizzard successfully. Four-wheel drive vehicles worked well in the snow and the chain saws used during hurricanes were useful in removing trees from roadways. This innovative thinking and use of a plan not designed for the specific incident showed an agile thinking process and the ability to adapt to a novel incident. Fortunately, few injuries and no fatalities were reported. Most of the residents stayed home as few knew how to drive on snow covered roadways, and few motor vehicle crashes were reported. The incident was challenging in other ways as a major structure fire involving a large warehouse facility occurred during the blizzard. The fire was started by a homeless person building a fire inside the structure for warmth.

Chapter 7

Evacuations

In some circumstances, officers are faced with the need to evacuate. These events range from bomb threats, civil disorder, and hazardous material incidents, to hostage or barricade situations, severe weather events, and fires. Law enforcement officials must be familiar with their agency's policy regarding evacuations and the laws from which the authority to evacuate is derived.

The policy should be based around the existing state or local law. Research should be conducted to determine what statutory authority officers have in the regulation of vehicular and pedestrian traffic during an incident. Research should identify the authority that officers have to forcefully evacuate individuals or close businesses in relation to an evacuation or curfew. If no authority exists to evacuate, those individuals must be left. The officer, when feasible, should note the name, address, next of kin contacts, and GPS position of those remaining. This information should be relayed to the command post.

Many jurisdictions have the statutory authority to regulate vehicular traffic and pedestrians at emergency scenes. This will address many circumstances. In situations in which persons refuse to leave, officers must have a clear understanding of who has the authority to remove them. The officer must also know what constitutes a situation in which an evacuation is mandatory. Officers may not have authority to forcefully remove citizens from their homes or businesses unless a state of emergency has been declared at the state or local level.

Many situations present a visible hazard, such as a wildfire or rising floodwaters, while in others the hazard may not be seen. This may produce hesitancy to evacuate in a hazardous material release when no hazard is visible. A frequent situation in which officers are requested to offer advice or make a decision regarding evacuation is a bomb threat. The logical approach to this situation is the ranking supervisor of the facility should make the decision based upon the totality of the circumstances. The best response when asked for advice is not to provide advice. Officers could make themselves liable if injuries result to persons evacuated, or worse, if the officer recommends no evacuation and a bomb explodes, causing injuries. The situation changes if a suspicious item or package is present. Then evacuation, at least in the vicinity of the item, becomes a necessity. The risk presented by the item compared with the potential risk of evacuating should be determined. It may be feasible only to evacuate a portion of a structure or have persons shelter in place.

When officers arrive an evaluation of the situation should be made. When approaching the incident an approach from uphill and upwind should be made if feasible. If a toxic material is involved, this should be considered in any evacuation routes selected. If a barricade situation is present or a shooter is involved, safe lanes out of the line of fire and vision of the shooter are needed.

Interfacing with other agencies, such as the fire department, facility management, and bomb squad, may be necessary to evaluate the potential threat and to establish the area in need of evacuation. Once the evacuation is started, an exclusion area should be established and marked with a tangible barrier such as traffic barricades or crime scene tape. The barrier should be manned and only those persons essential to public safety operations should be permitted inside the exclusion area.

If many persons or large facility must be evacuated, a staging area for public safety vehicles and equipment will be needed. Vehicles may be needed to transport displaced persons to shelters. Some agencies have agreements with public transportation entities or school system for buses to serve as a mode of transport. The law enforcement agency must designate an incident commander or operations commander and establish a command post or attend the command post if a unified command is used. Other agencies, such as the emergency management agency, the Salvation Army, and the American Red Cross, can provide or coordinate shelter support for displaced persons. Some agencies use their school district for transportation resources with school buses and may use schools as an initial shelter for displaced persons. Animal control and the Humane Society may be needed to assist with displaced pets. Some persons will refuse to evacuate unless they can take their pets with them, so this issue must be addressed and steps taken to house pets. Some areas use pet-friendly evacuation shelters. One agency in the southeast houses companion animals including horses at a pet-friendly shelter.

The situation becomes a major event if facilities to be evacuated have residents with special needs. Many emergency management agencies have a plan for sheltering those with special needs, such as the infirm or those with ongoing medical needs. If a nursing home or hospital must be evacuated, the risk to patients may be substantial. An option to consider is to shelter in place with a partial evacuation if feasible. A recent hospital evacuation in the southeast was required because a large transformer could not be replaced and power restored for more than 24 hours, as the transformer had to be shipped from a distant location. A major regional effort was required to move patients to other hospitals in the area.

This tactic of partial evacuation and shelter in place may be used in a bomb threat in some circumstances; the drain on resources will be large enough in some instances to warrant the recall of off-duty personnel, reserves, and mutual aid.

Factors that will affect the degree of evacuation include:

- The type of threat and its credibility
- Environmental conditions
- The type and degree of evacuation required
- The routes available
- The number of individuals requiring evacuation and their mobility
- The availability and types of transportation
- Shelters available
- The estimated time shelters will be needed
- The danger presented to law enforcement

Some evacuations can be conducted by the orders transmitted via telephone, but many will require door-to-door contact. The use of interactive automated notification systems that provide a text message, email, or message via landline telephone to the affected residents and delivers a pre-recorded message are an excellent tool. Some areas use fixed or mobile public address systems, while others use outdoor sirens to alert residents to check the local media. The broadcast media can be used along with the emergency alerting system to deliver the emergency message. The local emergency management agency (EMA) may be able to authorize the emergency alert system, which has the media and cellular telephone providers deliver an emergency message. Law enforcement supervisors should be familiar with this process and have the authority to use the Emergency Alert System (EAS) and cellular text message alerting systems. The labor-intensive method of door-to-door notification should be anticipated.

In some circumstances, such as large hazardous material releases, the hazardous material, particularly those that present a respiratory hazard, may preclude law enforcement officers from entering the contaminated area to perform evacuations. Critical structures that will present a significant difficulty to evacuations should have a pre-plan. This may include hospitals, nursing homes, schools, large industry, jails, auditoriums, or arenas. High-rise structures may also present a problem if elevators are not available for use, such as during fires or power failure.

The key to any successful evacuation is pre-planning and a coordinated effort. This makes a written plan controlled from a command post crucial.

Lessons Learned from Others

Perhaps the evacuation failure most remember is Hurricane Katrina. The video of dozens of school buses underwater attest to the failure to remove thousands from the affected area. The "blame game" was substantial following the event. The key is to pre-plan for the worst-case scenario in which the area becomes untenable and people must flee.

A major university learned that a door-to-door evacuation of structures on the campus took almost an hour after the public address and external warning systems failed. The same university found that the emergency lighting on campus only lasted for 20 minutes after several disabled persons on upper floors of structures had to be evacuated down stairwells in the dark after the emergency lighting failed during an areawide loss power. A quirk in the building codes allowed this public structure to escape the requirement of emergency generator power to elevators and emergency lighting. These situations caught university police officers unaware as they were responsible for the evacuations. They lobbied for generators, but since the building codes did not require them, university administration declined the request. The police agency was forced to purchase battery-powered headlamps for officers and purchase enhanced stair chairs for movement of the disabled from upper floors of buildings on campus. The continuing concern was that a power failure made the evacuation less time sensitive, whereas a fire would require a quick evacuation, which might be beyond the capability of the officers present.

Chapter 8

Epidemics, Pandemics, and Quarantine

Law enforcement will play substantial roles in events involving disease outbreaks and quarantine. The first necessity that is law enforcement must be able to staff its own operations through a continuity of operations plan. This will entail load shedding by delaying or not responding to some routine calls for service, using cross-trained personnel, and adopting expedient methods of operations. The agency must also consider the need for large quantities of PPE for officers. This may include nitrile gloves, N99 filter masks, hand sanitizer, eye protection, and gowns or chemical-protective clothing.

The law enforcement agency should look to the local health department or state health department for information regarding epidemics. These entities should be able to provide recommendations for the use of PPE and provide training. Many transmissible epidemic diseases will be transmitted via airborne droplets from coughs or sneezes or contact with these droplets on environmental surfaces (fomites). Some of the more concerning diseases include SARS, MERS (the novel coronavirus emerging in the Middle East), influenza, and the viral hemorrhagic fevers such as Lassa fever or Ebola. The transport of those who were ill from Ebola to the US and its transmission to medical personnel was a startling development for many. Many facilities were not equipped to handle this situation, especially from the aspect of mental preparation. The conventional strains of influenza kill far more people than Ebola, yet the novelty of the unknown surrounding a "new disease" caused more anguish than needed. The transmission of most communicable diseases can be through fomites or droplets (from sneezes or coughs). The number of organisms required for successful transmission is usually high and normal techniques like the use of nitrile gloves, N99 masks, fluid-resistant gowns, sterile techniques, and proper doffing can prevent the transmission of these diseases. The use of APRs or powered air-purifying respirators (PAPRs) are a convenience but are not required in most circumstances.

This makes the use of nitrile gloves and N99 masks essential in any setting where a communicable disease may be present. When body fluids can be an issue, eye protection and a water-resistant gown or chemical suits may be required. Officers will need to modify their activities to operate while wearing PPE. Officers will need to learn social isolation, not to approach anyone closer than six feet, and not have contact with any person unless needed for officer safety. Officers should avoid crowds and those obviously ill. Officers must doff PPE following any contacts and use antiseptic hand cleaner followed by hand washing with soap and water when feasible. Most officers are familiar with using protective gloves, but N99 masks and gowns or chemical suits will be a new experience to many. This makes exercises prior to an event important to familiarize personnel with the procedures to don, use, and doff PPE.

The CDC has published data that suggests up to 40% of the workforce may not be available during an epidemic. Many will be ill, others will be caring for ill family members, and some will be too frightened to come to work for fear of acquiring the disease. The agencies which will fare the best are those which have developed and exercised continuity of operations plans and trained personnel in the use of PPE along with the tactics to avoid exposure.

The more likely event in the US will be an influenza outbreak like the 1918–1919 outbreak. During this epidemic many cities were devastated, and some lost power because no one was present to operate the power systems. Some had no available physicians, nurses, pharmacists, police officers, or postal workers, as they were ill or caring for someone ill. Quarantines were imposed, and even expedient burials were necessary as some areas had no coffins available because of the large number of deaths. This disease was transmissible via airborne droplets. One misconception is the pandemic of 1918–1919 occurred in one wave. What occurred was an initial outbreak and subsidence followed by additional outbreaks. One can expect waves of the illness rather than a discrete period of illnesses. This may make the epidemic a long-lived event.

Law enforcement will play several roles. The primary role will be to maintain order. Other roles will include guarding infrastructure such as hospitals and medical clinics, which will likely be overwhelmed with patients. Expedient sites may be established to distribute drugs, food, and water. Law enforcement will play a key role in this process.

Another role may be to assist in epidemiology investigations. This is the investigation conducted by the federal, state, or local health departments to track the origin of the outbreak and the method by which the disease spreads.

These public health investigators have a variety of authority and broad powers in some locales. An important facet in the agency's emergency plan is to have a memorandum of understanding prior to an event occurring. This should address what each agency's role is and what assets will be provided by each agency during the emergency. This is a good plan for foodborne outbreaks, as some of these events have involved intentionally ignoring regulations in food processing, which may rise to the level of a criminal offense. An example is the recent contamination of peanut butter. Executives of the offending companies were indicted on criminal charges when they chose to ignore reports of their brand of peanut butter was contaminated with salmonella bacteria. The bacteria later caused the deaths of several individuals, resulting in criminal prosecution of the executives. The investigation was a multidisciplinary investigation involving law enforcement, public health investigators, epidemiologists, and bacteriologists, along with other scientists and technicians in a complex, multi-state criminal act.

Epidemiology investigators may take biological and environmental samples for testing and will likely interview large numbers of people. Their role is to track the origin and nature of the illness and identify the causative agent. Some of the terminology is different as these investigators refer to a "case," which means an individual displaying signs and symptoms of the disease. Law enforcement's role is likely to be limited to supportive measures such as assisting with interviews, obtaining and serving search warrants, and providing security.

Continuity of operations will be the larger challenge to an agency. This makes cross-training of personnel essential. Personnel may have to fill multiple roles and operate outside their normal job duties. Many routine functions may be deferred or stopped to allow more urgent calls for service to be answered. The agency will need sufficient expendables to operate for a long period with little or no outside support. This should include fuel, food, water, vehicle repair, sleeping quarters, PPE, and other daily use items. The transportation system is likely to be disrupted in the areas quarantined, preventing the flow of goods and services. Agreements should be in place with local vendors to acquire the needed goods and services even if the facility is closed because of a staff shortage or quarantine. The sustained loss of electrical power should be a consideration. Facilities without generator power to essential equipment plus the building HVAC will likely become uninhabitable. If the water supply or sewer system fails, the need for sanitary bathrooms will become an issue.

Questions the agency needs to answer regarding continuity of operations are:

- How will employees be recalled to duty?
- Are measures in place to shelter or protect law enforcement families?

- Can the agency operate for an extended time with no outside resources?
- What calls will be answered?
- What expedient steps will be taken regarding those officers who need to make an arrest (such as note identifiers and obtain a warrant after the emergency for less serious offenses)?
- Should non-violent offenders be arrested during the crisis period?
- What shifts will the agency work?
- What cross-training is needed prior to the event?
- Who will staff communications and 911?
- Who can fill empty civilian positions?
- Who can supplement officers (civilian employees, reserve or auxiliary officers)?
- If available, how will the agency interface with federal assets, National Guard, or state-level agencies?
- What steps will be taken for civil disorder, riots, or looting?
- Will the jail release prisoners because of staff shortage, and if so, which prisoners should be released?
- How will prisoners be fed and who will provide medical care for them?
- Where will the agency obtain fuel, food, water, medical care, vehicle repair, and other expendables?
- Will officers be allowed to return home or will they have to stay in protected sites to sleep and rest?
- If power fails how will communications, jail, and radio system operate?
- Are alternate locations available for agency operations, jail, communications, and 911?
- Does the agency have a backup communications plan should the primary radio system fail?
- How will the agency communicate with the media to issue information to the public?
- If power is not available, how will the agency communicate information to the citizens?
- Who will liaison with outside agencies?
- Who will staff the emergency operations center?
- How will contact be maintained with elected officials?
- Is the chain of command intact? If not, who has the authority to operate the agency?

- Does the agency have access to prophylactic drugs for personnel to take if directed by public health authorities (antibiotics, antivirals)?
- How will personnel be paid?

Security considerations for hospitals, clinics, and other critical infrastructure will be needed. The potential for looting will be substantial. Routine arrests may have to be curtailed as jail space may not be available or jail staff limited. Some agencies have contemplated releasing those prisoners in jail on misdemeanor violations or awaiting trial for misdemeanors or non-violent felonies should a shortage of jail staff or jail space occur. Another issue will be the number of inmates who become ill. The potential for release of large numbers of inmates should be a consideration.

Quarantines may be imposed to restrict travel or isolate individuals. The enforcement of these may fall to law enforcement. The key is to understand who has the authority to declare quarantine. Officers must know what to do with individuals who violate the quarantine. In most states the violation of quarantine is a criminal offense. The key question is if the person is potentially ill or a disease carrier, one does not want to place this individual in jail. One important question is where to house those violating quarantine and who pays their care. Another issue is whether employees still receive pay if they are ill or quarantined. The agency needs to know these answers and prepare for such questions prior to the event.

Legal implications should be investigated. Questions for each jurisdiction which need answering are:

- Who can declare a state of emergency?
- Who can declare quarantine?
- What legal authority does the agency have to enforce the quarantine?
- Where will quarantine violators be held and who pays for it?

Another issue law enforcement may play a role in is the need for body disposal and expedient burials. The agency should have a full understanding with public health officials and the medical examiner as to how bodies will be handled. In many instances mortuaries will be full or not available. Expedient burials may be required. The questions regarding expedient burials which should be answered are:

- Who can authorize expedient burials?
- In what manner should the body be buried in terms of locale, container, depth, and identifying the site and person buried?
- How should this be reported and to whom should this be reported?
- Who is responsible to conduct expedient burials?

Lessons Learned from Others

The 1918–1919 influenza pandemic saw many of these incidents occur. Some communities enacted quarantines, some conducted expedient burials, and the flow of commerce stopped. During this time communities were more self-sufficient. Today most communities are dependent upon the transportation system to provide the needed resources with little inventory kept in businesses that use the "just in time" delivery system. Many large chains and grocery stores use this method to avoid keeping an inventory. With the loss of the inflow of resources, the community may use the available food, fuel, and other expendables quickly. Some businesses indicate they have, at most, 24–72 hours of merchandise through normal use and less than this period during an emergency. Areas which experience hurricanes see this "stripping of store shelves" in just a few hours when hurricanes approach. Within a short period, businesses see their supplies sold, including batteries, battery-powered radios, flashlights, candles, oil lamps, non-perishable food, tarpaulins, plastic sheeting, plywood, generators, fuel, bottled water, and other building supplies. Agencies should not depend upon external sources for supplies but should have at least a 72-hour stockpile of expendables.

Chapter 9

Mass Fatality Events

An issue which has become more frequent is that of multiple fatalities at an event. Most mass fatality events involve law enforcement but not as the lead agency unless a motor vehicle crash or crime has occurred. Mass fatalities involving crime scenes are a once-in-a-career event. While double and triple homicides are not uncommon, homicides with four or more victims are unusual. Even these numbers will tax a small agency's abilities to deal with such a crime scene.

What issues will the supervisor face during a chaotic multiple-fatality scene?

- Which agency is in charge?
- Is mutual aid needed, if so, what is needed?
- Is the scene safe?
- Are responders likely to be attacked?
- What hazards are present?
- How can hazards be mitigated or eliminated?
- Is this a crime scene?
- Are victims alive and needing aid?
- How does one know the victims are dead?
- Is the scene secure from external intrusion?
- How is the scene to be documented?
- How is evidence to be collected?
- If this is a long-lived event, what onsite support is needed?
- When can one move the bodies?
- How is identification made?
- What happens to the bodies and any personal items?
- Who makes next-of-kin notifications?
- Who talks to the media?

Flatiron US Army Helicopter evacuates several injured from a motor vehicle crash with multiple victims. Photograph by Jim Smith.

- Who cleans up the scene following its release?
- Will officers need mental health assistance afterwards? If so, how is this provided?

In events involving crime scenes from a common source such as a shooting, law enforcement is familiar with the issues and can undertake the needed task of verifying death, processing the crime scene, transferring control of the bodies to the medical examiner, securing personal items, and dealing with the media. The operations may need to be sized upwards with a large number of victims.

Some common issues in this type of event are overwhelming the morgue and medical examiner. Expedient body storage may become an issue, as will sufficient body bags. Some areas have mobile morgues to handle several victims, but agency procedure should identify additional sources of expedient body storage and body bags. Some agencies use disposable cardboard stretchers and body bags to move the bodies and store them as part of their crime scene operations equipment. Both these items have a long shelf life. Remember, when feasible, human remains should be treated with dignity.

Another substantial issue is PPE. The conventional booties and gloves may not be sufficient. Officers may have to don chemical protective suits with chemical boots and use respiratory protection in some scenes. Most scenes will present a biological hazard requiring that PPE be used. Officers must use care to avoid contact with body fluids. Where will the needed equipment come from and have officers been trained in its use?

Aircraft crashes can produce multiple fatalities with bodies scattered over a wide area. Law enforcement's primary role will be to determine the extent of the scene and secure the scene. Primary investigative efforts will be from the federal level with the National Transportation Safety Board. Some considerations are:

- This will likely be a long-lived event requiring on-scene support such as a mobile command post, protection from weather, portable toilets, and lighting.
- A secure perimeter is important, as sightseers, souvenir hunters, the media, and looters can be an issue.
- If a military aircraft is involved, one may find live ordinance present. When fire is present, some military aircraft present unusual hazardous materials threats from materials the aircraft may be constructed of, and fuel and exotic chemicals such as hydrazine could be present. The carbon fiber structure of some aircraft presents a substantial skin and respiratory hazard. If the aircraft is suspected of carrying ordinance, the incident commander should consider a 1,500-foot diameter exclusion zone. If feasible, those within this zone should be evacuated upwind. When feasible notify the nearest military facility of the crash or if the base of origin is known, notify this facility. The law enforcement branch of the military service is a good contact point. Ensure that the military explosive ordinance disposal (EOD) is dispatched if live ordinance is suspected.
- If a military aircraft is involved, unless rescue efforts are needed within the scene, fight fires defensively and stay upwind and uphill while securing a large exclusion area. When feasible do not enter these crash sites. Some of these crash sites involving military aircraft may require chemical suits and SCBA to enter because of the hazards present. The components of the aircraft may also be of national security interest, which is another reason a large and secure exclusion area is needed.
- The primary investigative agency will be the National Transportation Safety Board if a civilian aircraft is involved. If bodies are removed prior to NTSB investigator arrival, make certain their location is documented to assist the NTSB investigators.

- If fire was not present and the crash was a high-impact event, body fluid contamination is likely to be widespread. Bodies will likely be fragmented and distributed over the site. If the aircraft broke apart prior to impact, the debris field may be very large, as in Pan Am Flight 103 in Scotland (the Lockerbie bombing, 1988).
- Sharp objects and torn metal present substantial hazards, as do unburned fuel and hydraulic fluid.
- Crashes in austere terrain may present access issues.

Expedient body storage can be challenging. Some agencies have agreements with trucking companies who provide a refrigerated trailer for body storage. If this is used make certain the name of the company on the trailer is removed or covered. One agency with 10 shooting victims recently used this expedient method to store and transport the bodies to the state crime laboratory. Care should be used to keep the temperature above freezing so as to avoid damage to the bodies. Other agencies have used nearby structures to serve as a temporary storage site. The problem arises that if private property is used, remuneration for the use may be a factor, plus most individuals would be hesitant have a facility used as a morgue, even temporarily. If a structure is used, publicly owned structures are recommended. The issue of body fluids and odors of putrefaction are another issue in a temporary morgue. If identification is needed, digital photographs of the face are suggested (if recognizable), rather than direct viewing.

Evidence collection on a mass fatality scene can be challenging. The sheer volume of evidence to be collected can be overwhelming. Some agencies will not have sufficient evidence collection containers for a large scene with multiple fatalities. Access to these items from other sources should be noted in emergency plans. Some states have regional evidence response teams, as does the FBI. Another consideration is a state or federal Disaster Mortuary Operational Response Team (DMORT). These teams have the equipment and expertise to assist at mass fatality scenes.

Events involving toxic materials, radioactive material, or a communicable disease will present special challenges. The investigation of the scene, evidence collection, body handling techniques, and decontamination will be factors. Public health officials will have a role in determining what protective steps are needed in the event of a communicable disease. If contamination from chemicals or radioactive materials is present, hazardous materials specialists, health physicists, and public health officials will need to establish a plan to mitigate these hazards. If the event involves a bombing, bomb technicians may want to collect evidence from clothing and bomb fragments at autopsy, or even during surgery on living victims. Another challenging situation will be if explosive devices are projected into a body. Although rare, a live piece of ordinance or IED present on or within a body is not unheard of in suicide bombings. One regional bomb squad faced this issue when a military ordinance collector was attempting to demilitarize a 40 mm grenade and the round discharged and lodged in his thigh. EMS providers transported the victim to a large university medical school hospital emergency department but were refused entry. The EMS providers were stuck with a seriously injured patient they could not transfer to a higher level of medical care. The regional bomb squad assisted on scene and determined the round was not high-explosive incendiary but a smoke round. The patient was still refused admittance, but physicians directed bomb squad members in the surgical procedure to remove the grenade while complying with bomb squad procedures. The patient survived.

Long-lived scenes will also have issues with scavengers eating body parts. Officers will need to take steps to guard the scene from ground and bird scavengers. One agency uses "bird bangers," which are fireworks launched from a plastic device which make a loud whistling noise followed by an explosion to discourage scavengers on such scenes. These devices provide an audible and visual distraction and scare both ground-based and avian scavengers away. The devices do leave some powder and paper residue. Nocturnal scavengers such as feral dogs, feral pigs, coyotes, and opossums may enter a scene. Most bird scavengers, such as crows, buzzards, and vultures, will be limited to diurnal incursions. Use of firearms is discouraged, as shooting a scavenger on the site may contaminate the site, and if the site is in an urban area, shooting may not be feasible for safety reasons.

Health considerations for those working these scenes include a current vaccination for hepatitis B and tetanus. Some agencies have added hepatitis A vaccinations to this regimen because of exposure to fecal materials on such scenes. For officers, heat illness and dehydration while wearing PPE are substantial threats in warm environments. N99 masks and masks rated to screen putrefaction odors are recommended as a minimum for responders.

For those working such stressful scenes, the offer of the services of a mental health professional acquainted with law enforcement operations and PTSD is recommended along with Critical Incident Stress Debriefing/Management (CISD/CISM) services. Although group debriefs are helpful, some agencies have found the "one-on-one" debriefs with a mental health professional familiar with public safety operations provide more long-term benefits and assist in identifying those employees who need additional services. Stress reactions to such scenes including loss of appetite, sleep difficulties, intrusive images, flashback to the scene, hyper-vigilance, distracted behaviors, and loss of interest in normal activities are common. The key is that if any of these symptoms persist more than a few days, the officer should seek professional mental health assistance. Disguise the treatment from mental health professionals as "stress abatement" to remove the stigma.

Lessons Learned from Others

Residents in a rural area of Florida reported a loud explosion during a severe thunderstorm. The sheriff's office receiving the calls initially dismissed the calls as lightning strikes as deputies found no evidence of an "explosion" or other event. The next day a helicopter known to have been operating in the area of the reported explosion was reported missing. The weather was clear, and the sheriff's helicopter conducted an aerial search while deputies conducted vehicle, ATV, foot, airboat, hand-paddled boats, and horse-mounted searches. Much of the area is swamp and thickly forested with cypress and other trees. Deep within the swamp deputies in the helicopter spotted debris believed to be a crash site. The site was not amenable to lowering personnel on a "jungle penetrator," and the crash was so severe that the likelihood of survivors was nil. Airboats and even small hand-paddled boats were too large to fit between the thickly wooded cypress trees in the swamp waters. The local county department of transportation cut down trees and built a clay and gravel road over a several-day period to the crash site. The road was large enough to accommodate off-road all-terrain vehicles to gain access to the site for investigation and body recovery. Body recovery was conducted but the remains of the aircraft not removed by the NTSB investigators were abandoned. Severe weather was listed as the likely cause of the crash. Deputies in boats near the crash site had to contend with scavengers attempting to gain access to the bodies. They used periodic gunfire to discourage alligators, vultures, and other scavengers from the site during the construction of the roadway. The landowner demanded restitution for the damage to his property from governmental entities who constructed the roadway to the crash site and from the company operating the helicopter. The litigation is still in progress.

Chapter 10

Agricultural Terrorism

Many agencies operating in rural areas will be familiar with the needs of agriculture and the operation of farms. This includes not only plants but animals used in agriculture. Many operations are susceptible to attack to induce panic and fear in the public, damage the operations economically, and consume resources. The introduction of plant or animal pathogens is not new. The Germans during WWI targeted mules in use by the Allies with glanders disease to render them unavailable for use. The introduction of plant pathogens or animal pathogens is a little exploited but valuable mode of attack.

Many states' economies are based around agriculture. Even the threat of the introduction of a pathogen could cause a tremendous cost in terms of quarantine and inspection. The loss of confidence in consumers could cripple the market with a simple threat. Most threats to contaminate food products have not been credible, and few acts have been successful. However, the random attacks with the cyanide in Tylenol capsules that occurred in 1982 induced fear nationwide and costs millions of dollars in investigative efforts and product recalls. This attack prompted the use of anti-tampering and tamper-evident packaging for over-the-counter products.

Few safeguards are in place to prevent or detect the introduction of a plant or animal pathogen. The US borders are porous and only cursory attention is paid to the prevention of infected foodstuffs entering are undertaken.

Many natural pathogens exist which if introduced in the US could devastate agriculture. Avian influenza or velogenic Newcastle disease could easily require a strict quarantine and the culling of millions of chickens. The same is true with foot-and-mouth disease in cattle. A strict quarantine with disinfection of farm equipment and sterilization of areas where these diseases are present would be required and could cost billions of dollars. Wheat smut or rice blast could be introduced via aerosols and cause billions of dollars in damage to many crops.

The role of law enforcement will be supportive of those agencies engaged in the investigation and quarantine of such an event. The US Department of Agriculture and state department of agriculture would be the lead agencies in identifying and ordering quarantines. Quarantines might include strict decontamination of vehicles, packages, and other items leaving a quarantined area plus the culling and burning of plants or animals potentially contaminated. The economic losses could cause bankruptcy for those farms involved in such an outbreak.

Some farmers might resist the efforts, requiring force be used to achieve compliance. Local law enforcement will be thrust into the center of such disputes. In some instances, violence has been used to resist compliance with orders to cull and burn infected animals and plants, as such measures will likely bankrupt the uninsured farmer.

Chapter 11

Unconventional Weapons and Tactics

Law enforcement must deal with a large spectrum of threats. However, recent advances in technology, the expansion of threat groups, and the availability of information regarding law enforcement tactics has led to individuals and groups to use unconventional tactics and weapons. Their purposes may be to further a criminal goal or for political reasons. The use of surveillance and countermeasures to defeat the operational security of law enforcement is becoming common.

Some of the tactics may include the covert use of cellular telephones to record or photograph law enforcement operations. These same cellular telephones can be used to intercept law enforcement communications or to use social media to assemble a flash mob. Law enforcement has been slow to realize these hazards exist and even slower to adjust tactics and take countermeasures. Another issue is the use of radio jamming devices, which may jam law enforcement radios, cellular telephones, and GPS systems. Although illegal, these devices are available via the Internet and can work in up to a several hundred-foot radius around the device.

The use of improvised explosive devices (IED) or improvised incendiary devices (IID) is an issue. Bomb threats and suspicious objects must be considered a valid threat if the threat is credible. When a bomb threat occurs, make certain the threat is not a ruse to have employees leave the relative safety of the structure to be engaged by concealed shooters. The evacuation areas should be inspected for pre-placed IEDs and to confirm they are safe from assault with firearms. This tactic was used in the Jonesboro, Arkansas, school shooting in which the shooters activated the fire alarm and shot students and teachers as they emerged from the school building. Conferring with local high-risk businesses, schools, and government facilities regarding their bomb threat plans is essential to assure they have adequate plans to cope with bomb threats and suspicious items.

Letter bombs or threat items, or even hoax threats via mail, remain a simple method to attack a specific target in an anonymous manner. Postal regulations have made it more difficult to send larger devices, but a small letter bomb or incendiary device is not difficult to send. Law enforcement should assist high-risk businesses, schools, and government facilities in developing mail and package screening plans. Suspect items such as unknown letters, unexpected packages, or those items that meet letter bomb criteria should be isolated and inspected by the bomb squad.

Vehicle-borne improvised explosive devices (VBIEDs) remain a threat. They are a favorite modality to deliver a large quantity of explosives to a target. Maintaining a standoff distance between structures and vehicles is advisable. Another issue is the VBIED delivered by a suicide driver. Forcible entry with a vehicle into a restricted area or densely occupied area should be a consideration. A standoff distance of 300 feet is optimal but not achievable in most locales. However, any standoff distance will lessen the impact of VBIED. The Oklahoma City bombing remains an example of the damage and destruction a VBIED can cause, plus it illustrates the ease of construction and delivery of such a device.

Even a vehicle without an IED can created multiple casualties, as evidenced by the increase in vehicles used to attack crowds and pedestrians. Pedestrians exist in every city and are a soft target. One can easily attack them with a vehicle, causing injury, and even potentially escape on foot in the confusion or in the same vehicle used in the attack. Other forms of attack include the use of edged weapons such as knives, machetes, or even kitchen knives. These attackers have been able to rival attacks with firearms in terms of numbers of deaths and injuries in crowds, especially if more than one attacker is present. These attacks are seen in areas in which firearms are difficult to acquire. These type of attacks are difficult to guard against and stop once started. Inevitably, the attack is over, and the attacker stopped or escaped prior to police arrival.

A checkpoint security program with a magnetometer and x-ray system for individuals and packages prior to entry into a sensitive area is recommended. However, when feasible this "checkpoint" should be located as far away as possible from the sensitive area in case an active shooter event occurs or an IED is detected. Law enforcement will be called upon to assist in establishing this type of security on occasion and will need this type of security to protect the law enforcement facility.

Terrorists and threat groups will usually have well-planned methods of attack. They may use a bomb or active shooting to lure public safety onto a scene to attack them with pre-placed IEDs, attack with PBIEDs, or ambush with firearms. PBIEDs are common in other areas, and a few events involving PBIEDs have occurred in the US. However, this form of attack should not be discounted. Venues with large numbers of people will be an attractive target, as will law enforcement operations. Soft targets such as sporting events, hospitals, hotels, restaurants, shopping malls, or other densely occupied settings are likely targets. Any explosion or shooting at this type of venue should be considered the prelude to a swarm attack or a lure for public safety to attack them on the scene. Plans should be developed to allow small unit tactics and provide for logistics during swarm attacks. Officers may not have traditional tactical assets or backup available in such events. This is the reason the officers need active shooter and small unit training, patrol rifles, and substantial amounts of ammunition to engage individuals conducting a swarm attack. The police in the Mumbai attacks lacked sufficient training in small unit tactics, had inferior firearms and limited ammunition, and experienced sporadic communications. Backup units with superior training and firearms took hours to arrive. Similar issues should be expected in this type of attack in the US, as evidenced in criminal attacks during the North Hollywood bank robbery and the Norco, California, bank, which found police "outgunned" by better-armed adversaries who had trained for the attack. Even though police outnumbered the attackers considerably, the attackers were able to keep police from arresting them, injure numerous officers, and escape (at least temporarily).

Another trend by conventional criminals is the use of military-type weapons and tactics. Criminals are now conducting surveillance, identifying rally points, and establishing ambush tactics, and some have sophisticated plans to conduct robberies. The Norco, California, bank robbery in 1980 and the more recent North Hollywood shootout (in 1997) are examples of what a small group of individuals can achieve. The "rogue cop" Christopher Dorner is an example of a trained individual targeting law enforcement. In 2013, Dorner killed at least two officers and wounded several others after killing two civilians. His tactics of fleeing and ambushing officers consumed law enforcement assets over a substantial portion of the western US. His tactics and actions mirror those used by terrorists, such as in the San Bernardino attack where two terrorists killed a large number of people in 2015. The Boston Marathon bombing (2013) and search for the terrorists paralyzed a large area. The explosions taxed public safety and medical resources. Several deaths and serious injuries were inflicted not only by the bombings but also by firefights with law enforcement. In 2017, the well-planned attack in Las Vegas by one well-trained and well-armed shooter was able to immobilize the city, kill dozens, and wound hundreds. Imagine several individuals conducting similar attacks simultaneously. The commitment of substantial resources is needed to isolate, contain, and neutralize such events. Although officers heavily outnumbered the robbers in Norco, in the Dorner incident, the Boston Marathon bombers, and the robbers in North Hollywood, these criminals and terrorists were still able to inflict numerous casualties on law enforcement and the public with superior weaponry and tactics. The use of body armor by criminals is becoming common, and officers must adapt targeting tactics to take into account the potential use of body armor. Targeting of unprotected body areas such as the legs, pelvis, and head should be considered if center mass shots do not incapacitate the suspect.

The use of distraction tactics is becoming more commonplace, such as calling in a bomb threat to a school or high-risk facility to distract law enforcement while a robbery or attack occurs. Some criminal elements have used arson fires or the explosion of bombs to distract law enforcement. The number of ambushes of officers has increased. These appear to be hasty and unplanned, but a few have been planned and well-constructed. Criminals have sporadically used hoax calls to ambush officers. The use of rifles with precision optics has occurred. Officers must be cognizant of this threat and have training to disengage and retreat from an ambush while on foot or within a vehicle. Protesters and anarchists have learned to defeat police less-lethal projectiles with the use of improvised body armor (magazines and newspapers) or by wearing body armor. These same groups have begun to use air-purifying respirators (military surplus gas masks or commercial APRs) to defeat OC and tear gas. They use the countermeasure of hand-thrown Molotov cocktails, slingshot-launched steel ball bearings, and other weapons to injure and impede law enforcement operations. Law enforcement now faces a well-trained and "smarter" criminal. Anti-abortion groups have used malodorants such as butyric acid against abortion clinics. This liquid smells like vomit and is an effective denial-of-use agent. Officers should realize that items contaminated by the malodorant will not likely be able to be cleaned. The use of exotic weapons such as biological or chemical agents has occurred in US and will likely continue. The anthrax attacks in 2001 created terror and public concern out of proportion to the threat. Even the 2013 ricin attacks caused concern but were overshadowed by the Boston Marathon bombings and other concurrent events. A newer toxic agent, abrin, is more toxic and just as easily obtained as castor beans. Several incidents have occurred with abrin, which is also known as *Abrus precatorius* seed, jequirity bean, rosary beads, Indian licorice, and others. These beans are easily obtained and transformed into a toxic agent for which no antidote exists.

Many agencies found their resources taxed by the large number of anthrax reports which were not credible during the 2001 events. The first sophisticated chemical weapon use in recent times was the sarin attack in Japan in 1995, al-

Castor Bean Plant. Photograph from FEMA.

though it appears that nerve agents, chlorine, and perhaps other agents have been used in the conflict in Syria. Nerve agents are difficult to manufacture, but substitute chemical agents such as organophosphate insecticides can be obtained. The use of toxic industrial chemical such as chlorine, anhydrous ammonia, or phosgene is feasible. These chemicals are common and theft prone, as they may have only a chain-link fence securing the site. These are lethal chemicals but would only affect a small area. However, attacks of fixed or enclosed structures such as a building, subway, or a stadium could produce a large number of casualties. The ease of simply releasing chlorine or anhydrous ammonia cylinder upwind of a crowded stadium is attractive. The ensuing panic would produce causalities even if the exposure to chlorine or anhydrous ammonia did not. OC could produce a similar result, as seen in stampedes induced in nightclubs following its use.

Another biological agent which is easy to produce but more difficult to dispense is ricin. Ricin is a deadly derivative of the castor bean and has no antidote. In 1994, a plot by a right-wing radical group proposed to use ricin mixed with dimethyl sulfoxide (DMSO), a powerful solvent, to contaminate and kill federal agents when they contacted doorknobs or door handles. Only a very small amount of ricin is required to kill, but the issue is the ricin molecule is so large the DMSO would not have allowed it to penetrate the skin. However, hand-to-mouth contact or non-intact skin might have allowed the toxin to be ingested or absorbed. This type of research and planning shows that law enforcement faces a more intelligent and sophisticated foe. The recent attacks involving ricin demonstrate this is a viable method to induce terror and perhaps denial of use of facilities.

The use of military-type improvised weapons in the form of projected IEDs from mortars has long been a favorite Irish Republican Army (IRA) tactic. The

Pipe bomb with booby trap mechanism. This is a re-creation of a booby trap used to guard a marijuana field and is typical of booby traps in drug related operations. Photograph by Jim Smith.

IRA tactic allows a stolen vehicle to be converted for use as a base for the improvised mortars. The vehicle is driven to the site and the motors activated to attack the target. The IRA would booby trap the vehicles and, in some cases, designed the vehicle to self-destruct. Individuals in the US have been arrested for selling kits with readily assembled hand grenades, while other individuals marketed IEDs attached to arrows as expedient grenades. These well-designed devices were being sold on the Internet along with other booby traps and explosives. Shotgun-launched grenades were used against law enforcement in the Norco, California, bank robbery, and rifle fire shot down a law enforcement helicopter during the robbery. The Riverside County Deputy Sheriffs Association has an excellent video concerning the event on their website.

The use of unmanned aerial vehicles (UAVs) or drones, to observe police, conduct preattack surveillance, and even deliver IEDs is a threat. The small and inexpensive UAVs, which can be purchased anonymously, can be converted to a flying IED and under the control of an individual some distance away. The media and others routinely use UAVs to observe police operations; even curious citizens do this. The problem is law enforcement does not know if the UAVs present a threat or surveillance of operations by an adversary. The neutralizing of such a threat is not simple. Several companies market devices to detect and defeat UAVs and range from sophisticated fixed equipment used to jam the UAV control signals, to counter UAVs to attack the intruding UAV, to handheld launched nets from a shoulder-fired weapon. Some police agencies have used shotguns with small shot to defeat UAVs, but the issue becomes whether such a tactic is safe and what liability is incurred by the crashing UAV. This is an issue the agency must clearly consider and have a procedure as to

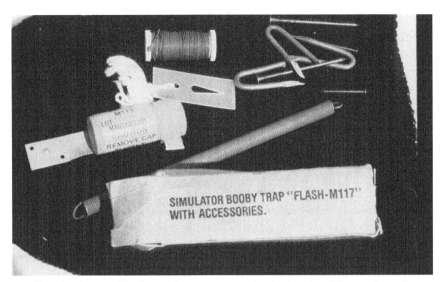

A military booby trap kit adapted for use to guard clandestine drug laboratories and marijuana grows. Photograph by Jim Smith.

A booby trapped light bulb filled with smokeless gunpowder which detonates when the light is turned on which was found in a methamphetamine laboratory. Photograph by Jim Smith.

the actions to take if a UAV is present on a scene. The recent attack against the Venezuelan president by UAVs carrying IEDs is an example of the application.

Booby traps of an explosive nature or using chemicals have long been a part of clandestine drug laboratories. Care should be taken in the raid of any suspected threat group or what appears to be a methamphetamine laboratory for booby traps. Another issue is that the laboratory may be an explosive laboratory making very unstable explosives such as triacetone triperoxide (TATP) or could be a laboratory for the deriving of toxins such as ricin. Many of the same chemicals used to make methamphetamine can allow explosives to be made. The white powder present may be methamphetamine, TATP, fentanyl, abrin, or ricin.

Laser pointers have become a source of harassment and potential harm. When a laser light is observed the law enforcement officer does not know whether he or she is being targeted or harassed. Officers must react as if they are targeted with a firearm. Research and industrial lasers present a threat of eye injury if used. The lasing of aircraft has become more common and affects the vision of the pilot, endangering the safety of the aircraft. Obtaining a laser of industrial or research grade (types IIIb or IV) is not difficult, and these lasers do present a substantial risk of eye injury if used improperly.

Threat groups, terrorists, and criminals are now planning and practicing tactics. They may even recreate the structures involved to hone their skills. These rehearsals and training make them a much more sophisticated adversary. Their training and equipment will likely exceed that available to law enforcement field personnel. Further, these groups may have conducted surveillance, listened to radio traffic, tested law enforcement response, observed the equipment and tactics in use by law enforcement, and designed countermeasures to defeat them.

Chapter 12

Emerging Threat Groups

Sovereign Citizens

Perhaps one of the more dangerous emerging groups is sovereign citizens. They believe the existing government is not legitimate and twist many legal findings and the Constitution to fit their beliefs. This group has emerged as a progeny of the Posse Comitatus groups which existed in the 1970s. Some areas of the southeastern US have been dealing with them since the mid-1990s. However, their status has changed from nuisance to a substantial threat to law enforcement in the last several years. Their efforts to evade income taxes and refusal to comply with laws, or recognize the existing government at any level, are the basis of their philosophy and operations.

Sovereign citizens have combined the best of tax evasion, government conspiracies to regulate behavior, and control of government by the rich into a palatable package swallowed by many. One might consider that only the uneducated would be attracted to its message. However, this is not correct as the frustration level with the government, especially the federal government, has led many to believe the propaganda of the sovereign citizens movement. Some sovereign citizens have operated pyramid schemes to generate income while others teach members the techniques to file bogus liens and how to harass local officials. In some instances, prospective members may have to pay for this "knowledge."

Indicators of activity of this group include their own government, which includes an executive branch with a president, vice president, cabinet, congress and senate, their own currency, travel documents, driver's license, and vehicle tags. What is more of a concern is these groups use their law enforcement branch and court system to issue warrants. Officers encountering unusual vehicle tags, unusual identity documents, and individuals claiming they are law enforcement officers from non-existent agencies are indicators of the sovereign citizen movement.

Sovereign citizens are sufficiently educated to use the court system to attack elected officials and law enforcement with false liens. Until recently the filing of these documents was not illegal in many areas. This required those served with the liens to retain legal counsel to disprove the lien and have it removed at their own expense. Now several states have made the filing of such documents a crime and the removal of the lien possible through criminal action against the person filing the false lien.

Sovereign citizens have been known to impersonate police officers and make arrests. Some have even presented the "prisoner" to local jails. The sovereign citizens may recognize the authority of the local sheriff since he or she is an elected official but only as long as it supports their belief system.

Sovereign citizens may spell or punctuate their name in an odd manner and indicate they are a "free man." They sometimes quote portions of the Uniform Commercial Code to support their position. The language used is reminiscent of the secret language of the Ku Klux Klan. Sovereign citizens are known to "squat" on foreclosed properties. They may use the tactic of paying off a large debt with a small number of silver dollars. Some occupy fenced or barricaded compounds. One sovereign citizen in the south of Alabama refused to pay his bills and dug a deep moat around his residence, which prevented law enforcement from evicting him from his foreclosed residence. Officers resorted to a raid via helicopter to evict the sovereign citizen. In another raid of a sovereign citizen's well-barricaded residence, more than 200 firearms, food, water, diesel fuel, and other survival supplies sufficient to last for several months were discovered. A large quantity of gold coins was also recovered. This particular sovereign citizen was sent to federal prison for income tax evasion, and his assets were seized.

Tactics used by sovereign citizens when dealing with law enforcement include delivering a rehearsed speech to distract officers and handing officers documents. This group uses phone trees, mass emails, and social media to assemble a flash mob. In many instances these individuals are armed and have practiced the tactics they will use against law enforcement. If one is encountering what is believed to be a sovereign citizen, the following steps are suggested:

- Do not become distracted and stay alert, as this individual is likely armed.
- Stay focused on the reason for the stop in the conversation.
- Do not accept items the suspected sovereign citizen attempts to hand you but watch their hands, and remember other sovereign citizens are likely responding to the scene.

- Obtain backup prior to making the stop if feasible.
- Expect the suspect to be armed and well trained in the use of firearms.
- The firearms used by sovereign citizens are likely to be of good quality.
- Expect other sovereign citizens to arrive to support the person stopped.
- These individuals will likely be armed and will harass and interfere with stop.
- These individuals record video and audio of stops.
- The person stopped will likely not cooperate.
- Expect violent resistance if an arrest is attempted.
- If outnumbered consider a tactical withdrawal.

More than a dozen law enforcement officers throughout the US have been killed in encounters with sovereign citizens. Sovereign citizens have a strong presence in the southeastern US but have supporters and active members throughout the country.

Militias

Militias are another emerging threat group. These tend to be insular groups with only a few members. They tend to be survivalist in terms of mentality and are planning for a failure of order. When government fails these groups will emerge to take control and fill the power vacuum. They have been known to construct refuges in remote areas which are well equipped to remain self-sufficient for extended period. Some have been known to construct bunkers or "storm shelters" within or near to a residence.

Many are disaffected individuals who gain a sense of power and purpose from membership in the militia. These groups are sometimes well armed and some are well trained. The concern for law enforcement is their plots to accelerate the loss of government control. Law enforcement is a common target and some militia groups have planned to attack law enforcement to start an apocalyptic cascade to destroy the existing government.

Some combine other philosophies such as white supremacy or other beliefs into their philosophy. Many of these groups are more of a social club who enjoy paramilitary training and the use of firearms. However, one should not discount the threat posed to law enforcement or government officials as several plots by militia to attack law enforcement or government officials have been disrupted.

Officers and agencies should stay abreast of the intelligence regarding these groups. Information from the local level is important but information from the state fusion center, joint terrorism task force, and local FBI office is valuable. Officers encountering anyone they have reason to believe is associated with one of these groups should follow agency policy regarding completion and submission of Suspicious Activity Report to the state fusion center. Officers should not confuse militias with state self-defense forces or state militias, which are official, governmentally sanctioned groups with legitimate disaster roles.

Chapter 13

Special Considerations

Operational Security

Many law enforcement agencies take a blasé attitude regarding operational security. However, in the current environment of sophisticated criminals and potential terrorist activities the role of operational security must be a priority.

Law enforcement operational methods and sources should remain confidential. Reality television has been a positive "learning experience" for the public, but it also provides a school for criminals and terrorists.

In a 2007 event in Florida in which the wife of a sheriff was kidnapped and killed during a gun battle between law enforcement and the kidnappers, the criminals in this case had watched television programs regarding crime scenes and read textbooks to defeat forensics. Their intent appeared to be to kidnap and kill the sheriff's wife and obscure the scene with hypochlorite (bleach) to prevent any DNA they might have left behind from being detected, and they carried protective clothing to be donned while they were on scene. During the gun battle the suspects killed the wife and a deputy before they were killed. The event stemmed from the sheriff's investigation of the death of the wife of one of the suspects under unusual circumstances in which sufficient evidence was present to deny the life insurance payment, but it was not sufficient to indict him for her murder. Criminals do read and watch television; many are savvy enough to use the Internet for information. The North Hollywood shootout and the Norco, California, bank robbery both were well-planned events in which law enforcement was outgunned and outmaneuvered by suspects who had taken the time to study the target and law enforcement tactics.

After studying law enforcement methods and conducting surveillance of the bank they chose to rob in Norco, California, the robbers engaged deputies responding to the robbery. During a running gun battle with deputies, the robbers managed to kill one deputy, wound eight deputies, destroy 33 patrol cars with rifle fire and shotgun-launched grenades, and shoot down a police helicopter. Eventually two robbers were killed and three captured. The key is these two bank robberies were executed by a small number of individuals who confronted a much larger number of officers but were able to inflict serious casualties using better weapons, better tactics, and better equipment than the officers possessed. These cases are salient examples of what research, planning, and training by criminals can produce.

To discover how law enforcement agencies plan, collect intelligence, conduct raids, respond to high-risk calls, one can watch television programs or research using the Internet. The methods used by forensic science in collecting trace evidence are presented, allowing countermeasures to be developed.

Some of the sources that criminals or terrorists can use to gather data about an agency include the agency press releases and media stories which explain new equipment or tactics in use by the agency. Agencies brag on operations or accomplishments and release crucial data as to methods of operation and what resources were used.

Agencies have extensive information about the agency and its special response teams on the agency's website. The CEO should review what is presented. One agency shows their special response team in full equipment. This photograph provides a criminal or terrorist a good idea of the number of personnel available, type of body armor worn, firearms used, and similar information. Public display of photographs of law enforcement personnel other than command-grade personnel should be avoided. The same agency displayed their extensive homeland security and bomb squad equipment during public relations events. This allowed anyone wanting to gain an inventory of the equipment and the deduce the capabilities of the department by simply attending the event. The tactical and bomb robots were used to demonstrate their capabilities and armored vehicles such as an MRAP vehicle were open to display, as were the various weapons in use by the agency's tactical team, including low-light imaging equipment, thermal imaging, and similar equipment. An adversary would have a good idea of what to use to defeat low-light and thermal imaging equipment. This information is readily available on the Internet and YouTube, whereas an adversary not knowing this equipment was available would be less likely to conduct countermeasures.

Some agencies have department photographs taken and posted in public places within their building. Some have removed their photographs of officers from public view after undercover officers were recognized in these photographs. Email should not be presumed to be secure, and in some states, emails may be discoverable as a public record. One should presume that email is not secure, especially if a public server is used. Some officers keep sensitive material in non-secure areas, such as their home, on a non-encrypted home computer, or even in the patrol car. The use of chat groups online can be another security issues as one never knows who might be in the chat room. Social media presents the same issues. Some officers may indicate they are about to engage in a sensitive operation by a change of their status. Many agencies prohibit officers from indicating their employment and agency affiliation, while other agencies allow officers to pose in uniform on social media. This is a security issue for the agency and the officer. Several groups have purposely targeted officers at their homes by using information gathered from social media.

Other methods used to gather information include surveillance of communications by agencies using non-encrypted radios. Some areas have civilian websites and social media devoted to posting police activities as they are overheard via radio on the website or through social media. They encourage website and social media users to send in cellular telephone photographs of police scenes. Some applications for cellular telephones allow individuals to report the location of officers engaged in traffic enforcement or surveillance. Some agencies now have to move traffic safety checkpoints several times during a shift as their location is promptly reported on social media. In some locales officers may be able see the motor vehicle crash scene on the website or social media prior to their arrival as a passerby has uploaded a photograph or video of the scene. Cellular telephones are private but with adequate resources can be intercepted. Another indicator that an operation is underway is the sudden switch from unencrypted radio traffic to encrypted radio traffic by officers. Some agencies randomly switch to encrypted traffic as a countermeasure.

In some agencies when a special operation is imminent, the assembly of a large number of officers donning raid vests or loading equipment at the station is seen. Meetings between command-level officers and special operation team commanders in a public place are a sign of an impending special operation. Changes in jail staffing patterns when a "round up" or mass arrests are planned telegraphs a special operation is imminent. In some instances, these schedule changes may be made weeks prior to the event. Some agencies now make certain they have officers don equipment at the station prior to training and at random times to defeat this observation.

Trash can be a fertile source of information as important documents are discarded. Some agencies' trash is handled by inmates who have access to some of the most sensitive documents the agency produces. Trash should be shredded with a professional-grade shredder. Mundane items such as purchase orders or telephone call return notes can compromise an investigation.

Law enforcement agencies love paper documents. Document security is another issue, as plans and vital data should be marked as confidential or law enforcement sensitive. These items should not be stored on a server outside control of the agency. For security reasons and to remind personnel that the information on the document was sensitive, one agency used a brightly colored paper for all law enforcement sensitive material. They found this tactic to be counterproductive as officers still discarded the unshredded documents in the trash. The inmate laborers emptying the trash were retrieving the brightly colored paper with the sensitive information. The information provided home addresses in which criminals targeted police vehicles, stealing firearms, munitions, and body armor.

Special steps should be taken to secure rosters that contain the names of personnel, their home address, telephone numbers, and other vital information. This can be seen on duty rosters, personnel records, or gained through computer intrusion into the agency's personnel computer records.

These rosters may identify members of special response teams, which could provide information as to their composition and size. Special protective measures must be taken regarding criminal histories and information from NCIC or state criminal justice information systems such that no unauthorized disclosure takes place. Several officers have been prosecuted by state-level criminal justice information agencies for failing to control protected information, criminal histories, and worse—selling such information or sharing the officer's password with civilians for money.

Counter surveillance should be conducted by law enforcement personnel as some threat groups have used surveillance to identify law enforcement, their residences, personal vehicles, and even family members. Holding sensitive meetings in public locations, like restaurants, where sensitive information can be overhead, is not recommended. The discussion of sensitive law enforcement information with family members is a problem, as they may unintentionally release information. This same admonition applies to non-law enforcement acquaintances as one never knows who this information might be leaked to in an unintentional manner. Social engineering by planting operatives in "cop bars" or "cop restaurants" is an old trick, as sensitive information is discussed and easily overheard. One regional intelligence sharing group meets in a restaurant and discussed law enforcement sensitive material within the hearing of non-law enforcement personnel within the restaurant. Even though this security breach has been pointed out the group, which contains civilian, military, and even federal agencies, still conducts these meetings in the public venue of the restaurant.

Security of firearms and other weapons is critical. The unauthorized access to a pistol, TASER, flash-bang munitions, OC or tear gas dispensers, or patrol

Law enforcement drill using explosive entry. Photograph by Dr. John Wipfler.

rifle could be lethal to the uneducated, or at the least embarrassing to the officer and agency. One agency had negative media reporting when a SWAT member left an automatic carbine on the top of his vehicle and drove away. The automatic carbine was later found and stolen by a passerby. The weapon was recovered and a suspect arrested prior to any harm. The loss of several pounds of explosives by their bomb detection canine handler was faced by another agency until the explosives were recovered. The handler simply left the explosives in the training location, a commercial concern. Cleaning personnel found the explosives and called police. In another, a specialty team member had explosive grenades that dispensed rubber buckshot and tear gas stolen from a storage shed at his residence. Why the officer was storing the items at his home was never adequately explained as this was a clear violation of procedure. The items were recovered prior to their use by a juvenile who possessed the grenades on a school campus. Firearms and munitions must be stored in a locked, theft-resistant location, preferably alarmed. Some agencies have installed theft-resistant vaults in vehicle trunks which are alarmed.

Inmate labor is common in the law enforcement setting and, in some instances, is the only janitorial labor available. The agency must ensure the inmates are restricted from access to sensitive areas. Even material placed on bulletin boards can be of use to these criminals. Imagine the chagrin one agency experienced when an inmate was able to retrieve an agency credit card from an investigator's desk and his keys to an unmarked patrol car containing several firearms. The inmate was later captured several hundred miles away using the credit card to gas the unmarked patrol car. One must remember these are criminals, and they must be supervised.

Other agencies operate with law enforcement, and as a rule their employees are trustworthy. One issue which should be considered is that the background investigations required (if any) are not as stringent as those for law enforcement. One may find persons with criminal records, even convicted felons, working for emergency management, fire service, or EMS agencies. Information sharing should be minimized regarding law enforcement sensitive material or attaching them to specialty team without a background check. One agency discovered a firefighter-paramedic operated as a member of a right-wing extremist group and was in consideration for an EMS role on their special response team. Clerical and IT personnel should also receive scrutiny. They have broad access to law enforcement sensitive information and background checks are needed to assure they are not security risks. The background checks should not be a one-time event but should occur periodically to ensure that the status of the person has not changed. Outlaw biker gangs specifically target law enforcement by attempting to insert a female into a clerical position. A dissatisfied employee or dishonest employee with access to sensitive data can do tremendous harm to an agency. A consideration during disciplinary issues is the suspension or removal of computer privileges, electronic and physical keys, radios, firearms, and other sensitive items.

Adversaries can be smart enough to identify law enforcement capabilities, plans, and operations, as one agency learned during a raid. Vice officers found photographs of unmarked and covert police vehicles with license plate numbers belonging to police officers' personal vehicles. The drug traffickers conducted counter surveillance of the police agency and identified officers. One group followed officers home and waited until the officer departed and broke into their patrol car to steal firearms and body armor. One sheriff's department discovered building plans and photographs of the exterior of their complex, the local courthouse, and the newspaper while investigating a suspicious person at a barn. A threat group unknown to the agency was conducting surveillance. The group was unhappy with recent article relating to the group's philosophies published by the newspaper and espoused by the agency's public information officer.

Indicators such as the type of vehicle, antennas, and radios located inside vehicles can be used to identify unmarked police cars. Pizza services report they know when the military is conducting special operations when they receive large orders of pizza from the Pentagon after normal business hours.

Some of the Local Emergency Planning Committee (LEPC) and SARA Title III records are open sources for the location, storage, and protection methods of hazardous materials. Although more stringent protection of the information has begun, this can be a fertile source for those contemplating the theft of toxic industrial chemicals or the attack of such a facility. The LEPC is important in coordinating response to various emergencies including terrorist threats that could involve hazardous materials. This information could be of use to groups contemplating the theft or use of hazardous materials in criminal acts. Each political jurisdiction is required to keep an updated Pre-Disaster Mitigation Plan to be eligible to receive federal funding. Such plans may be public record, and many list critical infrastructure locations within the plan.

The necessity of personal security should be a concern for law enforcement officers. The officer should be careful to not publish any telephone numbers or email addresses and use banking institutions for loans and credit. Using initials or an initial, last name, and no middle name on forms is another. Avoid social media and do not post photographs of oneself or family on any site. Have law enforcement magazines sent to the agency address. Remember, providing your telephone number or email to any group, whether social or fraternal, is the same as publishing it. Officers should consider checking information sites available to the public. Most sites will have a mechanism to remove information. Although time consuming, removing one's data from these sites is recommended, as some allow such requests on the site while others require a letter requesting the removal.

Agencies should take countermeasures that include a comprehensive operational security plan addressing how documents are handled and the methods to assure that sensitive information is not discarded. Secure communications are a necessity with the precept of limiting sensitive information to only those "who need to know." Specialty team commanders should consider methods to reduce "indicators" of operations. A comprehensive plan scaled to the individual agency needs with proactive steps to assure operational security is a necessity.

Canine Deployment

Litigation involving police canines has become a common source of legal problems for many agencies. Lawsuits alleging excessive force in the use of canines are common. Some agencies have responded by adjusting their policies to mirror court decisions and some have retained their current policies, while others have elected to disband their canine unit.

Canines have long been used for detection and apprehension of suspects, detection of illegal drugs, detection of trace accelerants in arson cases, tracking of human scent, and the location of cadavers. Recent Supreme Court cases involving the use of canines for drug detection on the curtilage of a residence (land immediately surrounding a home) should be reviewed. The areas litigated frequently are that of detection and apprehension. Usually the allegation is that

Appearances can be deceiving. Although this large Alsatian Wolf Dog appears intimidating, Tarby is a nursing home therapy dog who accompanies officers when they visit nursing homes. Photograph by Jim Smith.

the canine represented excessive force during apprehension, or the training or certification of the canine during detection may be attacked as in *Florida v. Harris*, 568 U.S. 237; slip op. 11-817 (2013). In many instances of apprehension, the canine may inflict some injury, but rarely serious or fatal injuries. An important decision within any policy would be the Ninth Federal Circuit Court of Appeals *Vera Cruz v. City of Escondido*, 139 F.3d, 659, 663 (9th Cir. 1998). This court held that as applied in *Tennessee v. Garner*, 471 U.S. 1 (1985) the deployment of a canine is not considered deadly force. One case that documents the fatal injury of a person apprehended by a canine is *Robinette v. Barnes*, 854 F., 2d 909 (6th Cir. 1988). If *Garner* were to be strictly applied canines could only be deployed when offenders potentially presented a threat to officers or others with a weapon or had committed a crime involving the threatened or actual serious physical injury. *Graham v. Connor*, 490 U.S. 386, 109 S.Ct. 1865 (1989), established a single standard to determine if excessive force was used. The standard is whether the officer acted appropriately and whether the action taken by the officer was objectively reasonable under the circumstances faced by the officer at that time.

Looking at these decisions in light of *Mendoza v. Block*, 27 F.3d 1357, 1362, (9th Cir. 1994), the deployment of a canine is a use of force. The objectively reasonable standard must apply, and if an officer would not be permitted to use force in the circumstances then a canine should not be deployed for detection and apprehension. The canine is simply another tool in the officer's armamentarium but can constitute a significant use of force. Some agencies classify the deployment of canine for apprehension purposes to be a step down from deadly force and the equivalent to less lethal alternatives such as shotgun-launched beanbags or other less lethal techniques.

The policy should clearly allow the canine officer to deploy the canine under circumstances based upon the severity of the offense, whether the suspect poses a threat to officers or other persons, and whether the suspect actively resisted arrest or is trying to elude officers. An important factor to note is many agencies consider the use of a canine for apprehension to be a high degree of force. The deployment must be in line with department's use of force policy.

Department policies that address detect-and-hold approach by the canine should be based around the three-pronged *Graham v. Connor* test. This provides a basis as to whether the suspect should be exposed to potential injury. Usually justifiable deployments include:

- Building searches for serious felony offenders or armed misdemeanor offenders.
- Effecting the arrest or preventing the escape of suspect involved serious offenses or violent suspects.
- Protecting officers from serious injury.

Some agencies do not send canine units to routine calls but hold them in reserve for specialty calls where the canine is most likely to be deployed and utilized efficiently. Other agencies cannot afford this luxury, and canine units answer routine calls for service. Canine officers will be subject to recall on a frequent basis and must perform certain aspects of the canine's care such as grooming, cleaning, and feeding off duty. This means there is usually significant overtime pay associated with this program, and the canine officer will usually have a take-home vehicle to transport the canine. Some agencies run canines on every shift while others only deploy them during high probability times such as night shift, when the canine is more likely to be utilized.

The selection of a canine handler should be carefully considered, and the potential handler should have an exemplary work record. A history of citizen complaints and excessive use of force should be disqualifiers. An essential factor is that the handler have a positive attitude toward police work, is patient in temperament, is dependable, and is in good physical condition. The recommended officer should have a minimum of three to five years of police experience in the patrol setting. A suitable location for the canine's kennel at the officer's residence is another issue that must be addressed. The handler must be willing to handle the increased overtime involved in the care of the canine and for recalls, although some agencies house the canine in an agency kennel. In some instances, the socialization of the canine in the family setting may be an advantage, especially for canines which are not used for apprehension.

Patrol officers and supervisors should be educated as to the canine unit's capabilities. The canine officer on scene should be the determiner as to if the circumstances are appropriate to deploy the canine. If a conflict arises, it should be resolved by the canine supervisor and the field supervisor. *Rodriguez v. United States* says that a traffic stop cannot be prolonged to bring a canine for a drug sniff unless articulable reasonable suspicion exists that illegal drugs are present.

Canine training and selection are critical factors. The canine selected should have good temperament and socialize well with humans. The best method of acquiring a canine is by purchasing from a reputable source that professionally trains canines for law enforcement work. Basic training is followed by continuing training on a regular basis and its documentation is critical. In *Robinette v. Barnes*, 854 F., 2d 909 (6th Cir., 1988), the court ruled that even though the canine killed the suspect, a properly trained canine apprehending a suspect does not normally constitute deadly force. The court closely examined the training records, making documentation of training essential in any litigation, as seen in several Supreme Court decisions regarding the detection of illicit substances. *Florida v. Harris*, 568 U.S. 237 (2013) examines the training records of canines used to detect illicit substances and what records must be kept and the needed training. This case is worth reading as it delineates clearly the needed records and training to meet the Supreme Court's standards.

There exists a debate over the method used for apprehension. Some agencies have adopted a find and bark regimen as opposed to a find and hold technique to reduce the potential for injuries. Significant justification exists for using this technique, as it allows escalation of force if the suspect resists or flees as opposed to find and hold, which almost always results in injury to a suspect. The find and bark method reduces the number of bites and therefore litigation alleging excessive force. There remains an unresolved issue as to which method is safer for the canine handler and officers with excellent arguments for both methods. A procedure not recommended is that canines be deployed to find suspects who do not present a threat to officers, have not committed a serious offense, or are not actively resisting or fleeing. Some agencies do allow the use canines to apprehend passively hiding suspects who do not meet the enumerated criteria. This is legally risky, as justification for this use of force can be difficult.

The maintaining of documentation of canine activities including training, searches, bites, apprehensions, and the like need to well documented and tracked as these records will allow the periodic evaluation of the canine's abilities and will assist in defending litigation. A negative illustration of this situation is *Kerr v. City of West Palm Beach*, 875 F.2d 1546 (11th Cir. 1988). The suit alleged excessive force involving a canine bite. The city was alleged to have inadequate training, insufficient policy regarding the use of force and the utilization of canines, and inadequate methods for tracking the performance of the canines particularly in relation to bites. The lack of records and documentation did not allow the city to defend itself effectively, as performance records were not kept permanently. Ideally, an ongoing record allows the canine supervisor to examine the bite ratio, bites versus total number of deployments, and bites to apprehensions to identify canines that need remedial training.

Training and supervision by the canine handler must occur to assure the canine is closely supervised and controlled. Several successful lawsuits have alleged inadequate supervision and control by the canine handler, resulting in injuries to the suspect. Usually visual contact should be maintained by the canine handler with the canine to assure adequate control. A bite ratio using bites versus apprehensions rather than total deployments versus bites provides a truer picture of the number of bites versus potential bites. Canine-produced injuries, particularly bites, should be well documented. The canine supervisor and field supervisor should respond. Immediate medical care should be arranged even if the injury appears minor. Photographs prior to medical treatment and following the injury cleaning should be taken to demonstrate the department's efforts to closely monitor such injuries and to document medical treatment. The canine handler should document with a use of force form providing the exact circumstances of the incident and how the suspect was injured.

An important aspect preceding the deployment of a canine is to warn the suspect that the canine is about to be utilized and that a bite or other injury may ensue. The warning may need to be repeated in a second language if non-English speakers are common. The use of force report should document the time the warning was announced, the language used, the time the canine was deployed, the time the canine contacted the suspect, and the time the canine handler arrived at the location with the suspect and canine. Some agencies transmit the warning via radio while broadcast via public address system such that an exact recording through the radio system can be maintained. The warning should be read from a written form to assure the entire warning text is broadcast to a potential suspect. If the structure has multiple floors the warning should be repeated on each floor, and if a building-wide public address system is available, it should be used. On some occasions it may be contraindicated tactically to broadcast a warning that would alert an armed suspect.

The first arriving officers on a scene where a canine may be used to search a building should confirm occupancy, security systems, and building layout. Care should be taken not to contaminate the scent paths the canine might follow. The canine handler may request the ventilation system be shut down to avoid scent track degradation. The use of a leash for the canine will be dictated by the individual circumstances and agency policy. Body armor should be worn by officers and the canine whenever feasible. The canine handler should work with a trained backup officer to ensure safety. When the suspect is located the canine handler will be engaged with the canine; the backup officer can handle securing the suspect. Usually the canine handler will need to the keep the canine in sight if the canine is off leash. Building search should be emphasized in canine training.

Canines are not recommended in crowd control because of negative perceptions by the public. However, the use of canines in riot conditions or unruly crowd conditions with supervisor approval may be acceptable. Policy should closely address this issue. If deployed the canines should be maintained on a short leash and typically used in a defensive posture. This does not prevent the canine being used for deterrent purposes while kept on leash at the handler's side.

Some canines are used for scent tracking to locate suspects or missing persons. Usually the canine should be trained in tracking prior to apprehension such that each find does not have to result in an apprehension. First arriving officers on a scene that a missing person or suspect needs tracking should determine the last site where the individual was seen and avoid contaminating the site with other scents. When possible, shut down vehicle engines to avoid contaminating scent tracks. If a vehicle is to be used for the initial scent track, officers should avoid contaminating it by entering or searching it. The preferred method is to keep the tracking canine on a long leash consistent with controlling the canine without impeding search efforts.

Canine care and safety are a function of the handler. He or she must be skilled in the routine care, grooming, feeding, and emergency care of the canine. Daily cleaning of the kennel and canine yard is essential along with disinfecting the facilities. Canine training should address the handler's abilities to provide routine and emergency care for the canine. Obviously, a veterinarian skilled at treating working dogs should be retained and periodically evaluate the canine on a set schedule, plus be available for consultation or emergency care after hours.

Canines used for detecting contraband such as narcotics are governed by a variety of decisions. The deployment policy should closely address the latest court findings. In airport settings the Supreme Court has ruled that the procedure of subjecting luggage and bags to a sniff does not constitute a search under the Fourth Amendment. There have been similar findings in sniffing luggage on conveyers and sniffing airport lockers. A prolonged detention of luggage may amount to a seizure, however, requiring probable cause. When searching public facilities, usually a recommendation is that luggage in the proximity to and control of a person is sniffed only upon reasonable suspicion. If feasible and part of agency protocol, obtain the facility manager's consent when private facilities are involved. The use of canines in schools has met with mixed results, with some courts ruling that the sniff constitutes a search. The use of canines in a school setting should be conducted with the utmost caution and with prior legal advice as to the manner and method by which the deployment should be conducted. The same is true of the exterior sniffs of residences, with the latest US Supreme Court decision requiring a search warrant being followed. Sniffs of motor vehicles should be limited to a detention for another valid reason, and the sniff should be contemporaneous to the stop. To detain a person longer than is needed to issue a traffic citation or perform a valid check of registration for a canine to sniff the vehicle may convert the detention into a search. However, if reasonable suspicion exists then the wait for a canine becomes less problematic.

The use of fentanyl and the potential to injure the officer and the canine makes the availability of naloxone (Narcan®) critical. The officer must be aware of self-administration and administration of the agent to a potentially contaminated canine. The feeling of stupor, lethargy, loss of motor coordination, and other signs and symptoms of opiate exposure should be an indicator of the need to use the naloxone nasal spray on oneself, another officer, or canine, if exposure to a powerful opiate such as fentanyl, or one of its analogs such as carfentanil, is suspected. The agency should have a policy developed and reviewed by the agency's medical director and veterinarian regarding the use of naloxone. The cost of naloxone is not substantial, and this pharmaceutical antidote is now a critical item for each officer to possess. The agency which fails to supply this antidote may incur substantial liability if an officer is injured by an opiate such as fentanyl because the antidote was not available. Further, agency personnel will view the stance of the agency in a very negative fashion if the agency fails to provide this vital piece of safety equipment.

Perhaps the most important aspect of any canine deployment policy is its documentation of training, deployments, bites, and general operations. The agency must require that the canine supervisors and handlers stay abreast of the latest court rulings within their jurisdiction, as procedural changes may be mandated by these decisions.

Communicable Diseases

Communicable diseases as a threat have been addressed by many sources but many within the law enforcement community still tend to take a cavalier attitude about limiting exposure or reporting potential contact with disease-causing substances. This is a hazard not readily visible nor does it have immediate dire consequences should it be disregarded. Law enforcement personnel are familiar and commonly deal with tangible hazards quite well but less familiar intangible hazards such as diseases are many times not viewed as a serious threat. Many officers still do not realize that contact with human body substances, animals, or contaminated objects can transmit the disease to the person contacted. The most critical aspect of disease transmission is prevention.

Law enforcement personnel work in uncontrolled environments where they may be exposed to various body substances or objects that may be contaminated with body substances. Of concern are human immunodeficiency virus (HIV), hepatitis types B (HBV) and C (HCV), rabies, and tuberculosis. These diseases are capable of transmission by body substances, particularly blood. Tuberculosis maybe transmitted via airborne droplets, particularly in confined spaces. Disease transmission can occur through mucous membranes such as the eyes, nose, or lips, or through non-intact skin such as abrasions, cuts, or puncture wounds following contact with body substances.

Officers should consider human, bat, or potentially rabid animals' body fluids, or excreta, as contaminated and potentially a disease-causing agent. This should include blood, saliva, urine, sputum, and feces. When handling any person, animal, or object with the potential to be contaminated, care should be taken to avoid contact with body substances.

These diseases are insidious. The ill person or ill animal may exhibit few or no symptoms or signs. Law enforcement officers, therefore, must assume that body substances can transmit disease and guard against contact. This is difficult in rapidly evolving exigent circumstances. Such incidents may include medical incidents, motor vehicle crashes, arrest situations, handling bats or potentially rabid animals, handling evidence or contaminated items, and crime scenes.

Agencies should encourage their employees who might be exposed occupationally to blood to take the hepatitis B vaccine. Many agencies provide this vaccine to their employees free of charge, as mandated by federal requirements enacted by the Occupational Health and Safety Administration in 1992.

Training should be undertaken to ensure that exposed personnel are familiar with body substance isolation techniques, are provided appropriate personal protective equipment, and can properly utilize the equipment. Written procedures need to address the program in terms of when, how, what type, and where protective clothing will be worn. Potential exposures and medical surveillance for those contaminated by body substances must also be addressed.

The procedure should address when and how to handle contaminated police clothing and equipment, spills, and contaminated suspects. Usually the minimum protective equipment should be gloves. Latex gloves should be avoided as sensitivity or allergies may develop to this material and latex is ineffective in stopping the penetration of some substances. Other gloves made of vinyl, butyl rubber, or nitrile materials are acceptable. Prior to searching any suspect, the officer should ask if the suspect has anything sharp on their person. Some agencies use the fluid-proof outer glove to cover an inner glove made of puncture-resistant material. Gloves should be carried on the officer's person. Several forms of containers exist that fit the duty belt or key chains, while some officers secrete the gloves in their headgear. Double gloving is recommended such that as the outer pair of gloves is contaminated, they can be discarded, and another clean set of gloves placed on over the protective set of inner gloves worn by the officer. Some officers triple glove, but this may reduce tactile sensitivity and restrict movement. Officers should also train to use their radio, firearm, and other equipment while gloved should an emergency arise. Regardless of how the item is carried it should be readily available.

When time permits and a situation in which splash hazards exist, or a substantial risk of contamination exists, additional protective clothing should be added. This may include fluid resistant coveralls, shoe covers, eye and face protection, and a bag-valve mask for circumstances in which CPR must be performed. In respiratory or cardiac arrest, a protective adjunct such as a bag-valve mask should be used during rescue breathing to avoid direct contact with the victim. However, with the new chest compressions-only technique, some agencies have eliminated mouth-to-mask ventilation or switched to bag-valve mask resuscitators. The bag-valve mask resuscitator is compact, inexpensive, simple to use, and reduces risk of contamination while affording a good technique to ventilate a cardiac arrest victim.

Contaminated items should be placed in a biohazard bag using gloves and with the gloves discarded into the bag. The biohazard bag with contaminated items should be discarded in the appropriate container. Many states and locales have specific regulations that prohibit these items discarded as household trash. It may be necessary to have a specific permit or contract a service for the disposal of biohazard materials. Check with your legal advisor and determine the appropriate disposal method for biohazard items.

Items that cannot be discarded are items of evidence. These items usually must be retained for court purposes or laboratory testing. They should be handled only with gloves and double bagged if potentially contaminated. The item should be marked as a biohazard and what type of contamination is known or suspected. Remember damp items bagged within a plastic bag will decompose rapidly. Usually damp items must be isolated, dried, and then placed in paper containers. Some evidence exists that infective viral fomites might exists for several days in blood contaminated items.

Contaminated items that must be sent to a laboratory should be packaged according to the shipping service requirements and appropriate federal requirements and labeled as a biohazard. Always check with the laboratory for their specific packaging and labeling requirements. Do not send potentially contaminated items unless they are appropriately marked as a biohazard. Do not comingle suspect and victim items in the same package, or comingle during drying, processing, or handling.

Various contacts with body substances have the potential to produce disease transmission. Contacts with intact skin by body substances should be washed with soap and water as soon as possible and documented. Any contact with non-intact skin, such as cuts, abrasions, or wounds produced by bites, or splashes or body substance contact with mucous membranes of the eye, nose, or mouth should be medically evaluated. The wounds should be flushed with water and washed with soap. Contacts with the mucous membranes of the eye, nose, and mouth should be flushed with water. Officers with non-intact skin should wear a fluid resistant bandage over the wound. Complete documentation is critical should disease transmission occur to protect both the employee and employer rights.

Other exposures that may require actions include contact with potentially rabid animals or their body substances. Contact with any of their body substances, including fecal material, should be avoided. Document and obtain medical treatment for bites, scratches, mucous membrane contacts, or exposure even with intact skin, with any body substance of a potentially rabid animal. Bites are particularly susceptible to rabies transmission. Once rabies is contracted, the disease is fatal. Officers should avoid contact with any animal behaving strangely, particularly wild animals. Even animal carcasses should only be handled with protective gloves. Animals that commonly carry rabies include bats, foxes, skunks, dogs, and raccoons. Some evidence suggests that bat guano and bat colonies may have the ability to transmit rabies without direct contact with a bat, possibly through contact with aerosol saliva or guano contaminated with the rabies virus. One bizarre case reported was a bat that flew into an open window of a moving police vehicle and managed to bite or scratch the officer, who almost lost control of the vehicle while distracted by the bat flying inside the car. Once the officer stopped the police vehicle, the bat flew from the car and could not be located. The officer took the rabies injections, as this was a potentially significant rabies contact.

Tuberculosis has made a return as a disease and is epidemic in some communities. Officers should avoid long periods of contact in confined spaces with persons suspected of having tuberculosis. Tuberculosis is transmitted via airborne droplets. Various state and federal regulations apply to persons with active tuberculosis when confined in a correctional environment, regarding how the ventilation system must operate, their contact with other inmates, and staff. If you have contact with a person who has confirmed tuberculosis, medical evaluation should be obtained. Usually a chest x-ray and skin tests are performed. Some agencies perform skin tests for tuberculosis annually. Persons with positive skin tests or suspicious x-rays may have to take a course of medication.

Other potential exposures also include contact with dried blood or other body substances. Officers routinely encounter dried blood handling evidence. Although no definitive evidence exists to demonstrate dried body substances can routinely transmit disease, the same level of care should be used to handle these items. The minimum protection should be the use of gloves. Some agencies have added protective coveralls and N99 mask for respiratory protection.

Human bites present a potential for disease transmission. This is especially true if blood is present in the suspect's mouth at the time of the bite. This injury requires immediate medical attention. The injury should be washed with soap and water. Medical evaluation may include prophylactic antibiotics. Some bites to the hand may require hospital admission, as the incidence of infection is high. It may be necessary to obtain a court order to gain access to the suspect's medical records or to obtain the necessary testing to confirm the presence of any transmissible diseases. Some states provide for access to medical records whenever a documented exposure consistent to disease transmission can be demonstrated. Check with the agency medical and legal advisor to assure the procedures follow local protocols for obtaining this information.

Cleaning contaminated items is an issue that must be addressed by procedure. Clothing items that belong to law enforcement officers should not be taken home and cleaned. The agency must either have approved onsite cleaning equipment or use a commercial vendor certified to clean body substance contaminated items. Some agencies discard contaminated clothing. The more common contaminated item is footwear. Officers either step in or have footwear splashed with blood at a crime scene. Tangible items such as handcuffs or web gear may tolerate cleaning or be cost effective to clean rather than to discard.

A variety of cleaning agents are on the market that kill the viruses and bacteria found in environmental settings. Whatever agent is used, assure the agent is effective against HIV, tuberculosis, and hepatitis. One of the least expensive agents is commercial 5% hypochlorite bleach. This is prepared using bleach and tap water usually in a 1:1,000 mix for general cleaning, with blood spills or other body fluid spills cleaned with a 1:10 mix. Protective gloves should be worn, and bleach should not be used on body surfaces. Unfortunately, many cleaning agents will discolor uniforms and damage web gear and handcuffs. However, little alternative exists to cleaning other than appropriate disposal of the contaminated item.

Spills of blood or other body fluids are quite common at crime scenes. Care should be taken to avoid contact with the fluids. It may be necessary to wear enhanced protective clothing such as shoe covers, fluid resistant coveralls, gloves, and facial protection or N99 respirator. Contaminated evidence must be handled carefully not only to preserve trace evidence but to also prevent contamination of the law enforcement officer.

Commercial biohazard kits are available that provide the appropriate protective clothing and spill cleanup items. Some agencies provide lists of vendors to property owners to facilitate crime scene clean up or, when the incident is on public property, contract with vendors to perform crime scene cleanup of biohazard materials.

Officers should always question suspects prior to searching asking if they have any sharp objects on their person. If needles and sharp objects are a common hazard officer may consider wearing puncture-resistant gloves under their fluid-protective gloves. Some agencies equip their officers with the puncture-resistant gloves for personnel in jail or corrections environments. Avoid searching in areas blindly in areas where you cannot see. This is true in searching under vehicle seats, in purses, or in packages.

With some effort many body substance contacts can be eliminated. However, officers must remain vigilant to protect themselves from yet another hazard.

Domestic Violence Involving Police Officers

No subject draws attention more than when a police officer is involved in domestic violence and is arrested. When convicted, this is typically a career-ending event. Usually domestic violence is defined as any threats of violence or physical violence committed by the offender in violation of local or state laws with a spouse, someone with whom they are in a dating relationship, or other household member. The definition of domestic violence will vary from state to state but is usually includes a person who resides in the household, who the offender has a child in common with, or who they are in a dating/romantic relationship with. Be familiar with your jurisdiction's law and its definitions.

One issue of significant concern is the early detection and prevention of do-mestic violence by police officers. Police officers lead a stressful life, which in turn places stress on their personal relationships. Background investigations following a conditional job offer should review for any incidents of domestic violence, elder abuse, animal abuse, or child abuse. A history of this behavior is very troubling and may exclude the prospective employee from employment even when no criminal conviction exists.

Recruit and continuing education should emphasize the appropriate response of officers to domestic violence and specifically address incidents involving police officers. Signs and symptoms of potential abuse include erratic behavior on the part of the officer, controlling behavior directed at the domestic partner, increased use of alcohol or illicit substances, increases in use of force incidents, frequent unexplained absences from work, performance deterioration, social isolation, motor vehicle crashes, on-the-job injuries, or other signs of stress.

There should exist a confidential method for family members or intimate partners to file a complaint with the agency. This method should be conveyed in writing to family members, usually at a family orientation class. The agency must respond quickly and appropriately to allegations of domestic violence. Usually both a criminal and administrative investigation will be needed. Com-plaints that do not allege a potential criminal act require follow up, usually in the form of counseling if confirmed.

The intervention early into a potential domestic situation may well prevent its escalation and salvage the career. Usually counseling is recommended to correct the issues. Anger management and stress reduction may be coupled along with relationship management. Some agencies have employee assistance programs that formally address these issues and may provide financial assistance. A leave of absence or reassignment may be needed to assure the of-ficer complies with the needed counseling and to isolate them from potential work situations in which their behavior might be inappropriate.

A clear policy with defined sanctions for domestic violence is required as administrative sanctions need to be in place for those officers who commit an act of domestic violence or who become abusive to a family member. Careful attention should be paid to protect the rights of the officer while at the same time affording the victim due process and protection.

The policy should address the reporting responsibility of any member of the agency who becomes aware of an incident of domestic violence involving members of the agency or other law enforcement personnel that may live within the agency's jurisdiction. Notification of a supervisor through the chain of command to the chief executive officer is necessary. If the act has sufficient probable cause to warrant a criminal investigation, steps should be taken on scene to assure the safety of the victim. The policy should specify how and when an officer could be placed on administrative leave and his or her service weapons seized. If an arrest takes place, an excellent policy is to have the officer surrender any additional personal firearms if he or she will do so voluntarily. If a lack of cooperation exists, the agency should move to assist the victim in obtaining a domestic violence protection order or restraining order that prohibits the possession of a firearm by the officer until the incident is resolved. Officers should neither overreact or underreact when presented with circumstances involving law enforcement officers.

Victims of domestic violence should be offered resources and referral to local groups such as domestic violence shelters, victim advocacy groups, or counseling services. Victim safety should be a primary concern, as should his or her confidentiality. Be certain to advise the victim about the methods and manner to obtain domestic violence protection orders, restraining orders, or similar legal processes. Provide the victim with a contact point of a command-grade officer who can update the victim as the situation evolves.

Obviously two distinct investigations will be needed. A criminal investigation and administrative investigation should be separate and run parallel. Information can be shared from the criminal investigation to the administration investigation, but the reverse is not true. The best policy is to avoid sharing data whenever feasible. Even if the victim does not wish to prosecute and the criminal case is disposed of, the administrative investigation must be completed and its findings reported the agency's chief executive officer. The failure of a criminal case to result in prosecution or conviction should not deter administrative discipline in a well-written policy.

The chief executive officer should consider the administrative findings and proceed with the appropriate disciplinary actions if required. Prosecution criminally will take place in the courts and should have no impact on administrative findings. In fact, for administrative discipline to be meted out it should be able to withstand scrutiny even if the criminal charges are dismissed or the suspect officer is found not guilty. Administrative charges should be based around violations of policies, rules, and regulations, and the offender's conduct, rather than requiring a criminal act for discipline to be imposed. This is where careful crafting of the administrative rules is needed to assure that even with a failure to successfully convict an officer of domestic violence, the behavior can be disciplined administratively.

If a conviction occurs for domestic violence, then steps should be taken to terminate the employee. This officer is no longer eligible to possess a firearm and cannot function as a police officer without one, plus with the *Brady* rule and *Giglio* the officer would likely be disqualified as a witness in many court proceedings.

Hostage Negotiation for First Responders

Perhaps one of the more chilling and potentially lethal calls an officer can respond to is that of a hostage situation. Professional negotiators may not be available, and first responders may have to act initially. The priority in these circumstances is the preservation of life. Tactics should be used to contain the scene, isolate the hostage taker, and negotiate.

Containment will usually consist of an outer perimeter and inner perimeter. When feasible, do not to allow a hostage taker to become mobile, as containment and isolation is lost. Isolation should consist of removing contact with the outside except through law enforcement. In the age of cellular telephones and Internet this may be difficult. In one recent hostage taking the hostage taker with his hostage retreated to an underground prepared bunker where television was available to watch the drama unfold, plus the hostage taker had food and water prepared for a sustained siege. The hostage taker had booby trapped the location with IEDs. After a several-day failed negotiation a sophisticated rescue operation by federal law enforcement rescued the uninjured child hostage. This event happened in a rural area, and it appeared the hostage taker planned the event over at least a one-year period. Unfortunately, the hostage taker did not survive the encounter with law enforcement, as he attempted to harm the hostage.

Law enforcement personnel should wear body armor in these events. Those on the inner perimeter should remain in positions of hard cover and avoid displaying firearms.

The initial responding officers should take several steps:

- Confirm the location of the individual and how many other persons are present.
- Set up an inner perimeter based on the perceived threat (handgun, long gun, edged weapon, explosives, or flammable items). Remember interior non-masonry walls and vehicles do not provide significant ballistic protection.
- Evacuate those who can be safely moved.
- Gather information and intelligence on the suspect and the circumstances.
- Call for additional resources, including a supervisor and hostage negotiator.
- Consider calling for a tactical team.

- If appropriate under the circumstances, establish contact with the individual.
- Wear body armor and make certain officers are clearly identified.
- Establish an outer perimeter when feasible.
- Call EMS and have them stage.
- Call the fire department if a fire hazard is present and have them stage.

Bear in mind that once contact is established the hostage taker may make demands. Typically, items for comfort, food, and drink are negotiable. However, many agencies do not allow firearms, ammunition, body armor, alcohol or illicit drugs, or other hostages to be delivered to hostage taker. These would either enhance the hostage taker's tactical advantage or in the case of alcohol or drugs make his or her behavior unpredictable. The idea of contaminating food or drink with a stupor-inducing drug is not wise since the hostage taker may have a hostage sample the food and watch for ill effects. Transportation is usually not an option, as containment is lost. Trading officers for hostages is usually not an option and may just provide the hostage taker an additional hostage. Anyone coming out of a hostage situation should not be allowed to return.

Kidnapping is one form of hostage taking and is divided into two categories, one in which a demand is made, and the other in which no demand is made. Usually the location where the hostage is held is unknown. If no demands are made, the probability is high that the hostage is held for sexual assault, assault, or for a homicide.

Sieges occur in several varieties. The more common is the spontaneous siege, which usually encompasses a short intervention period, as the offender is ill prepared to sustain a long-term siege. This is an interrupted crime such as a robbery or a burglary in which the offender takes hostages as law enforcement arrives. The motivation will be personal, and drugs or alcohol are likely to be involved. The state of mind of the offender will be emotional and may be irrational at times. These crimes occur away from the offender's home.

Other types of sieges are deliberate siege and anticipated siege, and both are rare. Deliberate sieges usually occur in a public or symbolic location with a long resolution period. Significant preplanning occurs, and the motivation political or ideological. The state of mind of the offenders will be rational and usually more than one well-armed and equipped hostage taker is present. Anticipated sieges usually occur at the residence of the offender, and hostages may or may not be involved. These are usually well equipped and preplanned to some degree. The motivation may be religious or political. Expect a long-term event with offenders well equipped and heavily armed. Most of those involved will display rational behavior albeit using unusual values.

People in crisis states are influenced by their emotions, as they have been overwhelmed by events. Their coping mechanisms have failed. Some display self-destructive behaviors, substance abuse, reckless behavior, or related behaviors. They may experience narrowed thinking and tunnel vision. The more time that elapses, generally the more rational thinking may return once the adrenaline rush of the initial phases of the incident passes. The offender will become tired, hungry, thirsty, and possibly bored. Hostages may escape, or other tactical advantages may arise. The passage of time also allows investigators to gather information and intelligence on the offender and hostages and time for a professional hostage negotiator to arrive. Listening is important, as it may be possible to gain rapport with the hostage taker, gather information, and allow decompression from the rush of the initial events to occur. However, extended incidents can lead to not only an exhausted offender but also exhausted law enforcement officials. This may lead to poor decision making on both sides. Perimeters tend to degrade and officers tend to become bolder by leaving their cover, grouping up, and talking, while the leadership may demand an active tactical solution to resolve the incident and return resources to normal duties. If a deadline is imposed by the hostage taker, a tactical solution should be developed; however, that a deadline is imposed does not mean the hostage taker will act. If possible try to stall or allow the hostage taker an "out," if the deadline demands cannot or will not be met. If the deadline is not mentioned by the hostage taker, then do not bring the issue up as the deadline approaches or passes. Do not dismiss trivial demands as inconsequential, as they may be important to the hostage taker.

Usually the officer communicating with the hostage taker will not say no to any demand but will not say yes either. One technique is to say the information is passed up the chain of command and is taking time to decide. This is a common stalling method, while another technique is to counteroffer with a lesser form of the demand or request something in return if the demand is met. Some material items such as comfort items may be used to gain confidence with the hostage taker by law enforcement offering the item. As the incident progresses the hostage taker's needs should only be able to be met through the officer communicating with him or her. If possible find a subject matter common to both to use as a facilitation tool. This may allow the hostage taker to express unspoken needs and allows the building of rapport.

When speaking with the hostage taker be supportive while communicating at his or her educational level and vocabulary. Be relaxed, calm, and minimize background noise. Speak slowly and distinctly, concentrating solely on the task at hand. Avoid saying yes or no to demands but try to prevent disappointment when it becomes apparent that the demands will not be met. Remain honest and credible.

The primary purpose in hostage negotiation is to preserve life and resolve the incident without injury. Containment and extensive perimeters are essential. Establishing communications is important and initially may have to be via public address systems. Telephones or "throw phones" are more reliable and effective. Contact should be established early into the incident. One problem is the media may learn the suspect's name and preempt by calling directly. This is one reason it becomes important to isolate the telephone access the offender may have. This may not be possible if a cellular telephone is used unless the cellular vendor will cooperate and disrupt service or a cellular jamming device is used.

Intelligence about the hostage taker is critical. Make certain the intelligence is accurate and cross-verified. Some of the information needed is listed below.

- Suspect name, description, demographics, criminal history, photograph, and education level. The same information about the hostage or hostages.
- Any prior hostage-taking incidents or suicide attempts. Methods used, mental health history, medications and medical conditions, recent medical visits, history of impulsive behavior, temper, or insomnia.
- Medical information about the hostages.
- Drug or alcohol use, current condition, availability.
- Prior statements about this act or any special significance of today's date.
- Family history of suicide or domestic violence.
- Any current stressful events.
- How does the person handle stress?
- Availability of weapons, explosives, flammable items, and the individual's familiarity with them.
- Prior military or law enforcement service, and occupational history.
- Location of individual within the structure. Floor plan. Telephone number including cellular telephones. Locations of the telephones within the structure. Basement or attic access.
- Location of utility, natural gas, telephone, and electric power hook ups.
- Hobbies and interests.
- Relationship to hostages.

Make certain a chronological log is kept of events as they occur. This will assist the officer in tracking the passage of time and allow trained hostage negotiators a summary of the events that have taken place prior to their arrival.

Perhaps the most frustrating situation will be when officers have secured a scene and then cannot communicate with the hostage taker. A variety of problems may be present. The hostage taker may not be able to hear officers or understand the language. He or she may be attempting to elude detection or may not be able to physically respond. Some have made up their minds and will refuse to communicate in fear that the officer will be able to change their mind. At some point, after making necessary attempts to communicate, tactical options for entry may have to be explored. Covert observation to determine if the structure is occupied is important. Always confirm that you are at the correct location. Officers have been known to select the wrong locations.

If hostages have medical problems, it may be a priority to provide them medical assistance. The suggestion that the sick or ill hostage is a drain upon the hostage taker's resources to care for or guard may be suggested. This will also affect tactical options, as hostages with pre-existing health problems may limit the use of chemical agents.

Indicators of progress may come in the form of a change in the tone of the hostage taker, them using fewer obscenities, or them becoming generally more cooperative. Much of the progress will be from the subjective assessment by the officer communicating with the hostage taker. Some hostage takers will be less than communicative initially and become more talkative, which is a positive indicator.

The media may present problems, particularly if the hostage taker can listen to radio or observe television broadcasts live from the scene. This may disclose tactical information and the media may eavesdrop on communications with officers via scanners or parabolic microphones. In the worst-case scenario, the media may call the hostage taker by telephone and talk directly, tying up the line. Contacts with the Federal Aviation Administration (FAA) may allow the airspace around the scene to be closed to the media particularly if gunfire may present a hazard to aircraft.

Third-party intermediaries such as family or friends are rarely used to talk with the hostage taker. In most circumstances they are discouraged, as their behavior is unpredictable, they are untrained, and they may increase the stress on the hostage taker and may cause officers to lose control of the process. Some hostage takers have committed suicide in front of a significant other to harm the significant other emotionally. Their use is strongly discouraged.

If the hostage taker relents and discusses surrender, then several topics need to be addressed. The surrender process and what the hostage taker should do as they come out should be discussed in detail. Have a tactical plan to take the suspect down quickly and safely. Do not let your guard down, as some hostage takers have used the surrender process to commit suicide or force a suicide by cop. Address what is to be done with any firearm, explosives, flammables, or other weapons by the hostage taker. Emphasize exactly what steps he or she is take upon exiting the structure. Some may want the media present to document their surrender.

Hostage situations are a stressful process that takes an emotional and physical toll on those involved. Critical stress incident debriefing is a consideration for those involved.

Missing Juveniles

Most agencies define a missing juvenile as a person under the age of 18 years whose location cannot be ascertained. The missing child usually falls into one of four categories: non-family abduction, family adduction, runaway, or lost. The most serious of these is the non-family abduction, where the child may be in physical danger. Some experts believe that the first few hours following the taking of the juvenile are the most dangerous. Classification of the missing juvenile may be difficult, but it best to presume the worst-case scenario and direct the resources to mitigate it. A detailed plan using as a model the National Center for Missing and Exploited Children's *Missing and Abducted Children: A Law Enforcement Guide to Case Investigation and Program Management* is recommended. A detailed local procedure with checklists and a resource list is a valuable aid in this type of incident.

The family abduction usually happens following some significant event within the family structure, such as a divorce, separation, or physical move to another location. This may result in a parent or other family member fleeing with the juvenile to another state or location. There exist some cases in which harm has been done to juveniles followed by suicide of the abductor.

Juveniles who have run away present a different kind of issue. The voluntarily missing juvenile may have planned their flight such that a long period may have elapsed before his or her presence is missed. The juvenile may have prepared with money or other means of transport to enhance the distance he or she can flee. Those who leave on foot may require active searches, particularly if an austere environment is present. Those that have fled voluntarily may also actively attempt to elude searchers by hiding or fleeing.

Lost children require a different mindset. In rugged terrain the ambient temperature or other conditions may present an immediate life threat, as do other features such as bodies of water and lack of food, protective clothing, or potable water. The incident may become primarily a search and rescue (SAR) event with law enforcement considerations a secondary priority. However, homicides have occurred in which the child was reported to be missing with these circumstances as a cover story. Be familiar with the SAR resources available from your agency, surrounding agencies, state police, or the National Guard in your region.

The 911 call is usually the first contact that initiates a missing juvenile incident. The communications center should gather as much information as is practical and dispatch appropriate personnel. Some agencies respond the nearest patrol personnel while others immediately dispatch both patrol and juvenile investigative personnel. The basic facts should be gathered rapidly to include a detailed description of the missing child and broadcast on applicable police radio groups.

A call history involving the location, the missing juvenile, and parents should be checked, with this information relayed to the responding officers. One important piece of information is the circumstances under which the child is missing. A juvenile with a prior runaway history may not be in immediate danger versus a young child who has disappeared under unusual circumstances.

The initial responding officer should assess the totality of circumstances and if needed treat the location as a crime scene and protect the scene from scent contamination if a tracking canine might be used. The assessment should include any unusual circumstances. Some of these include:

- The missing child is 13 years of age or younger.
- The missing juvenile is out of his or her zone of safety based upon their age and maturity.
- The child is mentally or physically disabled.
- The child has been missing for an extended time, usually more than 12–24 hours prior to a report of the missing status. This is suspicious in and of itself.
- The juvenile has a possible life-threatening medical condition, or the child is in a life-threatening environment.
- The absence is outside the normal behavior for the child.
- The officer believes other conditions are present which present a serious threat.
- The caretaker or parents' behavior is inconsistent with what is expected.
- Other circumstances are present that warrant concern for the safety of the juvenile.

If unusual circumstances are present this should heighten the officer's concern for the safety of the juvenile and may indicate a crime has occurred. A supervisor should respond along with investigative personnel. Usually this is the time to begin the commitment of sufficient resources to resolve the incident.

One of the more critical functions of the initially responding officer is to gather information. Interview of the parents or caretaker is crucial. Inconsistent stories may indicate a crime or negligence. Another important facet is to verify that the child is missing. This may include initial hasty searches, bearing in mind that such may contaminate a crime scene or scent trails. Children may hide or play in obscure locations within a residence or structure. Another common event is for one parent or caretaker to take a juvenile with them and leave a residence without notifying the other parent or caretaker. Contact with appropriate persons is essential. Repeat searches of the same areas are recommended as additional searchers may find additional nooks and crannies that may hide a child missed during the initial hasty searches. This can be performed in parallel with other activities.

Determine the child custody status. Determine who is the person legally responsible for the juvenile. Parental abductions are common, but what are more frequent are crossed signals in which one parent or guardian picks up a child without the other's knowledge. This can be resolved with a telephone call and visit to confirm the child's safety.

Determine the circumstances of the disappearance and when, where, and by whom the child was seen last. This is critical information and may assist in identifying suspects or a location to begin a search. Interview those who last had contact with the child. This may provide inconsistencies or direct data that will shape the direction the investigation and search take. Another key piece of data is to obtain a detailed description with a photograph and forward the information to dispatch. A missing juvenile flyer should be developed; this information should be transmitted to working personnel and surrounding agencies and releasing the information to the media and posting on social media should be considered. If the agency has a website, the information should be posted along with contacting media outlets and posting on social media if this is deemed appropriate. An Amber Alert should be considered. This should be an expedited process with frequent updates as additional information is gathered.

Obtain verbal permission and written consent to search appropriate locations such as the home, vehicles, and outbuildings even if not involved with the scene. Searches should be repeated if not initially successful. Searches of the residence for a missing child should be repeated as children have been known to be overlooked during the initial hasty searches. A reluctant parent or guardian may signal a crime has occurred. Instances have occurred in which a child was killed in the home and reported missing at another location. It may be necessary to secure a search warrant to search the residence. If the child is missing in a location such as an apartment complex that can be secured, officers should search vehicles exiting the facility for the child. A policy with legal review is needed for this type of event.

During the search of the residence obtain items for evidence such as photographs, a hairbrush, a diary, items with physical evidence such as fingerprints or footprints, video, or a source of DNA. This may be critical in physical identification of the missing juvenile. Very early into the incident enter the child into the National Crime Information Center (NCIC) using the appropriate category. Remember to report the missing juvenile to the National Center for Missing & Exploited Children (NCMEC) and if warranted, broadcast an Amber Alert. As the case progresses, prepare local fliers or bulletins and distribute them widely in both hardcopy and via email. If the agency has an Internet site, post the information there. Wide distribution and coverage in the media can be critical in the rapid return of the child or identification of suspects and witnesses.

A supervisor should be notified and dispatched on missing juvenile cases under suspicious circumstances. The supervisor's responsibility includes an assessment and review of the steps taken and notifications made. He or she should prepare a plan or follow written agency plans and commit the resources needed to assure mitigation of the incident. This may include search canines, search and rescue (SAR) personnel for ground search, and aircraft with forward-looking infrared and thermal imaging equipment to assist in the search. A command post should be established near the incident site but be sufficiently isolated to allow confidential discussion of the incident. Coordination of the operations is another necessity. Another factor important to monitor is the crowd, as suspects and witnesses may be present. Photograph, record video, and identify as many onlookers as possible. If a search is made using bystanders use care to identify them, since if a criminal act is involved, the suspect may be present. Media interactions, particularly during the initial phases of an incident, can be important. The media can distribute the information regarding a missing child. Use the access to the media for this purpose.

The investigative responsibilities should include a detailed briefing from on-scene personnel. The investigator should then verify steps taken and review information gathered. The on-scene patrol commander should review and discuss the current plan of operations. A consensus should then be obtained on how to proceed. Investigative personnel should conduct background and criminal history checks of suspects and participants. This may produce valuable information and produce additional direction for the investigation. A critical review of the family history and dynamics is important. Interview of neighbors, friends, and business associates may be needed. A canvass of the neighborhood or the location the juvenile disappeared from may be required. This effort may identify additional witnesses and confirm the disappearance story. When the initial review and evaluation of the available information is complete an investigative plan should be completed. Areas that should receive consideration are repeating interviews, canvassing the area, establishing lead tracking using software developed for that purpose, and assignment for lead follow up. This may be performed by computer software that allows cross-referencing and rapid searches. Consider performing in-depth backgrounds on the affected persons, reviewing the scene and searches, making certain the residence and vehicles have been searched more than once, and obtaining search warrants as needed. As with any investigation, document the areas searched on maps, with photographs and video as needed.

Perhaps the most common mistake made in a missing juvenile case is the lack of adequate resources committed in a systematic manner early into the incident. Remember a detailed written procedure with task checklists for the first responding officer, supervisor, and investigator can assist in the initial hectic minutes of these incidents.

Suicide Threats

Unfortunately, suicide threats and attempts are a common law enforcement call. Some agencies will not intervene unless the person presents a threat to others while other agencies make the response a priority call. Officers are expected to respond and resolve the issue. In many instances the severity of the incident is underplayed. One facet that should be borne in mind in operations is that many people who threaten suicide are committed to killing themselves, they may be homicidal and kill anyone who interferes with them, and they do pose a significant threat if armed. The initial responding officers may be forced to negotiate with the individual who has threatened suicide until a trained hostage negotiator can arrive.

The initial responding officers should take several steps:

- Confirm the location of the individual and if any other persons are present. This may be a hostage situation.
- Set up an inner perimeter based on the perceived threat (handgun, long gun, edged weapon, explosives, and flammable items). Remember interior non-masonry walls and vehicles do not provide significant ballistic protection.
- Evacuate those who can be safely moved. If persons are present who cannot be moved and are in danger, then treat the circumstance as a hostage situation.
- Gather information and intelligence on the suspect and the circumstances.

- Call for additional resources including a supervisor and hostage negotiator.
- Consider calling for a tactical team.
- If appropriate under the circumstances establish contact with the individual.
- Wear body armor and make certain officers are clearly identified.
- Establish an outer perimeter when feasible.
- Call EMS and have them stage.
- Call the fire department if a fire hazard is present and have them stage.
- Avoid entry into the residence or approaching the subject if feasible to prevent a "suicide by cop."

Suicide intervention is especially difficult, as usually a person who has gone to the extent that law enforcement is involved may be well committed to the act. However, every effort should be made to resolve the issue without injury or death. Gathering information about the individual is important. Many persons will provide clues to their impending suicide attempt, but these clues may not be accepted as serious. These clues may allow the responding officers and hostage negotiator some idea of the mental state of the individual. Some suicidal clues are:

- Expression of feelings of helplessness and hopelessness.
- Visiting friends or relatives and saying farewells.
- Verbal wills and the "gifting" of cherished items.
- Reestablishing old or broken relationships.
- A period of severe depression followed by "getting better" with more energy and purpose. The individual may not literally have had the energy to commit suicide during the depressed state but once the decision is made and energy returns, they may act on the crystallized decision to kill themselves.
- Prior suicide attempts or a family history of suicide.
- Extreme insomnia.
- History of impulsive behavior.
- Under the influence of alcohol or drugs.
- In an isolated location.
- Detailed suicide notes, plans, or fantasies.
- Mental health history and if inpatient care was required.
- Acquisition of a firearm.

If contact is established introduce yourself by name and agency. Avoid the use of a rank. One of the questions that should be asked is, "Are you going to commit suicide?" If the answer is yes, then treat the threat seriously. Ask how and when the individual intends to commit suicide. The purpose is to establish the intent of the individual. Ask what he or she has done prior to your arrival (ingested poison, cut themselves, carbon monoxide, shot themselves, consumed alcohol or drugs). This will help determine the seriousness of the situation and commitment of the individual. Emergency medical services personnel can help by determining the lethal nature of the actions taken. Ask direct questions as this may establish rapport with the individual. Family or friends may have skirted or refused to discuss the issue of suicide. If the individual tells you he or she has feeling of helplessness or hopelessness, this separates him or her from those who may be depressed.

Part of the information gathering process should address the individual's history. Does he or she have a history of impulsiveness? Indications include: prior arrests for traffic violations such as speeding and parking violations, "flies off the handle easily," history of domestic violence, or violent offenses. An impulsive individual is a more substantial suicide risk. Is/are a firearm, explosives, flammable materials, or edged weapons accessible, and is the individual familiar with their use? A skilled hunter with a scoped centerfire rifle presents a far more substantial threat than an individual armed only with an edged weapon. Remember males are more likely to use firearms in a suicide attempt than females, but this does not rule out females using firearms. Is there a family history of suicide? If family history of suicide exists, this makes the suicide attempt more credible, as suicides do tend occur in the same family. If gunshots have been fired, the individual may be making test shots just as those armed with edged weapons may make test cuts, better known as hesitation cuts, prior to suicide. This is ominous.

Another ominous indicator is locating a suicidal person in a remote location such as woods, a park, an isolated road, or a similar location. He or she may be seeking solitude to kill himself or herself. They may have taken an overdose of medication or simply not want their family to find their body at home or interrupt the suicide attempt. A more prosaic explanation is they do not want to "mess up" their residence with blood and gore from a gunshot wound. If the individual is believed to be under the influence of drugs or alcohol, this makes them more impulsive, lowers inhibitions, and affects his or her judgment. This makes successful suicide attempts more probable. If the individual has related fantasies, has a suicide plan, or left a suicide note, then the suicide attempt is more credible. A history of extreme insomnia and prior suicide attempts makes the possibility of a successful suicide more probable. If the individual has a history of mental health inpatient care then they should be considered at high risk for suicide, particularly if they had a depressed period and suddenly "had gotten better." Be wary if talking with a suicidal individual and he or she suddenly seems less depressed and sounds much better out of context with the conversation. The individual may have made the decision to carry out the threat to kill himself or herself.

Police officers tend to view suicide as a problem, whereas those attempting suicide view it as a solution to their problems. Many suicidal people feel they have lost control of their lives and suicide is the ultimate option to regain that control. It may be an act of revenge aimed at a spouse, significant other, or family. Therefore, speaking with family members is usually not recommended. Their presence may be what is desired. Some vengeful individuals may kill themselves in front of a spouse or family members. Others may be suffering from a debilitating or painful illness and suicide is way to end their suffering. Suicide may be viewed as their only meaningful option.

In speaking with a suicidal person, try to determine what his or her motivation is for the suicide attempt. What is he or she trying to achieve? Some may be simply trying to escape their immediate problems in an impulsive manner. Most will be ambivalent about suicide. Try to stay grounded in the here and now. Remember that under stress people will literally interpret whatever you say. Avoid telling a suicidal person anything is "all right" as they may interpret this as your tacit approval of their suicide. Some may be angry, and officers should presume that individuals attempting suicide present a threat to themselves and officers.

A phenomenon becoming more common is suicide by cop. This is the individual who, for whatever reason, such as religious conviction or a lack of courage, cannot kill themselves. The person will place officers in a circumstance where the officers must shoot the person. Some will confront officers with a firearm that may not be loaded or other weapon, forcing the officers to defend themselves. The individual may challenge or otherwise place officers in jeopardy to force the issue. Some may set deadlines. A good clue to these circumstances may be a significant emotional event that recently occurred, such as a martial or relationship breakup, death of a significant other, loss of a job, or similar traumatic incident. A particularly traumatic situation will be the loss of a spouse and job as this destroys the individual's support system and may precipitate a suicide attempt. These individuals may also demand to speak with whoever is in charge, such as the mayor, chief, or sheriff. They may want to shoot this person to force officers to kill them. Occasionally those bent on suicide by cop may not even wish to talk but may confront officers shortly after their arrival, as their mind is made up and they have nothing to discuss. If the individual has access to a hostage or other person, they may place the other person in jeopardy or even kill them to force officers to shoot. Avoid face-to-face meetings with anyone bent on suicide if the person is armed.

If you can communicate with the individual, listen to what is said while exploring the person's feelings. Ask why he or she feels this way and allow the individual to vent his or her feelings. If the person becomes angry, this could be a positive sign to a resolution of the incident. Try to stay focused on the causes of the suicidal feelings. Ask what has happened to cause them to feel that suicide is the only solution. Do not be afraid to use the word suicide and ask them if they intend to kill themselves. Discuss openly the finality of death. Try to establish what is still meaningful to the individual and use this to try to change their mind about suicide. Do not be afraid to describe the awful consequences of suicide and the trauma it will cause their family and friends. Stall for time. Explore any possible options. Ask the person to put down any weapons or to stop the suicide process. Keep them talking.

Suicidal persons are impulsive by nature and may not have realized they have other options to suicide. Many may fear something worse than death such as pain, helplessness, poverty, or loneliness, and see death as a tranquil solitude. Offer options but be non-judgmental. Avoid delivering sermons or lectures. Remember trite statements like, "It can't really be that bad" serve no purpose and reveal the officer does not understand the situation. Avoid moral issues and providing advice, as your role is to assist the person in finding his or her own solution.

Listed below is some of the information that officers should gather for intelligence purposes and may prove invaluable to negotiators.

- Suspect name, description, demographics, criminal history and photograph, education level.
- Prior suicide attempts and methods, mental health history, medications and medical conditions, recent medical visits, history of impulsive behavior, temper, insomnia.
- Drug or alcohol use, current condition, availability?
- Prior statements about suicide, any special significance of today's date?
- Family history of suicide or domestic violence?
- Any current stressful events?
- How does the person handle stress?
- Availability of weapons, explosives, flammable items and the individual's familiarity with them?
- Prior military or law enforcement service?
- Location of individual within the structure? Floor plan? Telephone number including cellular telephones? Locations of the telephones within the structure? Basement or attic access?
- Location of utility, natural gas, telephone, and electric power to structure?

Be very cautious in allowing mental health professionals not trained as hostage negotiators access to the suicidal individual. The same is true of family and friends, as they may precipitate the suicide. Foremost in any suicide attempt is officer and citizen safety. Treat every suicide threat as presenting a serious threat to the public's safety.

Clandestine Laboratory Response

A common issue affecting many agencies is clandestine laboratories (CL) for the manufacture of methamphetamine, other narcotics such as fentanyl, explosives, and biological toxins. Many agencies have seen these laboratories, which present numerous hazards that range from explosive and toxic chemicals to armed operators. Booby traps and bombs are not uncommon, and many laboratories are discovered following a fire or explosion.

The CL may be found in rental property or motel rooms, or portable labs may be found in vehicles, purses, or vehicle trunks. Special training and equipment are required in dealing with clandestine laboratories, and the training ranges from 40 hours to several weeks in length. The training and equipment, which includes devices to measure toxic atmospheres, protective and fire-resistant chemical suits, chemical analysis gear, over packing materials, and transportation drums, are expensive. An officer with extensive chemical training or even a forensic chemist may be needed for the more sophisticated laboratories. If booby traps, bombs, or armed operators are a possible threat, a tactical team and bomb squad certified to operate in the laboratory setting will also be required.

A critical factor is that personal protective equipment (PPE) is worn. The early clandestine laboratory responders suffered a high rate of medical issues and many medical retirements for lung issues, liver problems, and unusual cancers have been observed. This makes the use of PPE, a respiratory protection program, and careful hygiene along with a medical monitoring program essential. The chemicals used these laboratories are often toxic, explosive, flammable, carcinogenic, or corrosive.

Intelligence regarding those involved, with an emphasis on past criminal acts, paranoid behavior, weapons availability, and propensity for violence, is essential. In many instances a raid is better postponed should a "cook" be in progress. A raid on an unoccupied laboratory is a good option. Paranoid behavior and violence are often associated with laboratory operators. Prior to each raid, a safety officer should be designated to determine the levels of PPE, type of hazards known or expected, potential contamination issues, need for atmospheric testing, and respiratory protection needed. The level of chemical and respiratory protection

Officers are shown in Level C personal protective equipment in preparation for entry into a clandestine drug laboratory. Note the officers are wearing air purifying respirators. Photograph by Jim Smith.

should be determined by the safety officer based upon the type of laboratory and whether armed operators are present. In concert with the chemist, the safety officer should make decisions regarding the need and intensity of decontamination of suspects and downgrade of PPE once the laboratory is assessed. The decision regarding air sampling and potential toxic atmospheres present should be a consideration in the PPE selected. When the hazards are not known, level B is the recommended level of protection, using fire-resistant chemical suits and SCBA.

Tactical considerations are important and may preclude the wearing of some PPE; however, when feasible the appropriate chemical protective clothing and air-purifying respirators should be worn as a minimum. Bullet-resistant SCBAs are an even better option. Fire resistant outer clothing is a must. The safety officer should have the final authority in proceeding with a raid.

Infrequently officers may find a laboratory while investigating an unrelated event or may stop a boxed or active "shake and bake" mobile laboratory. When such occurs, the officers should secure the suspects and evacuate upwind. An isolation zone should be created based upon the size of the laboratory. A simple "shake and bake" may require only a 50-foot evacuation zone (further on the downwind side), whereas a large fixed laboratory using anhydrous ammonia or a laboratory producing fentanyl or a fentanyl analog, or worse, a suspected explosive laboratory, may require a several hundred-foot evaluation zone downwind.

Planned raids should be carefully staged with assets such as fire and EMS at least alerted if not staged upwind nearby. The priority in a raid of an occupied laboratory is securing suspects followed by a hasty laboratory assessment. Suspects should be removed from the laboratory and initial decontamination should consist of at least removal of clothing and redressing in disposable paper coveralls. The safety officer can decide regarding the need for technical decontamination. Some agencies perform the wet decontamination on site while others transport the suspects to jail after their clothes are discarded and paper coveralls donned, where they are showered for decontamination purposes. Agency procedure and the safety officer's recommendations should be followed. Upon arrival at the jail they are thoroughly showered. No contaminated items should be removed from the site except for samples to be tested or materials packaged to be disposed of as a hazardous material. Some agencies because of loss of federal funding for laboratory cleanup have sent officers through DOT and RCRA training to allow them to identify, segregate, and disassemble laboratory components. These items are packaged for storage and stored at an approved location for shipment later to an approved vendor for disposal.

The safety officer will determine the levels of contamination and what steps are needed for decontamination of not only suspects but also law enforcement personnel. Pre-approved decontamination procedures should be followed to assure that equipment and personnel are decontaminated properly.

Physical Hazards

Numerous physical hazards are present in a CL. This can include armed persons under the influence of methamphetamine, toxic and explosive atmospheres from solvents or reagents used in the cooking process, and incompatible chemicals. Most CL operators are not trained in chemical safety nor do they have any regard for safety.

Booby traps and bombs are a hazard that may be present, making intelligence important in determining if such hazards are present or if the operators have the requisite knowledge or training to construct them. Trip wires with audible devices or electronic devices such as passive infrared sensors to notify the operator of intrusion are common, as are low-light and infrared (IR) cameras. Some booby traps, such as fishhooks on monofilament lines, chemical booby

Simulated clandestine drug laboratory entry by officers wearing personal protective equipment. Note the officers are wearing powered air purifying respirators. Photograph by Dr. John Wipfler.

traps producing cyanide gas, explosives or firearms connected to trip wires, and bombs are less common but are documented hazards of clandestine laboratories and marijuana grow operations. The bomb squad is essential when such hazards are suspected or discovered. In some instances, the bomb technicians perform the initial assessment of the approaches and the unoccupied laboratory to identify and render safe such devices. Those on the entry team should be alert for trip wires and booby traps and not tamper with switches or wiring.

If a clandestine laboratory is below ground level or well sealed it may be oxygen deficient, especially if the Red P method is used, producing phosphine gas. Tactics for such an environment include ventilating the areas and testing the atmosphere prior to entry, use of SCBA, and a standby confined space rescue team with equipment.

Other hazards include the following:

- Electrical wiring with switches may present an explosion hazard.
- Solvent vapors are heavier than air, presenting an explosion hazard, but may also displace oxygen, making ventilation and atmospheric testing essential.

- The labs may be crowded, have wet floors, or have obstructions on the floor, making movement difficult while presenting fall and trip hazards.
- Compressed gas cylinders may be leaking or not secured.
- If anhydrous ammonia is used, it presents an immediate inhalation and explosion hazard, plus it presents a cryogenic hazard.
- The use of PPE will cause heat stress, limiting the time team members can work. Usual work times are limited to 30 minutes or fewer.
- EMS personnel should assess officers prior to and following entry to assure hydration and body temperature are within limits.
- Many agencies limit officers to balanced work and rest periods of equal times with officers requiring a below 100-degree Fahrenheit body temperature and less than 100 pulse rate for reentry.
- The use of cooled IV fluids to rehydrate and drop body temperature is recommended.
- Some agencies use ice water with the officer's forearms submerged to reduce body temperature.
- Some of the signs and symptoms of heat-related illness include nausea, vomiting, high pulse rate, weakness, pale and clammy skin, dehydration, light headedness, dizziness, dry mucous membranes, hot and dry skin, high or low blood pressure, or feeling faint.
- Any officer experiencing these symptoms or signs should be withdrawn from the operation and excused from any use of PPE or heat exposure for at least 72 hours.

Chemical Hazards

Chemicals found in the clandestine laboratory can include flammable, explosive, reactive, incompatible, corrosive, caustic, toxic, and acidic chemicals; high-pressure gases; those producing toxic atmospheres; pyrophoric chemicals; water-reactive chemicals; and carcinogens. The threat may also include toxic materials such as fentanyl, ricin, or abrin. Toxic materials of that nature require only micrograms of exposure by inhalation or dermal absorption to affect the ability of the officer to function and may depress respiration sufficiently to kill. Intelligence should provide what type of clandestine laboratory is in use, which will provide some idea as to the chemical and hazards to expect.

- Chemicals in any clandestine laboratory are toxic and may include cyanide, red phosphorus, phosphine, mercuric chloride, ether, chloroform, fentanyl, ricin, abrin, and methanol. These materials require respiratory and skin protection.

- Any solvents present are flammable and require testing for lower explosive limits (LEL). If the LEL is at 10% or higher, this mandates immediate ventilation to reduce the LEL. Some agencies ventilate if any explosive solvent is detected. Anhydrous ammonia and hydrogen present explosion hazards.

- Acids and caustic materials such as sulfuric acid, hydrochloric acid, sodium hydroxide (lye), or the intermediate lithium hydroxide can cause burns or may explode in contact with incompatible chemicals. Bases should not be mixed with acids or water.

- Some chemicals, such as hydrogen peroxide, a strong oxidizer, or hydrogen, present reactivity hazards, and contact with other chemicals can cause an explosion.

- Sodium and lithium when exposed to water will ignite and explode. During the "shake and bake" process, lithium can be seen sparking while submerged in solvent. Even though the solvent is flammable, the liquid solvent is too rich to ignite. A container failure with exposure to air will provide sufficient oxygen in this circumstance to cause ignition and an explosion.

- Some chemicals if overheated will produce toxic gases such as phosphine from red phosphorus.

- Acid generators use sulfuric acid mixed with rock salt to generate hydrogen chloride gas. These are usually plastic gasoline and pump sprayers containers with plastic tubing. Hydrogen chloride gas is toxic and can cause serious eye and lung injuries if the individual is exposed to the vapor or liquid.

Laboratory Types

Shake and Bake, One Pot, or Cold Cook

- Pressurized container with a plastic bottle soft drink container is common.

- The container may have a muddy appearance, it may be bulged, or the container may have bluish colored particles floating on the surface of a clear liquid. If there are bubbles and the liquid and particles are "rolling," this is an "active cook," which is generating pressure and heat. If the bottle is capped, an explosion hazard is present.

- Flammable solvents such as petroleum ether will be present in the container.
- Any black floating strips of particles are lithium, which will generate heat and hydrogen if exposed to water and likely explode or ignite any organic solvent present.

Look for:

- Plastic soft drink or other containers possibly bulged from pressure
- Lithium batteries
- Ammonium nitrate from cold packs or fertilizer or ammonium sulfate fertilizer
- Ether from starter fluid
- Sodium hydroxide or lye
- Rock salt
- Sulfuric acid
- Acid generator
- Sudafed or ephedrine and a blender or pill grinder

* If the container is bubbling, contents "rolling," pressurized, or bulged, this is an extreme overpressure explosion hazard followed by dispersal of the solvent and subsequent explosion with thermal event (fireball) following. Soft drink containers may tolerate upwards of 100 pounds of pressure before failing. Do not handle this container, evacuate the immediate area to at least 100 feet, notify the clandestine laboratory response team, and request the fire department and bomb squad. Differing protocols exist for dealing with such a hazard, as some agencies allow the container to progress until the reactions stops (which may be several hours), while others remotely open the container using a water disrupter or robot (a few agencies shoot them with a pellet rifle), and a very small number have a clandestine laboratory specialist or bomb squad member wearing a SCBA and flame resistant chemical clothing perform a hand depressurization and render the bottle safe. This latter method does preserve a substantial amount of product for prosecution purposes while other methods may waste or destroy the product. The downside to the last procedure is that the individual performing the hand render safe is in substantial danger from the pressurized container and potential explosion with resultant fireball and thermal event.

Red Phosphorus Laboratory, Red P, or "Beavis and Butthead" Lab

- Flammable solvents such as acetone, toluene, charcoal lighter fluid, starter fluid, ether, or white gasoline are used in this method.
- Red phosphorus, which can produce phosphine gas if heated, is used. Phosphine gas is very toxic and in a well-sealed CDL can create an oxygen-deficient atmosphere.
- Red phosphorus if overheated can produce white phosphorus, which may ignite and produce toxic fumes. White phosphorus fires can only be extinguished by submerging the white phosphorus under water. This material also adheres to flesh and may require surgical removal and inactivation with aqueous copper sulfate.
- Iodine and hydriodic acid are corrosive and toxic.
- Sodium hydroxide or lye, which is corrosive, is used with this method.
- Sulfuric acid or hydrochloric acid may be present. They are corrosive and may explode if mixed with sodium hydroxide or metals.

Look for:

- Heating source such as a microwave oven, hot plate, or gas stove
- Solvent containers
- Matches with the striker strip removed
- Red stains or red powder from red phosphorus
- Iodine, iodine tincture, peroxide for crystallizing iodine from tincture of iodine, or purple stains or gray to purple solids.
- A very heavy reddish liquid, hydriodic acid, which is corrosive and toxic
- Lye or sodium hydroxide
- Sulfuric acid and table salt
- Acid generators, plastic containers such as gasoline cans or spray containers with plastic tubing
- Hydrochloric acid or muriatic acid (brick acid)
- Hypophosphorus acid (rare but a substantial explosion hazard)
- Sudafed or ephedrine and a blender or pill grinder
- Red-stained coffee filters or other improvised filters
- Containers, microwave, or hot plate stained red or purple

Discarded red phosphorus methamphetamine laboratory found on the roadside. Note the indicators of a red phosphorus laboratory, matches with the striker strips removed to obtain red phosphorus, pseudoephedrine, and tincture of iodine, camp fuel, and hydrogen peroxide. Photograph by Jim Smith.

Red Phosphorus Variant "Volcano Method," Red P Dry Cook, or 30-Second Meth

The dry components of the red phosphorus method are mixed in a glass vessel (red phosphorus, iodine, and pseudoephedrine). A propane torch is used to heat them until charred. Chloroform is mixed with the resultant mixture along with sodium hydroxide. This process, if performed correctly, will yield methamphetamine, amphetamine, and amphetamine analogs.

* Phosphine gas is a very dangerous hazard if produced from heating red phosphorus as it displaces oxygen and may not have sufficient odor to be detected. Very small amounts of phosphine gas can kill if inhaled.

Officers in level C personal protective equipment enter a red phosphorus methamphetamine laboratory. Photograph by Jim Smith.

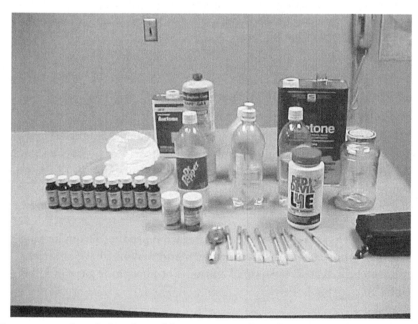

Components of a red phosphorus laboratory. Note the iodine tincture and the hydrogen peroxide used to crystallize the iodine. Photograph by Jim Smith.

Ammonia Laboratory, Birch Method, or Nazi Method

- Solvents such as toluene, lighter fluid, white gas, petroleum ether, or acetone. These are flammable.
- Lithium from lithium batteries. This is a gray soft metal typically in strips (may explode if mixed with a solvent and water is present).
- Anhydrous ammonia stored in an LPG gas cylinder. Look for bluish discoloration of the brass valve. This is a toxic and explosive gas which is an extreme respiratory hazard. It may also be stored in a thermos or other improvised container.

Look for:

- LPG or compressed gas cylinders of ammonia with bluish discoloration of the brass valve or other improvised containers, such as a thermos containing anhydrous ammonia.
- Solvent containers such as lighter fluid, petroleum ether, starter fluid, or acetone are common.
- Lithium batteries with the strips of lithium stored in mineral oil or kerosene is common (keeps the lithium from reacting with water). Lithium may generate heat and explode if placed in water.
- Rarely, pressurized cylinders of hydrogen chloride, which is in a standard cylinder, may be found.
- Rock salt and sulfuric acid for producing hydrogen chloride gas is found commonly. These are usually made from plastic gasoline containers or sprayer bottles.
- Sudafed or ephedrine and a blender or pill grinder

* **Anhydrous ammonia is an extreme inhalation hazard. When inhaled it forms a caustic ammonia solution in the upper airway and lungs. It also attacks the eyes and skin, plus the liquid is a cryogen with frostbite hazards. Anhydrous ammonia is also an explosive gas. Remember: it may be stored in LPG cylinders, which will have a bluish discoloration of their brass valve, or may be stored in some improvised container such as a thermos. Exposure to anhydrous ammonia for even a moment may result in death or disabling injuries.**

Phenyl-2-Propanone (P2P) Laboratory, Biker Method (Infrequent)

- This method uses very toxic and corrosive materials: mercuric chloride and methylamine.
- Flammable solvents such as alcohol, toluene, acetone, or ether are used.
- Aluminum foil is used (if mixed with an acid it produces heat and hydrogen which can explode).
- Hydrogen chloride gas or hydrochloric acid is also used in acid generators, which are usually made from plastic gasoline and spray bottle containers with tubing.

Look for:

- Solvents cans such as petroleum ether or alcohol
- Methylamine or mercuric chloride, usually from laboratory-grade reagents in commercial containers
- Aluminum foil
- Hydrogen chloride cylinder, gas generator or hydrochloric acid, rock salt, and sulfuric acid in plastic gasoline or pump sprayer containers
- Lithium batteries (lithium when mixed with a solvent may explode if water is present). Rock salt and sulfuric acid for producing hydrogen chloride gas is found commonly. These are usually made from plastic gasoline containers or sprayer bottles.
- Sudafed or ephedrine and a blender or pill grinder
- Rarely, this process may use naturally radioactive materials such as uranyl nitrate or thorium nitrate.
- Triple-necked flasks and heating mantles or other heating apparatus

* This method produces a toxic atmosphere. Mercuric chloride is both toxic and corrosive.

Thionyl Chloride Laboratory (Uncommon)

- Flammable solvents such as chloroform, methanol, or ethanol may be used. Chloroform may be carcinogenic.
- Palladium black, which is a black metallic dust, may be used. This is explosive if mixed with some chemicals. In rare cases Raney nickel may be used.

- Hydrogen gas, which may be from a hydrogen generator made with plastic gasoline containers or plastic spray containers mixing a metal such as aluminum foil or zinc with hydrochloric acid.
- A paint shaker is used, providing the common name "shaker labs."

Look for:

- Solvent cans
- Thionyl chloride is necessary, and exposure to water may cause it to explode.
- Hydrogen in compressed gas cylinders painted red is common.
- Sudafed or ephedrine and a blender or pill grinder
- A paint shaker is the unique signature of this laboratory.
- Rock salt and sulfuric acid for producing hydrogen chloride gas is found commonly. These are usually made from plastic gasoline containers or sprayer bottles.

Phenylacetic Laboratory (Rare)

- Phenylacetic acid is used and mixed with acetic anhydride. Acetic anhydride is violently reactive with water. This will likely be in a reagent bottle or commercial container.
- Sodium hydroxide or lye is also used.

Look for:

- Phenylacetic acid and acetic anhydride in reagent bottles or containers
- Lye or sodium hydroxide
- Sudafed or ephedrine and a blender or pill grinder
- Rock salt and sulfuric acid for producing hydrogen chloride gas is found commonly. These are usually made from plastic gasoline containers or sprayer bottles.

Methylenedioxyamphetamine (MDA), MDA Analogs, or Ecstasy Laboratory

- Isosafrole is used as a precursor.
- Other chemicals to look for include formic acid, hydrogen peroxide, sulfuric acid and methanol.
- Benzene and ammonium formate may be present.

Look for:

- Isosafrole
- Hydrogen peroxide
- Benzene, a suspected carcinogen
- Ammonium formate

Phencyclidine (PCP) Laboratory

- Piperidine is a precursor.
- Cyanide may be present.
- Sodium bisulfate, magnesium, petroleum ether, and sodium hydroxide are used.

Look for:

- Piperidine, cyanide, sodium bisulfate, and magnesium
- Petroleum ether
- Magnesium fires are difficult to extinguish and explode when water is added.
- Cyanide gases are a threat.

Gamma-Hydroxybutyrate (GHB) Laboratories

- Gamma-Butyrolactone is a precursor.
- Lye or sodium hydroxide

Look for:

- Gamma butyrolactone
- Lye or sodium hydroxide

Fentanyl Laboratories

These laboratories may be beyond the abilities of the typical "cookbook" meth lab operator. However, these laboratories are found in the US. Advanced chemistry skills are needed to operate this type of laboratory. Usually the method used will be the Siegfried method, as this method is easier than the original Janssen synthesis route. Both are available from the Internet. This laboratory will likely not look like the typical methamphetamine laboratory. The rule is if one cannot identify the type of laboratory or the laboratory is "very dirty," a tactical retreat is a good course of action. Strong vinegar-like odors, strong fish-like odors, and strong odors of acetone are indicators of an explosive laboratory and warrant an immediate evacuation. Many of the chemicals and apparatus found in a drug laboratory can be found in an explosive laboratory.

Fentanyl and Fentanyl Analog Laboratories

These laboratories will likely not resemble the common methamphetamine laboratory, as the skill needed to operate these laboratories is beyond that of the typical "meth cook." Laboratory glassware and evaporators will likely be used.

- N-Phenethyl-4-piperidinone (NPP) as a precursor
- 4-ANPP, 4-Aminophenyl-1-phenethylpiperdine as a precursor

Look for:

- 2-Bromoethyl benzene
- Cesium carbonate
- Aniline
- Sodium triacetoxyborohydride
- Piperidineamine
- Propionyl chloride
- Acetic anhydride
- Lithium aluminum hydride
- Ether
- Toluene
- Exhaust systems
- Air-purifying respirators, chemical protective clothing, and chemical gloves

Explosive Manufacturing Laboratories and Homemade Explosives (HME)

These laboratories may be found mixed with others or could be a stand-alone laboratory. One can find refrigerators, which may be used to store temperature sensitive explosives such as triacetone triperoxide (TATP), hexamine-based explosives such as hexamethylene triperoxide diamine (HMTD), and ice for controlling temperature in some reactions, such as in glycol-based explosives like nitroglycerin.

Look for:

- Smokeless gun powder
- Tannerite® or other reactive target materials or binary explosives
- Cold packs, ammonium nitrate fertilizer, potassium or urea nitrate fertilizer
- Powdered metals such as aluminum or magnesium
- Acetone, toluene, methyl ethyl ketone (MEK), nitromethane, race car fuel
- Citric acid, sour salts
- Fuel tablets or hexamine bars
- Antifreeze or glycol in any form
- Hair products with hydrogen peroxide in strengths above 30%
- Iodine or tincture of iodine
- Ammonium hydroxide
- Pool chemicals, hydrochloric acid (HCl), sulfuric acid (H2SO4), nitric acid
- Potassium permanganate
- Metal pipe, metal pipe end caps (nipples), PVC pipe
- Grinding apparatus, mixers, blenders, mortar and pestle
- Heating apparatus with water-cooled evaporators and other laboratory glassware
- Thermometers, refrigerators, ice maker
- Red phosphorus, strike anywhere matches, match striker strips
- Stump remover, potassium chlorate, sodium chlorate
- Sugar, confectioners' sugar
- Petroleum jelly
- Small copper or metal tubing for making blasting caps
- Metallic mercury or any mercury compound
- Batteries, wiring, switches, remote control devices, soldering iron
- Air-purifying respirators, chemical protective clothing, chemical gloves

Biological Laboratories

Biological laboratories may be used to refine toxins such as ricin or abrin or grow/process bacteria or viruses. This type of laboratory is uncommon yet presents a tremendous threat to responders.

Look for:

- Castor beans, jequirity beans/rosary beans/abrin
- Incubators, egg incubators, ice bath, thermometers

- Petri dishes
- Agar, peptone, sugar, glucose
- Very strong odors such as rotting meat
- Microscope
- Pipettes, filtration systems, laboratory glassware
- Fermenter, nebulizer, bioreactor, sprayers
- Grinders, blenders, filters, hot plates
- Exhaust systems
- Air-purifying respirators, chemical protective clothing, chemical gloves

Chemical Weapon Laboratory

Although rare, this type of laboratory presents a serious threat to the responder. Exhaust systems and PPE such as air-purifying respirators, chemical protective coveralls, and chemical gloves, are likely to be present. Antidotes such as atropine and 2PAM injectors (Mark I, DuoDote®) may be present. If a chemical laboratory manufacturing any chemical agent such as sarin or a blister agent is suspected, immediate evacuation is recommended.

Look for:

- Chlorine containing compounds such as bleach
- Phosphorus trioxide
- Phosgene
- Potassium or sodium cyanide
- Sodium fluoride
- Hydrofluoric acid
- Dimethyl sulfoxide (DMSO)
- Arsenic compounds
- Thiodiglycol

Mixed Laboratories

Perhaps the more substantial threat is a mixed laboratory, which may contain components used to manufacture clandestine drugs and other materials such as explosives. This is the more common mixed laboratory, but others cannot be ruled out. This is the reason that testing of unknown materials or materials from an unknown type of laboratory is not recommended unless the personnel performing the testing are well trained regarding the various types of laboratories. Fentanyl and its analogs are extremely dangerous, and small quantities can kill if inhaled, just as small quantities of TATP may cause injury if detonated, or very small quantities of sarin and VX chemical agents can kill if inhaled or if the agent touches exposed skin.

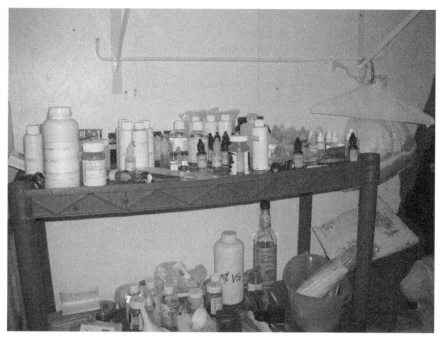

Synthetic marijuana laboratory with multiple unknown chemicals present. This type setting is challenging as the officer does not know what type of chemical hazards are present in unusual laboratories. This laboratory was found in a rural area. Photograph by Jim Smith.

Personal Protective Equipment

Personal protective equipment must include respiratory protection using a self-contained breathing apparatus or at least an air-purifying respirator. Skin protection should include chemical protective clothing and gloves rated to protect against the known chemicals. Many agencies elect to use air-purifying respirators (APRs) because of their ease of use and reasonable protection afforded. However, one must be certain the oxygen level is sufficient, the cartridges are rated against the chemical present, and the chemicals present have good warning properties. Chemical boots are a necessity in most laboratories as the floors will be contaminated. The use of APRs is not recommended in any laboratories except known low-risk illicit drug manufacturing laboratories. The threat must be known for APRs to be safe.

Safe In-Laboratory Habits

- No eating or drinking
- Frequent breaks for hydration
- Use of full PPE, including respiratory protection
- Shower as soon as feasible upon leaving the site

Decontamination

Decontamination is the removal of contaminated PPE and the washing of the hands and face. A full shower should follow as soon as feasible.

The typical decontamination sequence for CDL without substantial contamination other than the chemical boots and gloves is listed below. This is called dry decontamination.

- Place any equipment in appropriate location.
- Remove outer gloves.
- Remove outer chemical suit.
- Remove chemical boots.
- Remove respiratory protection.
- Remove inner gloves.
- Wash face and hands.
- Fully shower when possible.

The only items to be decontaminated by washing are the air-purifying respirator and chemical boots. The gloves and chemical suit will be disposed with the other hazardous materials. Some agencies discard the air-purifying respirator cartridges with the chemical clothing. Should chemical boots be contaminated in a "dirty lab," consider discarding them with other hazardous materials. Instruments should be decontaminated following the manufacturer's recommendation.

Wet decontamination may be used if approved by the Site Safety Officer. Wet decontamination requires control of runoff water and may require a hazardous materials team.

Site Cleanup

The agency should not assume responsibility for site cleanup. In the past the DEA used contractors to remove hazardous materials but in some instances these monies and services are no longer available. In many areas no funding exists at the state level to remove the hazardous materials. Familiarity with local, state, and federal regulations governing the handling, transport, and disposal of hazardous material is important. Some agencies have developed their own teams to deal with hazardous materials. If no mechanism exists for the agency to handle the laboratory hazardous materials, the agency should attempt to obtain assistance from state or federal-level agencies. The financial liability may be substantial if the agency has no means to dispose of the hazardous materials.

Notification of the Health Department and Environmental Management Agency

Some agencies notify the local public health agency or state environmental agency of laboratories raided. Be familiar with the requirements of the locale regarding such notifications. Some states have registries which track the locations and types of laboratories found. Some agencies post warning placards on the entries of the structure warning the site is potentially contaminated.

Role of Fire and EMS

Fires or explosions in clandestine laboratories do occur but with the increasing use of the "one pot" method, these explosions and fires are not as substantial as those involving the "Red P method" or "Nazi method." This may be the method by which the laboratory is found. Unexplained explosions with fire should be considered a clandestine laboratory along with an IED.

Fires in a clandestine laboratory will have a rapid spread of the fire following an explosion. Additional explosions may occur. The fire department may elect to fight the fire defensively to allow the chemicals to incinerate to avoid environmental concerns. Evacuation of the area, especially downwind is recommended.

Most medical emergencies on a laboratory raid will be heat related; however, exposures to ultra-toxic materials such as sarin, VX (a nerve agent), fentanyl, ricin, or abrin can be an issue. A good practice is to have EMS present once the scene is stable. They can perform pre-entry and post-entry assessments of the entry team members and treat any medical emergencies.

Heat-related emergencies will necessitate the immediate removal of the team member from the laboratory. An expedient removal of PPE may be required to treat the team member. This may require cutting off chemical protective clothing. Removal to a cool location, oral and IV fluids, and vital sign assessment is necessary. If skin contamination occurs the site should be flushed with water for at least 20 minutes. A garden hose or fire truck booster line may be used as an expedient method. Detailed decontamination should be delayed in serious medical emergencies until lifesaving care is rendered, except for laboratories suspected of producing fentanyl, ricin, abrin, nerve agents, or other chemical agents, as decontamination will be needed prior to definitive treatment. However, when feasible, decontamination should occur prior to delivery of the individual to the hospital unless the hospital has facilities for onsite decontamination. Substantial skin contamination, inhalation of toxic fumes, or other chemical exposures require decontamination and evaluation by a physician. Those exposed to chemical agents may require atropine and 2PAM.

Exposure to toxic atmosphere will require removal from the laboratory, expedient decontamination, and assessment by EMS. The nature of the chemical exposure will determine what type of medical care and evaluation are required. Especially dangerous exposures include anhydrous ammonia, phosphine gas, or hydrochloric acid. These agents produce an inflammatory response in the airway and lungs which may lead to delayed respiratory problems. Documentation of exposure for worker's compensation is a necessity, as officers exposed in clandestine laboratories have shown high rates of lung and liver issues along with cancer and leukemia. To be able to relate this to the laboratory exposure requires good documentation.

Confined Spaces

A confined space is defined as a location not designed for human occupation. These may have a toxic atmosphere and difficult entry or egress. Some of the typical structures include tanks, septic tanks, sewage lines, and even underground or well-sealed clandestine laboratories.

The reason for an underground clandestine laboratory is to reduce the signature of a large laboratory. The laboratory may in a basement or other expedient structure such as a buried septic tank or even a buried school bus. These are usually crudely constructed and ventilated poorly. This allows the potential for not only a collapse hazard but also toxic or explosive atmospheres and substandard wiring. Other hazards may include booby traps, mold growth, and restricted access. A few are discovered following collapse or explosion. Indicators of underground laboratories include wiring, pipes, or ventilation ducts that lead to no visible structure or have no obvious use. In some cases, one may see a structure placed above an area of disturbed soil to try to conceal the underground laboratory. These laboratories may be alarmed using motion sensors and video feeds. The above-ground structure camouflaging the structure will vary but some seen include a pump house, garden shed, and a dog house. Another clue is excavated soil with no apparent source. Other clues include dirt on suspect's clothing or the use of rubber boots, as the underground laboratory is likely to have poor or no drainage. Officers should be cautious in raids since crossing an underground laboratory with a vehicle or even on foot may cause a collapse. Raids of underground laboratories have a high risk factor as not only must officer deal with the operators but also the hazards of the underground laboratory. Above-ground apprehensions are preferred.

These laboratories will be larger laboratories and use the Red P or Nazi method. This means the potential for phosphine gas, an oxygen-deficient atmosphere, or anhydrous ammonia release are present. Access will likely be restricted to one location.

Entry to a confined space requires that officers meet a number of regulations from OSHA. These should be well planned and deliberate operations. A confined space rescue team must be available and those entering must be certified in confined space operations in addition to the clandestine laboratory safety. Some agencies have found it safer to remove the roof of the laboratory using excavation equipment than to enter it through conventional means.

Such an operation may require the assistance of a structural engineer and assistance from public works to provide equipment for the operation. Chemical suits and SCBA protection is the minimal PPE. The addition of EMS and fire personnel in support roles or in a staging area is recommended. A clear written plan must be undertaken. The removal of chemicals is another issue as the potential for a chemical event is substantial.

Forced ventilation to remove organic vapors and provide fresh air is essential and must be followed by atmospheric testing. The safety and state of the laboratory should be assessed and hazards mitigated. The laboratory should be documented and evidence samples collected. This can be followed by segregation of chemicals and finally the removal of chemicals and evidence.

Fentanyl and Use of Naloxone

Fentanyl was synthesized the early 1960s. Fentanyl is an opioid which is used to control pain and as an anesthetic. Per the US Department of Justice (USDOJ) website, fentanyl is roughly 100 times potent as morphine and 50 times more potent than heroin, but some of its analogs such as carfentanil may be 10,000 times stronger than morphine. Therapeutic dosages of fentanyl for pain via the intravenous route are usually no more than 50 micrograms in a field setting. Usually fentanyl is in a powder form, illicit compressed tablets, licit compressed tablets, or mixed with other substances and adulterants such as cocaine or heroin.

Some medical forms of fentanyl are transdermal gel patches and they appear like patches using nitroglycerin and nicotine. Some of the patches may deliver as much as 300 micrograms per hour. Several other medicines may also be administered by transdermal patches. If the patch is fentanyl patch, usually labeling will be visible on the patch, avoid contact with the patch as skin absorption can cause symptoms and clinical problems such as dim vision with pinpoint pupils, depressed mental functioning, slowed respiration, low blood pressure, collapse, respiratory arrest, and death. Any exposure to fentanyl or its analogs is dangerous and requires prompt transport to a medical facility for definitive care and potentially the administration of naloxone on scene and during transportation.

If any responder, including law enforcement canines, experiences the above signs and symptoms, with the more prominent issue decreased mental functioning and slowed respirations, the immediate use of naloxone is recommended by the USDOJ while following local medical protocols. The affected individual should be removed from the location, and if visible powder is present, removal of clothing and wet decontamination may be needed but act according to local hazardous material procedures. External support of breathing through use of a bag valve mask and oral airways can be required. Remember the effects of naloxone are short lived and additional doses may be required to keep respirations within the normal range.

Some agencies have issued naloxone in manual injection via syringe and needle form, nasal spray, and auto injectors to every member of the agency as fentanyl is found within the jurisdiction. Naloxone should not be used unless potential exposures to fentanyl or one of its analogs is suspected. Although a relatively benign drug, naloxone can have side effects. If naloxone is used on a person who uses opioids frequently, it may precipitate withdrawal and ruin the person's "high" with resultant combativeness and inducing withdrawal symptoms. Some medical protocols suggest using only enough naloxone to ensure respirations are within the normal range but follow local medical protocols for naloxone use. Some state health departments are providing naloxone to first responders at no cost and making the training/certification material available online in a short video.

Several first responders have been exposed to fentanyl from dermal contact or when the fentanyl dust is airborne. The minimum protective clothing is nitrile or butyl rubber gloves, an N99 respirator, and paper coveralls. Remember this ensemble does not afford any fire protection. It does afford some respiratory protection, skin protection, and can avoid contaminating a uniform. Use of this ensemble requires training in its use, limitations, donning, contamination control, decontamination, and doffing. This type clothing should not be used in a suspect fentanyl laboratory. Some agencies no longer test white powders on scene unless they are reasonably certain from the totality of circumstances that the powder is not a biological agent such as abrin or ricin, the powder is not an explosive such as triacetone tri peroxide (TATP) or Hexamethylene triperoxide diamine (HMTD), and the powder is not likely fentanyl. Some use the above cited PPE to collect the powder outside of a suspected fentanyl laboratory and transport it to the appropriate laboratory following local collection and transportation protocols. The sample should be packaged in the manner the laboratory requires. Do no deploy law enforcement canines in a setting where fentanyl is likely present as they can become ill from exposure to fentanyl and its analogs. Some veterinarians have suggested that two to four milligrams of naloxone be administered nasally in the law enforcement canine and such may alleviate the toxicity of opioids to the canine but follow up doses may be needed. Canine officers should follow local veterinary protocols.

Naloxone, the antidote for opioid overdose, comes in a variety of administration forms including liquid manually injectable via syringe and needle, nasal spray dispensed as an aerosol, and autoinjectors injecting the naloxone subcutaneously. Training is required to use naloxone in many locales, and according the USDOJ website, a prescription is required to obtain naloxone. This may necessitate acquiring a medical director for the naloxone antidote program. The typical starting dose is four milligrams (4 mg) via nasal spray and manual injection, however, auto injectors are two milligrams (2 mg) of naloxone as a rule. Autoinjectors should only be used following special training and the locations of injections is limited to the lateral portion of the thigh in the human for nonmedical personnel in a field setting. In some cases, several follow-up doses of two to four milligrams may be needed if respirations have not returned to normal range within two to three minutes after the initial dosing or if the patient still appears to be in distress. Make certain the training for naloxone use is followed, local protocols are followed, and package labeling material is followed. Naloxone is not usually effective during the cardiopulmonary resuscitation setting.

Suspected Fentanyl Powder Minimal Protective Clothing Outside the Laboratory Setting

- Nitrile or butyl rubber gloves for hand protection, double glove
- Fitted N99 respirator
- Paper coveralls

Symptoms and Signs of Fentanyl Exposure

- Dim vision
- Pinpoint pupils
- Depressed mental functioning

- Slowed respirations
- Low blood pressure
- Collapse
- Respiratory arrest
- Death

If a suspected fentanyl laboratory is present, the responder should retreat and request the clandestine laboratory raid team. Remember, signs and symptoms from fentanyl are usually rapid in onset, but some responders have not shown symptoms of the exposure for 15 to 30 minutes. In one case the white powder contaminated a uniform shirt during sampling and the officer was not affected by the until he later came into contact with the fentanyl laced powder at the law enforcement headquarters.

Operating a Safety Checkpoint

Safety checkpoints (SCP) must be operated legally and safely. Safe operation of the checkpoint is the most important consideration throughout the planning process. The SCP supervisor must assure legal guidelines are met and any department policies, local laws, or state guidelines are met.

Some of the general precepts of a SCP are to pick locations which meet the following criteria.

- Light to moderate traffic to avoid traffic back up, which can prompt rear end collisions
- Traffic from one direction is checked on a multi-lane unless a large area and numerous personnel are available
- The location and vicinity should have a history of traffic violations and DUI arrests or DUI-related motor vehicle crashes
- Areas to avoid include intersections, curves, hills, businesses, and high-speed multi-lane highways
- The location will require a wide area for parking and staging of vehicles
- Areas to avoid include those in which side roads provide an easy point to elude or avoid the SCP or areas with a decreased sight radius such as curves or hills
- A consideration must be the stopping distance for the speed, good visibility of the SCP

Identification of the checkpoint through signage, lighting, and traffic cones to channelize traffic is essential. Low-light operations require supplemental lighting such as generators with mast mounted lights. Times of poor visibility such as fog or rain should be avoided. High-contrast retroreflective signage is essential to identify the SCP in addition to warning motorists to slow. One recommendation is traffic be channeled to one lane with retroreflective traffic cones if the SCP is on a multilane highway. This will slow traffic and alert drivers to the checkpoint. A drive through by the SCP supervisor is recommended prior to operation of the SCP to assure visibility and function. The reaction to the cones provides officers with an assessment of the reaction time and potential impairment of drivers approaching the SCP. To meet federal requirements officers operating on federal highway or highways funded in part with federal monies should wear an ANSI-approved traffic vest.

The SCP should use a separate radio channel or group to facilitate rapid communications. If available a second channel or group should be used for communications to perform warrant and registration checks if such checks are not performed via in-car computers.

A pre-deployment briefing is essential and must address the below listed:

- Chain of command and radio designators for personnel
- Location, operational methods, and design of the SCP
- Vehicle placement
- Job assignments
- Vehicle selection and contact procedures
- Radio channel or group to be used
- Check of equipment
- Procedures of citing violators, arrests, and transport of prisoners
- Emergency procedures
- Procedures for the disposition of prisoners

Emergency procedures addressed should include:

- Pursuits toward or away from the SCP
- Back up and arrest procedures including those for resisting arrest
- How contraband thrown from vehicles will be handled and secured
- How attempts to evade or flee the SCP will be handled
- Procedure for a suspect with a firearm within the SCP
- What to do for emergency vehicles attempting to traverse the SCP
- What to do for a motor vehicle crash within the SCP or nearby

Safety checkpoints must have adequate staff with a minimum number of officers, about 12 for a light to moderate traffic flow area in good weather and daytime conditions. SCPs should be operated usually four hours or fewer because of fatigue of the personnel working. Some agencies operate for a short time and then move as the location of the SCP will spread rapidly. Very warm or cold settings may require cooling and warming points within the SCP for officers. Some agencies use propane-powered heaters for warming and large water misting fans for cooling.

The SCP supervisor should be responsible only for the safe and efficient operation of the SCP. He or she must monitor the traffic flow and back up and may have to order the flowing of traffic through the SCP with no vehicles checked to reduce traffic back up.

The supervisor should determine the criteria for vehicle selection for inspection. Some use a random number while others check every vehicle. Whatever is used the process must be consistent and random. However, this does not mean that officers cannot develop reasonable suspicion for criminal activity, observe license plate or lighting violations, and pull a non-selected vehicle for inspection. The supervisor should communicate with the counter and change the formula as needed to assure coordinated operation at the SCP. A diagram of the SCP location with each officer's position marked is helpful.

Additional personnel are officers assigned as flaggers whose role is to direct the selected vehicles into the inspection area. Officers must then inspect the vehicle using a standard greeting when asking for driver's license, registration, and insurance documents. The conversation allows the officer to detect the odor of alcoholic beverages, detect other narcotics, assess the driver's ability to speak, and consider the driver's demeanor.

If enough time and personnel are available, the vehicle tag and lights should be inspected. As space allows, some agencies move violators to another area to cite them. This may be dependent upon the driver's condition. Those who appear impaired should not be allowed to continue to operate the vehicle. A procedure for disposition of vehicles of those arrested should be available. Persons who appear impaired should be checked for weapons and have his or her field sobriety tests recorded on video. These checkpoints will produce DUI and controlled substance arrests, but officers must be alert for those who might be armed. Some agencies use onsite breath alcohol testing and a van for detaining those arrested, and some even have wreckers on scene to transport vehicles.

Safety vehicles should be placed on either end of the SCP to observe vehicles approaching, those attempting to elude the SCP, or those discarding contraband or switching drivers. A policy must be established to govern the process of stopping vehicles attempting to elude the SCP. This should follow local protocols. These officers should be observant because drugs and firearms may be discarded upon approaching the SCP. One agency in Alabama recovered a pipe bomb discarded by a driver approaching a SCP, while another recovered an improvised short-barreled shotgun. The potential for an impaired driver within the SCP striking vehicles or officers is present. The SCP supervisor and other personnel should be alert for such and a code word should be used on the radio frequency or group to alert personnel within the SCP. Areas in which officers can seek protection are required. Personnel operating within a safety checkpoint must constantly be alert for impaired drivers who may not respond appropriately. The SCP supervisor should make certain that if a vehicle approaches the SCP in a dangerous manner, officers are alerted and a safe location is available. Remember than traffic-related injuries and deaths remain high for law enforcement officers struck by vehicles. The local protocols and legal policy for the jurisdiction should be followed, but case law in several cases should be reviewed. This includes *Indianapolis v. Edmond*, 531 U.S. 32 (2000), *Terry v. Ohio*, 392 U.S. 1 (1968), *Delaware v. Prouse*, 440 U.S. 648 (1979), and *Michigan Department of State Police v. Sitz*, 496 U.S. 444 (1990). Care must be taken to not make the SCP a drug checkpoint. Drug detection canines should be available and even present but should not be deployed without reasonable suspicion.

School Crisis Response

The current attention to violence and incidents in schools mandates the development of a functional school crisis plan. The plan must address the interface of school administration, school police officers, and chain of command within public safety agencies.

The type of emergency will dictate the lead, with other agencies playing supporting roles. Where leadership becomes obscured are incidents in which multiple events, such as a shooting in which law enforcement is trying to secure the scene and contain and apprehend the suspect, emergency medical services (EMS) is attempting to gain access to patients to render aid, and school officials are evacuating students, are happening concurrently. Coordination of efforts is essential.

Many of the events will be within the purview of law enforcement, and most will be handled by onsite resources. These issues are not discussed.

As a minimum the school crisis plan should address:

- Bomb or other threat
- Assaults, shootings, or an armed person
- Hostage situation
- Disorderly persons, strike, or demonstration
- Fire or explosion, hazardous material release
- Mass casualty event

- Severe weather
- Transportation event such as a school bus crash
- Abduction of a student, staff member, or faculty member

The plan should clearly define who the law enforcement incident commander will be and the relationships among agencies. The school system administration should play a role in the decision-making process. Specialty teams that operate in a semi-autonomous manner, such as special response teams, bomb squad, and canine units, must have designated operational commanders with representation at the command post.

During the initial phase of the law enforcement emergency little or no coordination may exist. As the situation evolves, a coordinated effort must be undertaken to mitigate and resolve the event.

The plan should address the initial actions by responders:

- Determine the scope of the event and request additional resources
- Isolate, contain, control, and mitigate the event
- Establish an inner perimeter
- Evacuate as needed
- Establish a command post
- Coordinate with school officials and other responders
- As additional resources arrive, stage the assets and deploy as needed

The law enforcement incident commander should consider the following:

- Determine resources are deployed effectively
- Confirm students, staff, and faculty are evacuated or protected
- Determine whether resources present are adequate, if not request additional assets
- Designate radio channels or groups to be used
- Advise the chain of command of the event
- Determine if the command post is placed adequately and protected
- Confirm an inner perimeter is established and establish an outer perimeter
- Keep routes to and from the site open and deal with parents and onlookers
- Apply the available assets to mitigate the problem
- Designate a public information officer (PIO) and present a coordinated press release
- Keep a log of the events as they unfold
- If the event appears to be long lived, request additional logistical support

Coordination with the media and other responders to squelch rumors with accurate information is essential. Control access to the site, keep traffic flowing, and keep access for emergency vehicles clear. Considering requesting a NOTAM (Notice to Airmen) if gunfire might affect low-flying aircraft or if such will interfere with police aerial assets or aeromedical helicopters. The local FAA should be contacted and request a Notice to Airmen (NOTAM). A clear and concise argument for closing the airspace must be presented. If aeromedical evacuation is needed use pre-established landing zones. These should be out of sight of the school, out of gunfire range of shooters, and free of overhead hazards.

Each school should have close and distant evacuation sites. These evacuation sites should serve as evacuation sites for fire, and each location should be as far away from the buildings as feasible. Accountability is an issue as are communications once structures are evacuated. Portable radios and cellular telephones should provide school officials with the means to communicate. The school crisis plan should address the need to report unusual persons or situations that may indicate a fire alarm is a ruse to empty occupants from the buildings with the intent to harm them once outside.

Bomb threats require a different response, as the receipt of a credible bomb threat may require evacuation. The maximum distance possible should be used but no one should be less than 1,000 feet from a structure. The decision to evacuate in credible bomb threat scenarios should be made by school officials. Bomb threat evacuations should not be disguised as a fire drill as windows and doors are closed, which is not recommended in a bomb threat. Distant evacuation sites should be addressed in the plan as these sites would be used if students are transported away from the school site.

Hostage or barricade situations tend to be long-lived events with needs such as relief personnel, mutual aid, lighting and power, barricades, shelter, bathroom facilities, food, refreshments, and spare radio batteries. Even portable toilets may be required. Recall of personnel should begin early to facilitate a transition from routine to emergency operations.

The plan must be approved by the agencies involved and the school system. The school system must provide an executive-level decision maker to the command post. If the school system operates its own radio system, a representative with a radio should be present at the command post. Access to any CCTV or other surveillance system is a necessity as are plans for the school buildings. Keys, maintenance personnel, and information regarding the types of locks and location of utilities will be needed. If available, interior photographs are helpful if entry is made by officers along with other information available about the structure. The location and types of any hazardous materials is another vital piece of information.

The plan should include preplanned emergency medical services (EMS) triage and staging areas should a large number of injured persons be encountered. Another distasteful but necessary requirement is the provision for a temporary morgue. Some agencies use portable morgues or refrigerated trailers (with the company name removed) to store bodies. Some states have state mortuary disaster teams which may be of assistance should multiple fatalities occur.

Several situations could occur that require special considerations. Any suspected package bomb or chemical, biological, or radiological device should be addressed by the crisis plan. One must consider that many experimental bombers are juveniles, and the school chemistry and physics laboratories provide resources to construct such a device.

When the active phase of an event is terminated, the crime scene processing and body recovery and identification, along with recovery efforts by school officials, must be considered. An after-action report made in compliance with agency policy is recommended.

Lessons Learned from Others

During a recent FBI raid, agents stopped in the parking lot of a nearby hospital to don raid vests and check equipment prior to the execution of a search warrant. This telegraphed that a raid was imminent and was posted on social media and a police activities website at least 20 minutes prior to raid. Although the target was unknown, it had to be near the location of assembly of the agents. Local law enforcement was not aware of the raid but saw the posts and inferred it might involve a government entity near the location, and their surmise was correct. Had this been a raid against an armed adversary, the adversary might have gained time to evacuate or prepare to oppose the raid.

Chapter 14

Excited Delirium and Positional Asphyxia

Excited delirium is an ill-defined state which normally does not refer to a mental or psychological state but a clinical condition of end-stage drug intoxication. Officers are not likely to respond to these events frequently enough to understand, through experience, the hazards present. Some officers disbelieve the reports of superhuman strength and no feeling of pain by these individuals. The more common drugs implicated in this state are cocaine, methamphetamine, and methamphetamine analogs such as "bath salts." However, other drugs, alcohol, antipsychotic drugs, and polydrug abuse can result in a similar state. Some individuals experience this state for unknown reasons when no detectable illicit substances are present. In this condition the person has a hyperdynamic circulatory problem (rapid heartbeat and high blood pressure); their heart is susceptible to ventricular fibrillation from enlargement. The heart damage is likely from prolonged drug abuse and lack of oxygen. The person will usually be in a delusional and paranoid state mentally, will feel little pain, and may have hyperthermia with a body temperature sometimes over 105° Fahrenheit. This may lead to the person shedding their clothes. Their behavior is bizarre and combative. Their inability to rationalize their actions and lack of feeling pain allows them to engage in activities beyond normal behavior and makes restraining these persons difficult. They literally have used up their available energy and oxygen and their muscles begin to cannibalize themselves. This results in low blood oxygen levels, very toxic waste products in the blood system, a condition called acidosis and rhabdomyolysis, sensitization of the heart for ventricular fibrillation, and damage to the liver and kidneys. In other words, this person is in a death spiral. At some point law enforcement will have contact with the individual and will try to restrain them. In some cases, no matter what steps are taken by EMS or law enforcement this individual will suffer cardiac arrest.

Common findings for those in excited delirium include:

- Armed with a nearby weapon, such as broken glass, knife from kitchen, tree limb, etc.
- Pain tolerance of an incredible degree
- Hyperthermia and hyperventilation
- Incredible strength with seemingly no fatigue
- Will not respond to law enforcement commands
- Attack glass in windows, doors, and may use glass shards as a weapon, etc.

In attempting to subdue these individuals officers are likely to end up on the ground engaged in a struggle with a subject who has abnormal strength and feels no pain. This makes for a scenario in which both will sustain substantial injury. The use of a conducted energy weapon is recommended to restrain these individuals.

Positional Asphyxia

The reports of litigation and in-custody deaths from prone restraint (hogtie, four-point restraint) abound in the literature and courts. This prone (face-down) restraint does place a prisoner at serious risk for positional asphyxia and death. There have been numerous studies and reports in medical and law enforcement literature describing the process whereby the person restrained in this manner decompensates, suffers cardiac arrest, and dies (*Custody Death Task Force Final Report*, San Diego, CA Police Department, 1992; International Association of Chiefs of Police, *Policy Review*, "The Prone Restraint—Still a Bad Idea", Vol. 10, No. 1, Spring 1998).

What is postulated to occur and what has been reproduced in controlled settings is that an arrested person who is in a state of agitated delirium, when placed in a face-down position with four-point restraint, suffers respiratory difficulty. Drugs, alcohol, exertion or a combination of these factors usually induces this state of agitated delirium. If this person is placed in a face-down (prone) position with their hands handcuffed behind their back, they will have difficulty breathing and certain types of drugs and alcohol may suppress their respiratory drive. Physical difficulty in breathing is caused by the added compression of the chest by body weight, stretching of the diaphragm, and the awkward position of the arms behind the back. This does not allow full chest expansion to exchange air. When the handcuffed suspect's restrained legs are attached to the wrist, which adds additional weight and compresses the chest further, this causes restricted air exchange and aggravates the low blood oxygen, thereby contributing to the asphyxia. In some circumstances officers may additionally restrain the suspect by holding them down, which prevents them from adequately exchanging air. Several studies have shown that even normal individuals suffer some respiratory compromise when placed in this position.

Add to the fact that the person may be intoxicated with drugs that sensitize the heart to ventricular fibrillation, have struggled and already be oxygen depleted, and have been sprayed with a chemical agent that makes breathing difficult, and with the additional respiratory compromise sudden cardiac arrest occurs. This is a preventable in-custody death. Other factors that may predispose the restrained individual to positional asphyxia include obesity, a seizure occurring, and psychotic behavior related to drug intoxication. The simple maneuver of physically placing the person in the restrained position may cause claustrophobia and further aggravate their struggles, causing them to consume more oxygen. Officers respond to this more restraint, which further aggravates the situation. This is a downward spiral that can cause hypoxia (lack of oxygen) to a heart already drug-sensitized from cocaine, methamphetamine, or related substances, and can induce cardiac arrest.

Legal notice by the courts has been taken of agencies failing to take adequate steps to prevent positional asphyxia. Several lawsuits have added to the courts' findings that inappropriate restraint can be the proximate cause of an in-custody death and agencies/officers may be held legally accountable for their actions (*Gutierrez v. San Antonio*, 139 F.3d 441 5th Circuit, 1998, *Swans v. City of Lansing*, 65 F. Supp. 2d 625 W.D. Michigan, 1998, *Cruz v. City of Laramie*, 239 F.3rd 1183 10th Circuit, 2001). Litigation can be expected as a result of any in-custody death, especially a death involving positional asphyxia. An agency without a clear and enforced policy on preventing positional asphyxia may have a difficult time defending their actions. The act of restraining an individual using four-point restraint is usually not in and of itself an act that is considered excessive force or may not even be an unlawful seizure. However, the failure to properly position an individual restrained in this manner and obtain medical assistance may be tantamount to culpable negligence. Some speculation exists that failure to act appropriately in these circumstances might also result in criminal charges for negligent homicide.

Any policy addressing restraints should be clearly written such that if a suspect is restrained in the prone position, officers closely monitor their respiratory efforts. The prone position should be avoided whenever possible. In no circumstances should a person with a four-point restraint be placed in the prone (face-down) position. Any in-custody suspect with breathing difficulty should have emergency medical services summoned for an examination. If four-point restraints are to be used under no circumstances should the individual be placed prone, nor should officers compress their chest or in any manner interfere with their breathing efforts. The individual should be maintained on their side. This prevents compression of the chest, allows better expansion of the diaphragm but should still allow reasonable control of the suspect. This position also assists with keeping an open airway should the suspect vomit.

If emergency medical services (EMS) elects to transport the person to the hospital, assure that an officer accompanies the suspect to the hospital. Remind EMS personnel not to place the patient in a prone position while restrained. Medical care may require the removal of some restraints, and an officer must be present if needed to not only remove the restraints for treatment, but to assist in controlling the suspect. Do not send a suspect restrained to medical facility without an accompanying officer. EMS personnel may want to attach the suspect to a spine board for ease of movement or prevention of additional aggravation of suspected spinal injuries. This may require the removal of some restraints, but once again, avoid placing the patient face down while restrained. This can be avoided by rolling the spine board with the suspect attached onto their side. This will facilitate better airway control and make breathing easier for the suspect. This is well within EMS protocols, and many EMTs will be familiar with positional asphyxia but do not presume they are.

Officer may find it difficult to remember positional asphyxia after a long struggle with a drug-crazed suspect who has been handcuffed with substantial difficulty. But this is exactly the candidate for positional asphyxia, who officers must "pile on" to initially control their aggressive behavior. Procedure and policy should make the suspect's medical condition and respiratory efforts a priority once the suspect is under control. Avoid the prone (face-down) position with any person restrained when feasible, but do not place a suspect face down who has a four-point restraint.

Conducted Energy Weapons

There have been associated several deaths, probably from excited delirium, with conducted energy weapon strikes. The TASER functions by overriding muscle nervous impulses (T-Waves) and causes collapse. Whether or not the TASER contributes to the cardiac arrest is in dispute, with several studies showing a proper "take down" with the TASER has caused no deaths; however, the small number reported in the literature as opposed to the large number of drug-related deaths, estimated at 40,000, makes its contribution to the death unlikely. The persons exhibiting agitated behavior who present a threat to officers are those that the TASER was developed for use against. The conventional method of using impact instruments, multiple officer takedown, OC, or firearms to immobilize the suspect also carry a dramatic amount of risk for the suspect and to officers. As stated earlier, many of the individuals are already in a downward spiral and are very subject to cardiac arrest regardless of the intervention undertaken.

Warning Signs

Officers and EMS personnel should be educated to recognize the warning signs of excited delirium and be prepared to deal with a potential cardiac arrest.

- History of drug abuse, particularly cocaine and methamphetamine, combined with alcohol or other drugs. Cocaine and an alcohol mixture have been associated with this syndrome.
- Excited, combative, paranoid, and agitated behavior with restless movement, shouting, and fighting behavior
- Removal of clothes, which is common with hyperthermia and paranoia
- Profuse sweating with pale skin
- Rapid breathing
- Breathing-related complaint such as, "I can't breathe."
- Chest pain or complaints of an irregular pulse
- Rapid heart rate, high body temperature, and high blood pressure
- Obese or a big belly
- OC or TASER ineffective, or multiple TASER shocks required (likely because of poor electrode contact)
- Restraint by multiple persons required

If one or more of these warning signs is encountered, then officers should assure that EMS is available. Once the suspect is in custody there should be an immediate EMS assessment and transport to the hospital should be a strong consideration. Remember, regardless of the intervention the suspect may suffer cardiac arrest.

One suggested takedown technique is to have five officers and EMS to be present and when the suspect is immobilized by TASER the officers control the four limbs and head. The patient is rapidly immobilized on their side to a spine board, an IV is started, and a benzodiazepine or related tranquilizing drug is administered by IV, and, if the hyperthermia exists, immediate cooling takes place with cold packs and cooled IV fluid. Rapid transport to the hospital is indicated.

Chapter 15

Active Aggressive Behavior

Introduction

Mass shootings and active aggressive behavior have been an issue in the US for many years. According to FBI data and several studies, including one from the University of Illinois, these incidents have not become more frequent but have remained steady between the years 2006 and 2019, with shootings producing large numbers of casualties, such as the Las Vegas shooting, an anomaly. Violent crime in the US has been on the decrease since the mid-1990s (apart from in some major metropolitan areas), and recent research points to gun crime and mass shootings in the US occurring at rates like those in many countries in Europe when compared on a per capita basis, with the US below some European countries. Part of this perception is the "see it while it happens" media reporting, as many of the events are carried as they are in progress or during the immediate aftermath. Then they continue to run this information to fill the 24-hour news cycle. The media seeks high ratings and tends to report events in a sensational method, ignoring facts in many cases and even reporting rumors to enhance ratings. Some say gun control is the answer to prevention of these incidents, yet countries with stringent gun control measures have similar mass murders with similar numbers killed and injured using other weapons (e.g., United Kingdom, China, etc.). The other weapons vary, from vehicles to IEDs to edged weapons. Some do not consider the long-lived attacks with IEDs as part of active aggressive behavior or acute attacks with IEDs to be part of the active aggressive behavior spectrum. This textbook treats these events as active aggressive behavior because they do follow the patterns of active aggressive behavior, induce terror, and have similar motivations as shootings, acid attacks, and edged-weapon assaults, while injuring and killing large numbers of persons.

The problem of active aggressive behavior has no simple solutions, such as restricting firearms or incarcerating those with mental health issues. A holistic approach must be employed to reduce the threat. Those with mental health issues carry out many of these incidents. Serious mental illness plays a role in many of the incidents. When terrorist attacks are excluded, those aggressors with mental health issues tend to kill and injure larger numbers in workplace shootings. This appears to be based upon a revenge motive, as evidenced by data from FBI studies.

One must remember that these events are examined with "20/20" hindsight noting the information available. Many wonder why the information was not acted upon and what was the motivation for the attack. The reasons vary, but lack of reporting, tracking, and understanding of information is common to many of the events. The key that leaders and those responsible for the prevention, deterrence, and response to these incidents must understand, is that prevention is the primary goal but to achieve it a culture of reporting is needed to detect and deter internal threats. While target hardening and security is needed to discourage and prevent external threats, one must guard against the internal threats contemporaneously. Terrorist attacks must be a consideration in high-risk facilities and areas with a dense occupancy, but the internal threat of a workplace shooting must also be considered.

Motivation is another factor: revenge for a perceived wrong is a common motivator, and shifting blame to others to avoid admitting one is wrong is common in society. Those with mental health issues may have a motive which is apparent only to them. Then others will have no apparent motive. "Magnicide" is a term used to describe a person who commits suicide after committing an act that garners attention. As many of those engaged in active behavior do commit suicide, this may be a motivating factor.

Many consider active aggressive behavior as a person or persons in a dynamic situation attacking multiple individuals. The situation is not static, such as a hostage situation with a bank robbery interrupted by police, in which a barricade/hostage situation exists. Active aggressive behavior may involve more than one locale or movement through a large locale such as a large building, mall, or stadium, or involving several locales. This individual or these individuals present an immediate threat and are armed with firearms, IEDs, edged weapons, or other deadly weapons. The actor presents a clear danger, and the person is attacking those present. An immediate response by law enforcement is required to isolate, contain, and neutralize the threat. However, according to published FBI studies, about half of the events have concluded prior to law enforcement arrival. Another consideration is that a static situation such as a barricade situation with hostages can escalate and become an active aggressive behavior incident if execution of hostages begins. Examples would be the Bataclan theatre attack (in Paris in 2015) and Beslan school takeover (in Russia in 2004). Hostage execution began following the takeover; however, these tend to be terrorist-type incidents, as both these cases were.

Usually active aggressive behavior does not cease until intervention occurs. Normally, action by law enforcement occurs, the actor is overpowered by those present, or, if using a firearm, the shooter must reload or expends their available ammunition. Those events at multiple locations, or in a serial fashion within one locale, continue until one of the above occurs.

Targets will usually be sites which have little external security and are classified as "soft targets." Examples include malls, office buildings, theaters, restaurants, streets, mass transit facilities and vehicles, schools, and the like. Other targets that begin the transition to hardened targets may include government structures with magnetometers and armed personnel, airport terminals within restricted areas, stadiums protected by armed personnel screening those entering, and similar venues. The more external security and security measures are present, the less likely an attack is from an external source, but one must consider the insider threat which many would tend to ignore. This person has defeated external security because of trust placed in him or her. However, this does not exclude the actor attacking the entry points that could provide a dense group of persons awaiting screening for entry or for an "insider" to smuggle weapons into a secure setting. The paradoxical issue is that stringent external security at the perimeter creates an inviting soft target of those awaiting screening to enter a secure hardened area. Thus, the reason for suicide attacks against the American military at entry control points.

External threats are usually considered criminal threats, such as robberies, burglary, or theft. However, some active aggressive behavior, especially outside the educational setting, where almost every attacker has a connection with venue attacked, may be those with minimal or no connection to the entity. Some active aggressive behavior incidents involving external threats arise from domestic circumstances. These can be particularly dangerous events as the aggressor will likely be committed, well motivated, expect to die or be prepared to die, and his or her motivation will likely be driven by the perception of a wrong for which revenge is the only available avenue to resolve the issue. These attacks usually do not produce more than six casualties, excluding the shooter. This same issue is faced in many medical facility incidents. The aggressor is focused on a single target and will do whatever is needed to attack and kill the target. The motivation for these aggressors will be strong and focused. They will have likely conducted reconnaissance, and the targets will be soft. Those killed other than the target are bystanders who happen to be present. This is an aspect of many workplace shootings, as there exists a primary target but those nearby become targets of convenience.

Terrorist incidents have an entirely different aspect. These events are designed to provoke a terror reaction in the public. The more carnage and casualties that can be created by the incident, the more media coverage will result. These attacks are focused on specific targets, which may be a locale of a symbolic nature, and the people present, or a specific person or group. The attacks in Paris (in 2015), Pulse Nightclub (in Orlando, Florida, in 2016), and San Bernardino, California (in 2015), reflect these types of attacks. The attack on the Charles Hebdo facility (in 2015) was aimed at the Hebdo staff, while the attacks on Bataclan, Pulse Nightclub, and health facility in San Bernardino, California, were designed to kill as many persons present as possible. These attacks were executed in a manner to garner the desired attention. The attacks created terror, caused loss of use of facilities, generated a tremendous economic effect, and provided the terrorist an opportunity to show their attacks can occur anywhere regardless of efforts by the government. In doing so, this causes the public to respond to the incidents in a negative fashion and lose confidence in government. The terrorists in these incidents were not under active observation by any law enforcement agency; in the San Bernardino case and Pulse Nightclub they appear to have acquired the firearms through "straw purchases" or legal methods.

Therefore, the methods used in such an incident will depend upon the motivation of the aggressors. Incidents involving a person with a mental health issue or revenge issue in the workplace will likely be solo attacks focused on a discrete locale and group of individuals. The FBI reports that active shooters in the US are almost exclusively solo attacks. Terrorist incidents usually involve more than one person and are well planned, and the aggressors are committed and expect or want to die. No escape plan is needed. Further, terrorist attacks are more likely to involve IEDs and use military tactics. In some instances, one may see hybrid attacks, which use components of a typical terrorist attack combined with an active shooter with revenge motivation. Hybrid attacks in which homegrown violent extremist motivation is difficult to extract from the more common active aggressive behavior, and some attacks attributed to nonterrorist actions, may in fact be motivated by terrorism.

Another aspect of active aggressive behavior is the wide availability of information regarding the attacks and tactics used. The Internet is a fertile source of information regarding the tactics used and successful tactics, along with countermeasures taken by entities and law enforcement. Even countermeasures established by entities to protect personnel and venues may be available via the Internet. Sites operated by extremist groups also provide an extensive array of ideas, tactics, and exhortation to attack a variety of targets within the US and targets outside the country which have US interests. This can lead to radicalization of those present in the US and generate the evolving issue of homegrown violent extremists (HVE). Prisons are a good source of those who can be or are radicalized, with a grievance against the government and society already in place. Some of the HVE have traveled to foreign countries where they have received training in military tactics, IED manufacture, and covert operations. The line between international terrorism and domestic terrorism has become indistinct because of this radicalization of HVE within the US from sources outside the US or the self-radicalization of those present in the US.

Many consider the first modern mass shooting in the US to be the Unruh shooting in 1949. The incident occurred in Camden, New Jersey, with 13 killed and three wounded. This is a classic case of a mentally ill person committing mass murder. Many of the classic behavioral clues were present prior to the shooting. This incident will be discussed later in the text.

Active aggressive behavior evokes the image of a heavily armed gunman entering a school or business and shooting people randomly. Granted, in the United States this is the image, but one should not be lulled into the mindset this is the only method in which many persons can be injured or killed. A simple Internet search revealed numerous incidents not only outside the US, but also several in the US, in which as many as a dozen persons were injured and several killed with edged weapons such as knives, flammable liquids, and even incidents in which several individuals are bludgeoned with baseball bats and other objects. Vehicles being used to attack pedestrians has become a common method of attack and is difficult to guard against in urban areas, as large groups of pedestrians are present throughout these areas. The expense of placing vehicle-resistant bollards, barricades, or other barriers make it less likely that these countermeasures will be possible over wide areas.

IEDs have long been used to invoke terror and for active aggressive behavior incidents. Some of these events tend to be long lived and sometimes do not meet what today is considered an active event. Examples of long-lived bombing campaigns, which will be discussed, are the Unabomber, Eric Robert Rudolph, and the Mad Bomber, along with acute attacks such as the Oklahoma City bombing. One cannot discount the use of IEDs in concert with other weapons or as a stand-alone weapon.

The key is not to focus only upon firearms, but also to consider the use of edged weapons, blunt instruments, flammable liquids, vehicles, or IEDs. Mass killings have been an issue in almost every country and throughout history and not just isolated to the US. One must take a holistic approach in preparation, generate a culture of reporting, and assess known threats. The entity must train its employees to respond to such events and have a post-incident recovery plan.

Another issue is that preparation for an internal threat may not be adequate or even applicable in some respects to person(s) motivated by violent extremism. Preparing for what many characterize as a terrorist event is not the same as preparing for an internal threat from an employee, client, or student, or preparing for an external criminal threat. Those motivated and called terrorists or homegrown violent extremists present a more substantial risk, and preparation for this threat has some parallels. However, it should be differentiated from the internal threat and external criminal threat. Preparation for terrorist events and response to them will be different. However, these events may not be able to be separated from a conventional attack until after the event is concluded.

Actions such as establishing a culture of reporting and a behavioral intervention team, searching for "leakage," and recognizing "triggering events" can contribute to the prevention of such internal events. Reporting of behavior of concern by employees, staff, students, faculty, the public, and others is essential. Training of these individuals is key to the process so that the behaviors can be recognized. Leakage is the relating of plans, noting of purchases consistent with violent behavior, and behavior consistent with potentially violent acts revealed verbally, by actions, in writing, by email, through studying prior violent events, or even drawings and photographs.

Source Material

This material is derived from a variety of sources, including open-source material from the United States Secret Service (USSS) and the Federal Bureau of Investigation (FBI), material from Homeland Security Active Shooter resources, and open-source material from the US Northern Command, US Naval Postgraduate School, Bureau of Alcohol, Tobacco, Firearms, and Explosives (BATFE), and others. When feasible, official reports, such as the Connally Report from the Texas Tower shootings and the Jefferson County Sheriff's Department report on the Columbine High School incident, were used, but in some cases media accounts may have been the only source of information available at the time this text was written.

Case Histories of Active Aggressive Behavior Not Including Terrorism

Most of the active aggressive behavior incidents occur in medium- to small-sized communities, according to the *FBI Bulletin*.

Some statistical data published by the FBI is important:

- Most incidents occur in small- to medium-sized communities.
- Average incident is less than 12 minutes in duration, with about 40% less than five minutes.
- Almost every event is a single aggressor, usually a shooter.
- Almost every shooter is male.
- Slightly fewer than half commit suicide during the event.
- Very few bring IEDs.
- About 10% stop and leave.
- About 20% go mobile with his or her active aggressive behavior.
- Almost half of the events are completed before police arrival.
- About half are in progress when police arrive.
- Many shooters stop (commit suicide) when police confront them.
- Police can act in most events if in progress.
- About one-third of officers responding are shot if the event is in progress upon their arrival.

The message from this data is that active aggressive behavior incidents are over rapidly and that response by those present on site is critical to reducing casualties. The incident will produce several casualties. The average number of fatalities according to FBI data is three, with roughly three injured. Response following the incident stopping can also prevent death from hemorrhage, and methods to expedite treatment by those present are essential. Onsite medical equipment and training is another essential facet, as is interfacing with first responders and leadership during a crisis.

One interesting aspect is the data from the FBI did not link any temporal preferences to the events. The ability to create a "profile" of the typical person who will become engaged in active aggressive behavior is also not feasible at present. The data only indicates that commonalities exist. Many of the factors use in predictive algorithms are behaviors which will not lead to an episode of active aggressive behavior. An "over triage" factor exists in many instances. The need for professional threat analysts in assessment of these individuals is recommended.

A Brief Review of Selected Incidents

To understand these violent events, one must carefully study prior events to provide the context, tactics, outcomes, and thought processes of those involved. This can help in the construction of abstract and concrete concepts by the reader to provide a basis for developing plans and tactics for prevention and reaction to such events. Remember these are reviews conducted with "20/20" hindsight and not meant to be critical of those involved.

Educational Events

Bath School, 1927, Bath, Michigan

The Bath School was bombed by a disgruntled school employee, Andrew Kehoe. He is alleged to have placed 1,000 pounds of dynamite of which 500 pounds detonated. Kehoe's history included a severe head injury incurred during training in electrical engineering at Michigan State (College) University. Kehoe was also implicated in the explosion of a stove that killed his stepmother. The triggering event is the loss of an election by Kehoe. He was under stress because his wife was ill and his home and farm were about to be foreclosed. Kehoe, the school board treasurer, placed hundreds of pounds of dynamite in the school and detonated it. Kehoe killed his wife and burned his farm prior to the school bombing. The fire department responding to the report of fire at the Kehoe farm heard the explosion and returned to town to assist with the school bombing.

Kehoe then drove back to the school in his car, which contained a large amount of dynamite, and detonated it, killing himself, the principal of the school, and a student who had survived the initial blasts. Reports place the number of deaths at 45 with 38 listed as students. The dispute was related to a property tax issue. This is an early use of a vehicle-borne improvised explosive device (VBIED).

Texas Tower, 1966, University of Texas, Austin, Texas

Charles Whitman climbed the University of Texas Tower in Austin and began shooting. He killed 15 people, including an unborn child and a police officer, and wounded 31 people. Some of those hit by gunfire were 400 meters away. Whitman was found to have a brain tumor, which some believe caused the behavior. His marksmanship is likely linked to his status as a former Marine.

Whitman had a tumultuous childhood and recognized his increasing mental health issues. He sought help but only made one visit to a psychiatrist. He planned the events and chronicled his thoughts and preparations in notes and a journal. Whitman killed his mother and wife by stabbing them repeatedly and called their workplaces and reported them ill before proceeding to the tower. He wore work coveralls to disguise himself and used a false ID to gain access to the tower, while using rented hand trucks to transport his weapon-laden footlocker. He then assaulted and killed a receptionist, barricaded the stairwell to the observation deck, and shot spectators attempting to gain access to the observation deck. The observation deck was some 70 meters above ground level.

The Connally Report details many of the findings concerning the events surrounding the shootings. The psychiatrist who saw Whitman described him as "oozing with hostility." Whitman told his psychiatrist that he was considering going to the Texas Tower with his deer rifle and shooting people. This was not reported to law enforcement.

Whitman bought and took about 700 rounds of ammunition, several firearms, food, water, binoculars, amphetamine pills, and even toilet paper in his footlocker to begin his siege. He carefully planned the event over a period of at least several weeks. The failure to recognize leakage and the other behavioral incidents doomed many to die in this event. Whitman provided clear information to his psychiatrist that he would commit the murders. He had behavioral indicators including increased hostility and erratic behavior. These were ignored, but at the time, little was known about the tactics and indicators of such individuals and what behaviors constituted warning signs of impending violent actions.

Columbine School, 1999, Jefferson County, Colorado

The attack at Columbine High School changed the tactics used by law enforcement. In lieu of the "surround and wait for SWAT" philosophy, it became apparent that the first arriving officer should close with shooter to isolate or neutralize the threat. The "wait" philosophy likely contributed to the deaths of one or more of the injured at Columbine. This prompted changes in the manner EMS responded to these events and started the trend to use aggressive techniques in reaching the injured in active aggressive behavior incidents. On at least three occasions officers exchanged gunfire with Harris and Klebold, but no one was struck in the exchanges.

As with most events of a negative nature, no one factor caused the event. A multitude of factors contributed to this event. The apparent lack of law enforcement action on web-based threats posted by Eric Harris certainly played a role in the event. Reports indicate that Harris even stated he had made pipe bombs in his web posts. Why police did not react is not clear. The planning and preparation for the event took place over roughly a year.

Harris and Klebold were convicted of a felony theft and sentenced as juveniles. They were sent to anger management, and Harris began receiving psychiatric care. Harris complained of depression and was started on antidepressant drugs. Klebold was said to be depressed. Some considered Harris a psychopath and leader of the duo.

Motive for the attack remains unclear. The personal journals, notes, and videos revealed that they wanted the event to rival Oklahoma City. They documented their acquisition of firearms, construction of IEDs, and hiding places of firearms in their homes. They explained the tactics used to keep these activities concealed from their parents. They produced a video prior to the attack as a final statement and apologized for their actions to family and friends. Numerous theories have been put forth, but no definitive reason has been universally accepted as to a motive.

The attack killed a dozen students and one faculty member, while injuring an additional 21 individuals. Harris and Klebold brought at least 99 IEDs to the attack. They hoped to distract law enforcement and fire service personnel from the school with an arson fire. They secreted IEDs in the cafeteria to detonate during lunch and kill many students. They planned to shoot the survivors as they exited the cafeteria. Many of the IEDs failed to function, as did two large bombs in propane cylinders hidden in their vehicles outside the cafeteria. During the attack, they seemed to shoot students at random, targeted others, and taunted those they were about to shoot or who had been shot. They seemed to lose interest in shooting students about an hour into the event. They discussed other potential actions to kill individuals. They checked but did not enter locked classrooms and even had eye contact with students hiding within the rooms. Both offenders decided to commit suicide and did so apparently simultaneously. It appears they had little or no preparation for a long-term siege or escape plan.

Significantly, the persons providing the firearms are alleged to have some information regarding the attacks prior to their occurrence, and a student who had had a conflict with Harris was told to leave before they entered the buildings. This student left quickly and had an opportunity to notify school officials or law enforcement. He knew that Harris had said he had made pipe bombs and had made threats to use them.

University of Alabama at Huntsville Shooting, 2010, Huntsville, Alabama

At the time of the shooting, Amy Bishop, a 44-year-old female professor, shot associates at a meeting. The trigger was her denial of tenure. She systematically shot six professors, killing three. She was under suspicion for murder of her brother in 1986, arrested for an assault, and had been investigated for a bomb threat.

Her colleagues and students described Bishop as having mood swings from rage to empathy, being demanding, and being "always about to explode." According to some reports, Bishop stayed in conflict with peers and supervisors, had a less than adequate work product, and generated several student complaints.

Bishop allegedly went to a firearms range and practiced prior to her shooting incident. The university appeared to not have reacted to the complaints made in a coherent fashion to prevent this event. Based on the reports there appeared to be enough information from multiple sources to assess Bishop as a threat and to confront her. After the shooting, according to some reports, Bishop denied she had committed the crime.

A culture of reporting, a central point of tracking, and a behavioral intervention team are necessary components in most settings to assess and determine what threats need action to mitigate. This type of environment would afford the better chance to detect and prevent active aggressive behavior.

Virginia Tech, 2007, Blacksburg, Virginia

Seung-Hoi Cho, the shooter at Virginia Tech in 2007, was 23 when the event occurred. Cho had a history of unusual and disturbing behavior. According to reports, he managed to kill 32 and wound 23. Cho had a bizarre set of beliefs and believed that he was present to liberate the poor and oppressed. Cho was said to be paranoid and depressed, was suffering severe social anxiety, and was suicidal. He was undergoing outpatient mental health care at the time of the shooting.

The warning signs in Cho were missed, ignored, or not recognized. It appears that the threats to fellow students and professors he made were not passed to campus authorities or not recognized as a serious threat. No coherent plan was in place to encourage, assimilate, analyze, and track threats. No culture of reporting existed, and no central reporting point was available, according to various reports. This failure to educate students, staff, and faculty was one factor in the success of the attacks.

Cho had disturbing writings, including gruesome poems, stories, and plays. He exercised selective mutism and was a target of derision by students who knew him as the "question mark kid." Cho was an isolated loner. Between the shootings in the dorm and classroom building, he had the wherewithal to send his manifesto to NBC.

One of the comments attributed to Cho was, "Evil plan doing good," he viewed himself as the savior of the oppressed, poor, and those rejected by society. He likened himself to Jesus Christ but was antagonistic toward religion at the same time. This duality and conflict regarding religion has been seen in several shooters. He had been diagnosed with an anxiety disorder and had an extensive mental health history noted in some reports about the incident. The information from some mental health workers was not shared with Virginia Tech because of privacy laws. In 2005, a court declared him mentally ill after he stalked two females. This information was not reported or tracked at the federal or state level, allowing him to purchase firearms since he was not institutionalized.

His attacks were well planned, and he carried spare ammunition in additional magazines and carried a secondary firearm. He entered a locked residence hall and shot a female student, and when a residence hall student employee responded to the shooting, he was shot and killed. Cho then left and returned to his residence hall, where he changed out of his bloody clothes, deleted his emails, and removed his computer hard drive. This hard drive was never located. He went to the post office where he mailed his manifesto to NBC.

Cho then proceeded to Norris Hall, which contained classrooms. He carried two firearms, chains, locks, a hammer, and knife. These items along with the handguns and 400 rounds of ammunition were carried within a backpack. He chained three main entrance doors and left a note stating trying to open the doors would cause a bomb to explode. He peeked into one classroom twice and then entered and began shooting with a 9mm semiautomatic pistol. Cho went classroom to classroom shooting professors and students. Cho stopped to reload and began revisiting the classrooms in which he had shot individuals, and he was stopped by a barricaded door in two classrooms but was able to shoot through the door, killing at least one and injuring two. Roughly 10 minutes into the event Cho stopped and committed suicide by shooting himself. Speculation is that Cho detected police arrival inside the building and their approaching him. He had fired at least 174 rounds but had more than 200 live rounds available when he died.

Police arrived within three minutes but took five minutes to gain entry to the building because of the chained doors. Virginia Tech notified students via email roughly two hours following the first shooting in the residence hall, but the assessment was that this was an isolated incident and domestic in nature. No lockdown or cancellation of classes took place. Failures in prompt notification became an issue, as did the lack of coordination/assessment of threats, and lack in patient mental health treatment. Any of these areas might have prevented the event or reduced the number of casualties had the information been shared and acted upon by authorities.

Umpqua Community College, 2015, Roseburg, Oregon

As with most educational shootings, the shooter, Christopher Harper-Mercer, had a relationship with institution. He was an assistant in drama productions and a student. According to reports he was on academic probation and owed a substantial amount of money in unpaid tuition. His history included graduation from a school for the learning disabled with emotional issues. He was reported to have Asperger syndrome with behavior which included head banging. As with some shooters, he had a manifesto and was active online.

His neighbors told the media they "got bad vibes from him," and he seemed to be unfriendly. Another described him to the media as a "loner with a grudge." His online and email activities revealed he used the emails with phrases like "Iron Cross 45," and "Pro IRA," and some of the material noted him as mixed race. Harper-Mercer prepared for his attack, wore body armor, and took three handguns with an AR-style rifle with multiple magazines. His mother reported to the media he was fascinated with firearms. Harper-Mercer served a short time in the Army and was dismissed allegedly for a suicide attempt.

Some of his writings showed he was obsessed with Satan and did not want to die as a virgin or friendless. Harper-Mercer also wrote "The material world is a lie … our spiritual development has been halted"; on his profile he noted he did not like religion. Harper-Mercer had studied the Sandy Hook Elementary School shooting and the Vester Flanagan shooting of the female TV reporter and camera operator on live television. According to media reports, he wrote about Flannigan, "people like him are all alone and unknown … when they spill a little blood, the whole world knows who they are," "Seems the more people you kill, the more you're in the limelight," and he noted, "my success in Hell is assured." Upon police arrival some six minutes into the event and after about two minutes to arrive at the shooting site, they saw Harper-Mercer peek out of a classroom, and shots were exchanged. Harper-Mercer was hit and appeared to commit suicide.

However, Harper-Mercer has the characteristics and commonalities of many shooters. He was a loner (although many of those with active aggressive behavior are not loners), had impulse control issues with festering anger, and was fascinated with firearms and death. Harper-Mercer also had problems with a religion and seemed to have grudge against the world. The probable triggering events in this shooting were Harper-Mercer's poor grades and money owed to the college. The above factors are seen in many shooters.

Panama City School Board, 2010, Panama City, Florida

Perhaps one of the more difficult individuals to detect is a "lone wolf." Some are mentally ill, while others may seek revenge for a variety of motives. Clay Duke, 56, was a described as a failed ex-convict with bipolar disorder. Duke had a history of stalking and weapons use and had served time in prison. At the time of the shooting he was unemployed.

His connection with the school system was that his wife had been laid off from the school system and her unemployment benefits had run out. He wrote a farewell on social media about a week prior to the event and marked the day after the event on a calendar. Duke entered the school board meeting and walked to a podium, spray-painted a "V" in a circle, and warned bystanders and the media to leave. The event was recorded by the media and can be seen on video sharing sites. Duke displayed a firearm, made a rambling speech about his wife's problem, and said he expected to die. Duke is alleged to have posted on social media, "My testament: Some people (the government sponsored media) will say I was evil, a monster (V) … no … I was just born poor in a country where the Wealthy manipulate, use, abuse, and economically enslave 95 percent of the population. Rich Republicans, Rich Democrats … same-same … rich … they take turns fleecing us … our few dollars … pyramiding the wealth for themselves." This is obvious leakage and forewarning of the event.

Duke released the only female present but still held four male school board members hostage. Duke eventually fired one round at the school board chairman, missing, and appeared to unintentionally discharge another round. Duke then engaged in a gun battle with the school system security director and was hit, fell, and committed suicide with his own gun. No one else was injured in the event, and Duke's wife stated she believed he intentionally missed the first shot he fired, as he was familiar with firearms and a good shot.

Duke is an aberrant case in which one has difficulty predicting his actions since he has no obvious ties to the persons and facilities attacked. He apparently did not send threat letters or make threats to the school board. In these circumstances, one must depend upon infrastructure such as armed personnel at magnetometers to protect from such assaults. Unarmed security personnel staffing screening points provide a false sense of security, as will be seen in the Red Lake School shooting.

Red Lake School Shooting, 2005, Red Lake, Minnesota

In 2005, Jeff Weise, 16, used an illegally acquired pistol to shoot and kill his grandfather while he slept. The grandfather was a tribal police officer. Weise then took his grandfather's department-issued pistol, body armor, and shotgun. Weise also killed his grandfather's younger girlfriend. He proceeded to the Red Lake School, where he was a student, in his grandfather's patrol car. Weise was wearing his grandfather's body armor. He entered the school, where he shot an unarmed security guard at the entrance where magneto-meters were used to screen those entering the school. Wise then entered a classroom and proceeded to kill a teacher and five students. Wiese tried to enter other classrooms but upon hearing the gunfire, the classrooms had been locked down.

He managed to fire 45 shots in three minutes, before he was shot by re-sponding officers in areas not protected by body armor. Wiese then is alleged to have committed suicide.

Weise reportedly studied neo-Nazism and was said to have had admiration for Hitler. Wiese had been depressed and was using psychotropic drugs for his depression. He had a prior suicide attempt. His father was reported to have committed suicide, and his mother had been seriously injured in a car crash. This is the reason he was living with his grandfather.

Wiese had posted dark scenes of suicide, photographs of the Columbine shooters, Hitler, and Charles Manson. He had photographs of himself wearing his hair styled as devil's horns. Weise had adopted the dark "Goth" look and delved into morbid themes according to some of his writings.

These themes seem to be similar to the shooters from Columbine and some other younger shooters. These disaffected youth seem to be attracted to the neo-Nazi movement to have a sense of belonging.

University of Wisconsin, 1972, Madison, Wisconsin

Although a terrorist act, the Sterling Hall Bombing in 1972 on the University of Wisconsin-Madison campus is an interesting case as it involved a large ve-hicle-borne improvised explosive device (LVBIED). The explosion killed one person, a physics researcher, but injured as least three others with an estimated 2,000 pounds of ammonium nitrate fuel oil explosive in a van alleged to have been used by an anti-Vietnam war group called the "The New Year's Gang." The target building housed research facilities for the US military. This attack is significant as it was a precursor to the Oklahoma City Bombing and used a similar explosive in a LVBIED configuration.

University of Oklahoma, 2005, Norman, Oklahoma

In another bombing, which has an unclear motive, a student detonated a person-borne improvised explosive device (PBIED) near the Oklahoma Memorial Stadium. The explosion killed the bomber. The student is alleged to have had a history of depression and bomb construction. Some suggested the target might have been the stadium with a premature detonation while others speculate the explosion was a suicide. The alleged explosive was triacetone triperoxide (TATP), which appears to have been produced in the student's apartment. The cause and motivation of the event remains unclear.

Alabama, 1990s

Officers received information that a student was planning to construct a bomb and bring it to school. The adopted child, 14 years old, had a tempestuous relationship with his adoptive parents and his adoptive brother. Officers were unable to confirm the information regarding the threat but continued the investigation. Before officers could interview the parents and juvenile suspect, he killed his adoptive brother, shot one adoptive parent and injured the other adoptive parent and fled the scene. Officers responded to the scene and uncovered bomb components. When the adoptive father was interviewed, he stated that he had hidden the smokeless gunpowder to keep the suspect from building a pipe bomb. He and his wife had been hesitant to call police about the circumstances.

The juvenile suspect had a poor performance record at school, had disciplinary problems at school, was alleged to have an unstable home life, and had made multiple threats against fellow students and teachers, even telling them he would bring a bomb to school. A search of area around the suspect's residence uncovered multiple booby traps and dead falls protecting a "fort" he had constructed in the woods and equipped as a refuge to hide from police. He had water, food, a sleeping bag, insect repellent, ammunition for his shotgun, and a portable radio for entertainment. Although the pipe bomb to be assembled was crude, it could have killed or caused serious injury to any individuals nearby when detonated. The suspect eluded officers but was eventually caught hiding in the attic of nearby structure. The suspect was charged with attempted criminal possession of explosives and murder.

Alabama, 2000s

Parents called 911 to report their 21-year-old son had fired multiple shots in the residence, took a firearm, and fled. What disturbed the parents was a "hit list" of students, teachers, and administrators at his former high school. Although he was more than five miles away from the school, officers formed a protective cordon around the school and an immediate lockdown followed by evacuation of the more than 800 students attending school occurred. The shooter barely had sufficient grades to graduate, had just been accepted into the military, and was slated to leave the following day. The military career had been a long-time plan of the suspect. The parents indicated the suspect's behavior had become erratic in the previous weeks, and they were unsure of what the motivation was for the "hit list" or the shooting in the residence. The parents stated they knew of no mental health issues but were concerned with the recent erratic behavior and thought it might be related to his coming departure to join the military.

A search involving dozens of officers and a helicopter could not locate the suspect, presumed to be in a heavily wooded and swampy area between his residence and the school. The following day the suspect set fire to a vacant structure to distract police but was arrested by an officer as he crossed a street within 100 yards of the school. The suspect was arrested but failed to provide any rationale or reason for his threatening note, the shooting in his residence, or the arson fire. The suspect was convicted of making a terrorist threat and arson. His offer of employment by the military was withdrawn.

Teachers noted unusual behavior of the 16-year-old leader of a group of "goths." His followers had also withdrawn themselves from students at the school. An interview with some of the group revealed the leader was constructing a pipe bomb to take to school. Execution of a search warrant recovered pipe bomb components and an anarchist handbook along with ritual magic items. The individual never provided a motive or any type of explanation for his behavior.

Occupational/Commercial

2014 Workplace Active Aggressive Behavior Involving an Employee

The shooter in this case had an employee relationship with his employer, as with most workplace shootings, and was a former employee terminated the day before the shooting. The employee was a white male, roughly a 20-year employee, and 45 years old. The media reported that this individual had been fired previously but had been reinstated following the previous firings.

The trigger in this event appears to be fact the employee was not reinstated. The former employee had lost his final appeal the day before the shooting. The shooter wore his work uniform either to gain entry or for symbolic reasons, accosted his former supervisor, and shot and killed the supervisor and an uninvolved employee present in the supervisor's office.

As with many shooters, the employee used a handgun and committed suicide following the shooting. The media reported that several employees had warned the supervisor who was killed and other management figures that the shooter was likely to commit this type of violence. Further, the employees stated that many employees believed that this event would occur following the termination.

As with many incidents of active aggressive behavior, it appears these warnings were not passed along, not considered valid, or ignored. Warnings of this nature are seen frequently following such incidents. Some are "20/20" hindsight, but other warnings in many cases had reached the target or management but were not acted upon to mitigate the potential event. Usually no system is in place to encourage reporting, assimilate, analyze, and track the threats. Such a system is a requirement to detect the event during its phases prior to execution.

US Postal Service Facility, 2006, Goleta, California

This incident involved a white female, Jennifer San Marco, which is unusual. Most shooters are male, and many are white. The 44-year-old female was a former employee who had been terminated for mental health reasons according to reports. The media reported she suspected her former colleagues were conspiring against her, and she exhibited paranoid behavior. She attempted to publish a hate newspaper ranting about minorities.

She had prior police contacts for her bizarre behavior and had a past mental health commitment. She still managed to purchase a 9mm handgun. She had been on disability for roughly three years prior to the incident.

The shooting started with the murder of a female neighbor who had allegedly complained about San Marco's loud singing. San Marco was able to enter the secure facility by obtaining an employee's badge at gunpoint. She killed two employees in the parking lot and four more inside prior to committing suicide. It appears she targeted minorities in the shootings.

This event highlights the inability to link mental health records and commitments to the national database for the purchase of firearms. The same issue occurred with Cho at Virginia Tech, and in the 2015 Charleston church shooting, where mental health records were either not reported, not linked to the national database, or were missed in some fashion if reported. Although improvements have occurred in the background checking system, the issue of not allowing those with mental health issues purchase weapons, and of even more concern, how to impound the weapons of those exhibiting mental health issues, remains a problem.

Fort Hood, 2009, near Killeen, Texas

The shooter in this event was a member of the military and a psychiatrist. Hassan was apparently committed to Islam and did not desire deployment. He appeared to have conflicted feelings over his mission with the US Army and his religious commitment. During his residency at Walter Reed Hospital, he produced a presentation in which he suggested Muslims be granted conscientious objector status.

According to various reports his presentation was not well received. Hassan continued his efforts to avoid deployment but was unsuccessful. Other stressors included the death of his father and his belief that others were prejudices against him. Some reports indicate he received negative evaluations at work. He sought the guidance of an imam who advocated violence against the US through the Internet. This communication and counseling may have encouraged his belief in the need of violence. At some point, Hassan became convinced that his only option was to commit violence and potentially become a martyr. Hassan appeared to be isolated and frustrated, believed he was the target of harassment because of his religion, and, it appears, saw no other avenue out of his circumstance.

Leakage occurred as Hassan practiced firing on the range prior to his attack, and he presented his neighbor with cherished personal items. Neither of these events was reported. Hassan entered a crowded medical facility and began shooting randomly. He shouted "Allah Akbar" during his roughly 10-minute shooting spree. He was engaged by Army civilian police officers and managed to shoot one but was shot by the second officer and became unconscious from a head wound.

However, Hassan managed to kill 13 and wound 30 during the incident. According to reports, he fired at least 146 rounds inside the building and additional rounds outside for at least 214 rounds. He still reportedly had an additional 117 rounds in his pockets when he was shot by police. Hassan had no apparent escape plan. The controversy as to the status of Hassan as workplace shooter or terrorist remains. What this event likely represents is a homegrown violent extremist acting on religious beliefs.

Medical Facilities

Shootings in medical facilities usually involve a domestic issue, a workplace issue, revenge against a staff member, or a "mercy killing." However, some do have a random component.

An individual in the military reserve who was about to be redeployed to southwest Asia came to a "walk-in" medical care facility. He is alleged to have carried a military-style rifle and worn a helmet and some form of military body armor. The individual walked into the reception area and fired a shot from the rifle into the ceiling.

Visitors and staff members fled the building while others hid. Police negotiators were able to convince the shooter to surrender without further violence. His claim of mental health problems induced by his former combat service did not impress the court, and he was convicted and sentenced to prison. This individual had no apparent direct connection to the facility other than that the facility was near his residence. The motivation for this event is not clear and the individual was found competent to stand trial. Some speculated he did not want to return to a combat situation.

In 2012 a man walked into a hospital from which he had been ejected for his behavior earlier, which included a verbal altercation that allegedly included threats. The shooter's spouse was a patient in the cardiac care unit, and the shooter was displeased with the care rendered. Accordingly, the shooter took an unarmed hospital security officer hostage. When police arrived a gun battle ensued with numerous rounds fired. The shooter was hit by police gunfire and died but not before shooting two hospital employees and a police officer. Behavioral clues were either missed, not understood, or not acted upon.

In the 1990s, a female was injured by her live-in boyfriend and taken to a hospital and admitted. The boyfriend fled prior to police arrival. The boyfriend discovered the location of his girlfriend, took a semiautomatic rifle in an AK47 configuration, and managed to enter the hospital unobserved. Fortuitously, two unarmed hospital security officers encountered the suspect and were able to disarm him. The suspect allegedly told police he was going to shoot and kill his girlfriend. The reason security officers were able to disarm the suspect was that he was intoxicated.

Numerous cases have been reported in a variety of sources, including the *Annals of Emergency Medicine*, where family members have entered medical facilities with firearms to commit "mercy killings" of family members with terminal diseases. In many instances, following the killing of the relative, the shooter committed suicide.

Other events included individuals with a specific target of revenge where a negative medical outcome was blamed on a physician or other medical staff. These individuals usually have a well-planned method to gain entry and shoot the target. These individuals are well motivated and usually commit suicide following the shooting. These shootings may occur months or even years later, as seen in a recent murder of a physician in Texas, after the death of the family member. Since most medical facilities have minimal external security, gaining access is not usually an issue, and most of these shooters are familiar with the location because of prior visits or have conducted reconnaissance. In rare circumstances, terminally ill patients may commit suicide while in a medical facility.

Medical facilities, like any other workplace, do infrequently have workplace-related shootings. These are usually between employees and revolve around some unresolved dispute.

San Ysidro, California, McDonald's Shooting, 1984

According to reports, James Huberty, a security guard, believed he had mental health issues and told his wife he had issues. He telephoned local mental health hotline but, in a mix up, his call was not returned. This appears to be the trigger that sent Hubert "hunting humans." He is alleged to have made this statement to his wife and told his daughter he would not be coming back. He drove 200 yards to a McDonald's and began methodically shooting customers and staff. He gunned down arriving customers and juveniles on bicycles. Huberty was armed with a 9mm pistol, 9mm carbine, and 12-gauge shotgun. Ten minutes into the shooting, police had not arrived, but a fire engine staged within sight of the restaurant. Huberty fired at it, striking the engine several times.

Huberty is alleged to have carried additional ammunition. He killed individuals ranging in age from an infant to 62 years old. Huberty shot the victims repeatedly, with 257 rounds fired during the incident. He reportedly shot one victim 48 times. A police sharpshooter killed Huberty roughly 78 minutes into the event. This event prompted many police agencies to consider their ability to respond to such an incident and prompted changes in the way events of this type would be handled.

Huberty's mother left the family early in his life. He became progressively more concerned about the breakdown of society and Russian aggression. He bought non-perishable food and firearms. His paranoia appeared to increase up until the shooting event. The autopsy of Huberty showed no drugs or alcohol in his system.

The Aurora, Colorado, theater shooting, which injured and killed more than 70, appears to have been motivated by mental health issues. The shooter even booby trapped his apartment with IEDs to impair law enforcement in their search for evidence. Even though the shooter attempted to use an insanity plea, the court was not impressed and found him guilty of multiple murders.

Attacks with IEDs

In some incidents, bombing attacks may be used to distract first responders. Several bombings have been used to distract law enforcement while a bank or armored car robbery occurs. One failed bombing of a gasoline pipeline in Norco, California, in early 1980s was intended to distract law enforcement officers while the suspects conducted a bank robbery. This led to a shootout like the North Hollywood bank robbery. Even though the bomb failed to detonate, the group proceeded with their robbery. In the shootout with police, more than 1,000 rounds were fired. One deputy sheriff was killed, more than a dozen officers were injured, and the group managed to shoot down a police helicopter and destroy more than 30 police cars with gunfire. The suspects conducted extensive planning and created and used IEDs, including shotgun-launched IEDs. Some were hand thrown from the rear of a hijacked pickup truck while others were launched from a shotgun. This event demonstrated how poorly prepared law enforcement was to defend themselves against a well-armed and well-trained group. Officers were shooting revolvers and shotguns against perpetrators armed with semiautomatic rifles. The suspects were able to force police officers to stay a sufficient distance away from them to allow the escape into a forested area. This group was eventually captured, with one killed during the pursuit and another during apprehension. This was a salient lesson, but one which was not learned by law enforcement, as seen with the North Hollywood robbery, where officers faced similar armed and trained gunmen with shotguns and semiautomatic pistols. Norco should have been the Mumbai-type "wakeup" for law enforcement in the US, but many agencies, because of bureaucratic inertia and fear of appearing "militaristic" and offending the public, continued to arm officers with the needed semiautomatic long guns and have not increased firearms-related training. Officers need to not only fire more rounds in the current environment, but shoot in realistic settings with better accuracy and where small unit or individual tactics without outside support are emphasized.

Overview of Events with Three or More Fatalities (FBI Data)

- 98% shooters are solitary
- 96% shooters are male, almost half are white males
- Roughly one incident occurs per month
- 70% are in commercial, business, or educational setting

- 60% are over prior to police arrival
- Small number killed family member prior to event
- About half of the shooters committed suicide
- About 15% had shootings in more than one locale
- A very small number have IEDs
- 70% are over in fewer than five minutes, many in two minutes
- Similar risks by day of week
- If a commercial or business, about 70% have a relationship, former/current employee (an exception is open-air facilities, such as a mall)
  - Most were current employees, 70%
  - A few were just terminated, fired, or suspended, 30%
- In shootings in malls, shooters had no relationship to businesses
- Institution of higher education shooters were likely to be:
  - Current Students 30%
  - Former Students 50%
  - Employee or others 20%
  - Shooters age 18–62 years
- Incidents in schools K–12, 27 events
  - High school 50%
  - Middle school 30%
  - Others 20%
  - Two events occurred in school board meetings
- Open space shootings
  - Most involved the shooter in a vehicle at some point
  - Large portion engaged by police with gunfire
- Military and government
  - Large number of responding officers killed or wounded
  - Shooters age 23–63 years
- Houses of worship
  - Few but lethal results
  - Shooters age 24–69 years
  - Most commit suicide
  - Motives hard to ascertain
- Healthcare
  - Few but lethal in results
  - Shooters age 38–51 and almost exclusively male
  - Committed to take down specific target
  - Well planned
  - Distinct motive, "mercy" killing
  - Most in hospital setting

- About 10% of the total events involved a shooter-targeted female, with whom they were in either a current or prior relationship; many bystanders or those present were shot even if the target was not present
- 10% of the events were ended by unarmed citizens
- 2% were ended by off-duty law enforcement officers with gunfire
- 4% were ended by armed citizens with gunfire
- 28% of shooters exchanged gunfire with police
- High casualty rate among law enforcement officers who engage shooter

High School Shooting Overview

- 33% of casualties fatal (less than typical shootings)
- Ages of shooter range from 14 to 19 years
- 86% were current students
- 7% were former students
- Many were disarmed or stopped by principal, faculty, staff, or students

Events Planned

- **Violent behavior or potential for such is rarely new.**
- Usually *patterns* of negative thinking, feeling, and behavior are part of the history.
- **Triggers intensify** the negative elements.
- **Planning** for violent reaction usually takes place over some time (usually weeks, some months, rarely years).
- **Leakage** during this time, including signals, flags, and sometimes threats, *exist* but are **rarely seen as serious** or are *not reported.*

Stages

- **Fantasy*** (usually has a relationship with target, roughly 60% of victims know shooter per FBI data)
- **Planning*** (comfortable weapons use)
- **Preparation*** (may practice, e.g., Cho and Bishop)
- **Approach** (must depend upon infrastructure)
- **Implementation** (must depend on law enforcement response, self-rescue)
- * Leakage, opportunity to prevent the attack

Environment

Prepared for extended operations

- Negative Situations
  - Personal
  - Social
  - Political
  - Religious, many have conflicted religious beliefs
  - Philosophical
- Intense Feelings
  - Anger
  - Hostility
  - Retaliation
  - Vengeance
- Thought Process
  - Ideas
  - "Change is not possible in peaceful way"
  - "Violence is necessary"
  - "Violence is justified"
- Planning
  - Weeks/months/years
  - Violent Behavior
  - Firearms most likely
  - May come prepared
  - Handguns common
  - Long guns second choice
  - May use IEDs

If the Behavior Is Not Based upon Ideological Issues

- Hostile reaction to some frustration, loss, or **damage to ego**
- *Self-centered*
- Desire for vengeance "justifies violence"
- Seeks *psychological reward* through terrorizing others, sees this as "pay back"
- *Thrilled* by power of firearms, bombs, killing, and chaos

Planning

- Extra ammunition carried, multiple firearms
- Shooter often exhibits cold, calm, and expressionless appearance

- Mental rehearsals and practice firing to prepare shooter
- Avoidance and escape plans almost non-existent
- Bishop practiced at pistol range prior to shooting
- Cho practiced shooting targets on the ground and brought chains and locks to prevent escape/entry
- The Las Vegas shooter brought extra ammunition and firearms

The Target Matters

Those shooting or violent attacks in schools and institutions of higher education (IHE) almost always show a relationship with the offender to the facility. Former or current students or former or current employees with current far more common than a "former" status. The issue with schools and IHEs is that these have a threat spectrum which covers students, staff, and faculty. This is a broader threat spectrum than that of most institutions and businesses.

Businesses where the actor is an employee or former employee is common in terms of this person as an aggressor. In most instances some type of disciplinary action has been taken or the employee has been terminated. Some of the employees or former employees will be described as "vengeful." In many instances, fellow employees will have insight into the thought process of the former or current employee. The acrimonious dismissal or firing of an employee makes this type of event post termination more likely. Some have been seen months to a year later. The issue in this setting is that the employee knows the operating routine, security measures, and layout of the facility. This could be a general shooting exacting revenge on any person found or may target a specific supervisor with anyone nearby becoming a target. In some instances, the employee or former employee may allude to his or her intentions or exhibit leakage to fellow employees.

Domestic shootings can occur during or following the termination of a relationship. The aggressor in these events does not care what steps are needed to attack the former spouse or significant other. He or she is willing to sacrifice his or her life to eliminate the former spouse or significant other. These usually occur when a triggering event happens, such as finalizing a divorce or a former spouse/significant other starting a relationship with another. The danger in this type of event is the aggressor is committed and is willing to die, knows the layout of the target's home or workplace, knows habits, and the like. A determined attacker in this instance will eliminate anyone in his or her way during the effort to kill a former spouse or significant other. IEDs should be considered a threat in this setting.

In a healthcare setting the aggressor is likely to have a specific target, according to data published by the American College of Emergency Physicians. This could be to terminate the life of a suffering relative. It might be to target a medical provider for what the aggressor sees as a failure to properly care for a relative. These usually are well-planned events, but the planning cycle to execution can be short if the relative is still a patient. If the patient has expired, the planning cycle may be much longer and better planned, as demonstrated by a shooting of a cardiologist in Texas recently in which the event took place multiple years prior to the relative shooting and killing the physician. Homicide followed by suicide in the case of an older, terminally ill spouse is not uncommon, if the homicide is seen by the shooter as relieving suffering or preserving dignity.

Open-air or mall attacks are more difficult to characterize. Some may simply be a target of opportunity or easy target, since security is not likely to be substantial. Attacks can occur to make a statement and various weapons may be employed (firearms are more common but edged weapons are also used). The problem is that these facilities cover a large footprint and may have complex layouts with businesses. The open-air shootings, such as the Las Vegas shooting, may have the shooter at a distance from the event, and the motivations of this type of attack may not be obvious. The key is that the more resources and higher commitment of the aggressor, the more likely the attack will be successful. These are soft targets with a high density of potential victims. An attack method that would result in numerous causalities that has not been seen frequently is the use of an irritant agent, such as oleoresin capsicum (OC), or pulmonary agent, such as chlorine, phosgene, or anhydrous ammonia, being released upwind of an outdoor activity such as a football stadium during an game. This would cause many injuries or deaths because of the agent (if chlorine, phosgene, or anhydrous ammonia are used) and perhaps more injuries/deaths because of the stampede to escape the locale. This has occurred several times in closed facilities such as nightclubs, where security personnel or others have intentionally released OC. The ensuing stampede caused deaths and many injuries.

The following risk assessment tool is designed to "over triage" risks. Several factors are listed. When the factor is not known it should be scored as the maximum value. This is simply a tool and not designed to provide an absolute index of risk. However, the author has used it for many years, and it has provided a risk assessment that identified a potential school bomber and school shooter. Both incidents were mitigated. **However, formal vetting and research have not validated this material.**

General Risk Assessment and Target Unknown

Demographic Risks		Score
• Male	Yes	5
• Age 15–50	Yes	4
Category Score		_____
Relative Risk High: 4 or higher		

Historical Risks		
• Prior suicide attempt	Yes	3
• **History of violent behavior**	Yes	5
• Criminal history	Yes	1
• Prior history substance abuse	Yes	3
• Arrest for crime of violence	Yes	4
• **Arrest for weapons violation**	Yes	5
• Prior civil commitment	Yes	4
Category Score		_____
Relative Risk High: 14 or higher		

Current Risk Factors		
• **Diagnosed with mental illness**	Yes	5
• Not responsive or compliant	Yes	3
• Acting irrationally	Yes	3
• Showings signs of paranoia	Yes	4
• Showing signs of delusional behavior	Yes	4
Category Score		_____
Relative Risk High: 8 or higher		

Situational Factors		
• No family or other support system	Yes	3
• **Recent failure or loss** (trigger)	Yes	5
• **Access to firearms** (critical path)	Yes	7
• Exploring death, morbid themes/suicide	Yes	4
• Researching prior mass shooters/events	Yes	4
Category Score		_____
Relative Risk High: 11 or higher		

Imminence Factors		
• Showing signs of anger, bitterness	Yes	4
• Violent thoughts present	Yes	4

• **Has planned violence**	Yes	5
• Threatened violence	Yes	4
• Impulsive behavior	Yes	3
Category Score		_____

Relative Risk High: 8 or higher

Total Score		_____
• **Total Risk Extreme**		**>60**
• **Total Risk Very High**		**50–60**
• **Total Risk High**		**45–50**
• Total Risk Moderate		30–44
• Total Risk Less than Moderate		<30

When factors are not known, any three categories showing High Risk should be considered a High Risk

Risk Assessment and High School or Institution of Higher Education

Demographic Risks		Score
• Male	Yes	5
• Age 15–50	Yes	4
Category Score		_____

Relative Risk High: 4 or higher

Historical Risks		
• Prior suicide attempt	Yes	3
• **History of violent behavior**	Yes	5
• Criminal history	Yes	1
• Prior history substance abuse	Yes	3
• Arrest for crime of violence	Yes	4
• **Arrest for weapons violation**	Yes	5
• Prior civil commitment	Yes	4
Category Score		_____

Relative Risk High: 14 or higher

Current Risk Factors		
• **Diagnosed with mental illness**	Yes	5
• Not responsive or compliant at work/school	Yes	3
• Acting irrationally	Yes	3
• Showings signs of paranoia	Yes	4

• Showing signs of delusional behavior	Yes	4
Category Score		____

Relative Risk High: 8 or higher

Situational Factors

• No family or other support system	Yes	3
• **Recent failure or loss at school or work** (trigger)	Yes	5
• **Access to firearms** (critical path)	Yes	7
• Exploring death, morbid themes/suicide	Yes	4
• Researching prior mass shooters/events	Yes	4
Category Score		____

Relative Risk High: 11 or higher

Imminence Factors

• Showing signs of anger, bitterness	Yes	4
• Violent thoughts present	Yes	4
• **Has planned violence**	Yes	5
• Threatened violence	Yes	4
• Impulsive behavior, increase in disciplinary actions or absences, unexplained use of sick time	Yes	3
Category Score		____

Relative Risk High: 8 or higher

Total Score	____
• **Total Risk Extreme**	>60
• **Total Risk Very High**	50–60
• **Total Risk High**	45–50
• Total Risk Moderate	30–44
• Total Risk Less than Moderate	<30

When factors are not known, any three categories showing High Risk should be considered a High Risk

Post Incident and Recovery

One of the forgotten topics in crisis management is the post-incident phase. With multiple casualties, the storing of bodies, collection of evidence, and return to normalcy of the facility or locale should be considered. Crime scene operations may take days to weeks before the facility is released to the owner/operator. Remediation of biological hazards will be a priority as will repair of infrastructure.

One question that must be answered is whether it will be cost effective to reopen the facility and what aspects of any insurance on the property will be covered. Government-owned facilities are likely to be reopened, whereas some public facilities of mass shootings elect to cease operations.

Operations must be located at an alternative site; communications, computer systems, and data must be moved to the alternative location or purchased/leased until access can be gained to the original site. If this is a school, classes may need to relocate. Counseling can be a necessity for those involved through Critical Incident Stress Debriefing (CISD) group debriefings and follow-up sessions with mental health professionals on an individual basis. Legal advice is essential for leadership to ensure the appropriate steps are taken to protect the entity from litigation. The more common lawsuit will allege failure to protect on the part of the owner/operator of the locale.

The ensuing litigation is another aspect. Some entities elect to shut down and file for bankruptcy rather than face litigation and will raze the structure. For instance, Sandy Hook Elementary School was razed, and the Pulse Nightclub will become a site for remembrance, as did the bombing site in Oklahoma City.

About the Author

Jim Smith has more than 45 years of public safety experience and has served in every position in crises, from line officer to police chief to public safety director. He currently serves as public safety director for a rural community. Smith is a nationally registered paramedic and has served as a firefighter paramedic and tactical team paramedic for several years. He has commanded a medium-sized metropolitan police agency during several hurricanes, including a category three hurricane, several tornadoes, hazardous material events, mass causality events, riots, and evacuations. Smith served as public safety coordinator for a large university with multiple campuses and assisted in organizing and operating a behavioral intervention team and threat assessment team. While police chief in a rural community, Smith has coordinated public safety efforts during a category five hurricane, tornadoes, and areal flooding along with several large hazardous material incidents. He also conducted threat assessment of potential active aggressive behavior actors and potentially prevented a school shooting and school bombing.

Smith has a Master of Science in Safety from the University of Southern California, a Bachelors of Science in Biology and Chemistry from Troy University, and an Associate in Science in Emergency Medical Technology. Smith teaches homeland security, terrorism, and criminal justice courses for the University of Phoenix and Troy University. Smith has developed certification programs for clandestine laboratory entry, assessment, and safety, along with certification programs for response and mitigation of WMD related events. He supervised a regional FBI-certified bomb squad and regional clandestine laboratory entry/assessment team for several years. He also served on a federal counterterrorism task force for several years. Smith has served as a health physics and chemistry technician at an operating nuclear power facility. Smith published research regarding pipe bomb fragmentation and propagation patterns, pipe bomb fragment, and blast suppression. This led to the commercial production of equipment to fulfill the role. Smith has published numerous peer-reviewed articles in journals and has published five criminal justice, tactical medicine, and homeland security textbooks.

Index